Pit, Polo, Pulpit

An Autobiography

by

George Dudley Andrew Fox

Published by
Ogilvie Dickson MPD
Melrose, Scotland

© Copyright: Ogilvie Dickson MPD, 1997

Photographs by Hector Innes, Kelso

ISBN 0 9530924 0 2

Printed by Buccleuch Printers Ltd.
Carnarvon Street, Hawick

Dedicated to my wife Pat.

Dudley poses proudly with his favourite polo mounts, Merah, John Willie and Eriskay, and his Singapore groom.

Dudley, third from right, lines up before the first chukka, with the umpires, Lord Louis Mountbatten and Major Frank Harding, in the centre of the picture. Singapore circa 1954

A unique attraction as the Singapore Polo Club take on the might of the "Generals", mid 1955, showing left to right: (STANDING) Major General Peter Lindsay, Director of Operations; Major General Lewis Pugh, Brigade of Gurkhas; Dudley Fox; Michael Henigan, M.R.C.V.S. (SEATED) Major General Derek Tulloch, G.O.C. Singapore; General Sir Charles Loewen, Commander-in-Chief, Far East Land Forces; Major Frank Harding Major Roy Bennett, C.M.G. T.D., 21st Lancers.

Camborne-Redruth Cameo

Camborne Show I₂
Secretary

Mr. G. D. A. Fox For Upcountry Post?

ORGANISATION AND HARD WORK

CAMBORNE Show, one of the best in the county, is also its most miraculous in the way it overcomes crises and rebuilds after change. I don't know of any other organisation which has been faced with so many changes of top working officials and I doubt if there is another in the county which could have survived them so well.

When Camborne Show gets under

MR. G. D. A. FOX

way on Monday—its 20th year—it will be facing yet another handicap in the coming loss once more of a very capable honorary secretary. Two years ago it had to replace chairman, secretary and treasurer. This year it will have to find another secretary as well as another chairman of the organising committee.

In two years the present hon. general secretary, Mr. G. D. A. Fox, has done a great deal to improve on the organisation of the efficient officials who preceded him. Organisation has been his lifetime's study for it was as the head of the Holman Group invoicing and checking department that he came to this area in 1957. Two years later he took up-residence in Pendarves-road and from that time Camborne Show had him firmly in its grip.

How firmly can be seen in a glimpse of his study where we sat down to discuss this year's show prospects. It is the study of a busy man with Camborne Show its predominating feature. Charts cover the walls, from section arrangement to car parking, from grandstand accommodation to the president's luncheon. All have their place. All are fully organised as is every item down to the minutest point for Monday's event.

IMPROVED ON TRADITION

In this Mr. Fox has admittedly followed a tradition but he has also improved on it. There have not been many secretaries in the 20 years of this event but all have been masters of organisation. The first change was from Mr. A. M. Bray, founder-secretary who held office until some years after the war. He gave up to Mr. Desmond Hocking, now vice-chairman of our Urban Council, and Mr. Hocking in turn relinquished office to Mr. Jack Odgers. The latter had to give up when his bank promotion took him to Penzance and Mr. Fox appeared on the scene just at the right time.

This show will be his swansong because he has resigned from Holmans and will probably be going "up-country." So in the coming winter Camborne Show officials have to look round for another secretary. He will find things well prepared for Mr. Fox has added another system to the already good exhibition planning. He has prepared a book which gives monthly work essential to keep the show preparation running smoothly right from the end of one exhibition to the beginning of the next. So, week by week, whoever takes on the job will find advice from the departing secretary to guide him on his way.

Mr. Fox assured me everything was going smoothly—but it might well not have done so but for his experience in pulling together. Less than a month ago there was every danger Camborne Show might not have a cattle section this year. The previous section secretary was unable to carry on and there was a tremendous amount of preparation to do to get in the entries. Horse section secretaries Messrs. John Harvey and Philip Keverne, both young energetic men, were approached by the general secretary and agreed to add the cattle section to their burden. A notice appeared in the Press inviting cattle entries and the response has been so good that section will be well up to standard on Monday.

Mr. Fox commented last week, "Our regular supporters have shown themselves very keen to come in again. They have shown an interest in the continuance of a good section which is a tribute to their loyalty."

JUMPING CHAMPIONSHIP

Horses are well up in light, heavy and jumping with the Cornish adult jumping championship as the main attraction. Dogs have reached an all-time peak, pigeons, cage birds and rabbits are up. Horticulture we are not sure about as to numbers, but Mr. Fox agreed with me that the officials there will always make sure their entries border on the 1,000 mark.

Our secretary, soon to retire, has proved himself an exceptionally energetic organiser. Not only has he helped keep Camborne Show going but he has infused Camborne Rugby Football Club of which he is chairman with a new spirit of co-operation. Now in his second year with them he has applied his planning to their benefit as well. Here again something for which he has fought will probably be achieved just as he is leaving. This is the Colts headquarters on the Rugby ground, for which we expect to have the "All-clear" soon.

His knowledge of club and exhibition organisation came from years as honorary secretary of the Singapore Polo Club. He was there for 12 years and was both secretary and captain of that well-known institution. As a polo player he rode on the field against many top teams—as the mantelpieces of his Pendarves-road home testify with their myriad cups, tankards, silver salvers.

A Highland Scot, Mr. Fox will be sorry to leave Camborne and its people and organisations he has come to know so well. He will be leaving a lasting impression behind him of energy, organisation and friendship.

A cutting from "The Cornishman" of August 1961.

Laid out on display is an impressive array of Dudley's polo tournament trophies from his exploits in Singapore and Malaya.

Dudley, in his most rewarding post, as he preaches the Gospel from the pulpit of Kelso Old Parish Church.

Kelso Old Parish Church.

Contents

Lady Jane Grosvenor

Foreword

TODAY the peaceful countryside of the Scottish Borders tempts one to forget the region's dramatic past. In a similar way, Dudley Fox's quiet days of retirement in Kelso belie the active and often exciting life he has led – from soldier to Church of Scotland minister, giving dedicated service at all times.

It was in the latter capacity that he introduced himself to me some years ago. His amazing powers of persuasion drew me into an active involvement in what seemed a daunting project to repair and refurbish his church in Kelso. His leadership, his commitment and his faith ensured that the project succeeded and the beautiful building was saved for future generations.

Out of that experience of working together, my admiration and respect for this engaging and caring man became, and remain, enormous. I am truly delighted, therefore, that, through this book, Dudley Fox is sharing his wealth of experience, his wit and his observations with a circle of people far beyond his immediate friends and acquaintances. I have been privileged to hear some of his recollections at first hand and I know that his tale is one which is well worth telling.

Lady Jane Grosvenor   *Easter 1997*

Acknowledgements

M Y GRATEFUL thanks to Lady Jane Grosvenor for her very kind foreword.

This biography was not originally intended for publication and was written to share with members of the family, a few close friends, and colleagues of the rugby and polo clubs of which I was a playing member and club official. That it has been printed and published in this fine style is in no small measure due to the help and advice given to me over a period of several years by a few long-suffering "friends".

My son-in-law, Dr. Jeremy Sammes, of Texas Instruments Software, and Craig Stockton, Centre Manager of R.N.I.B., for their patient tolerance in assisting me to cope with the PC and WP, and to Professor Tony Sammes, Computing Science, Royal Military College of Science, Cranfield University, who eventually managed to translate my out-dated computer disks to a useable format.

Also to Scott Robertson of Buccleuch Printers and Elliot Renwick who gave me the benefit of their typographic experience and skills; and finally, to Ogilvie Dickson, my publisher, who provided the impetus and expertise to put this book onto the shelf.

G.D.A. Fox

Introduction

I T WAS ON the 18th of June 1990 that I received two letters from old friends, and both referring to the same subject, the writing of this biography.

One letter contained a magazine in which there was historical accounts of what had taken place at Gorebridge in Midlothian from the 19th century until the 1939–46 war, (WW2). This letter was from the minister who had been my minister when I was aged seven. Gorebridge was his first Charge.

The second letter was from a friend who had given me much encouragement in my attempt to rescue the Kelso Old Parish Church from closure and to have it restored to full status.

I will have more to say about Kelso Old in due course but for the moment I will record that it was removed from being on 'Terminal Appointment' to Full Status on the 16th of December 1984. (Presbytery of Jedburgh had permitted me to choose the date for this historical occasion and I chose Pat's birthday).

Under the friendly compulsion I commence this task. I may not be competent to make it interesting but without the Grace of God and divine providence most of what you are about to read could not have happened.

This is a personal account of what happened when encouraged by my mother who never admitted defeat; an account of what happened after leaving school at the age of thirteen and a half to work in a coal mine and return to night school until all certificates had been attempted. They were, fortunately, obtained.

The Lord is my light and my salvation;
whom shall I fear?
The Lord is the strength of my life;
of whom shall I be afraid?

And be not confirmed to this world:
but be ye transformed by the renewing of your mind,
that ye may prove what is that good,
and acceptable and perfect will of God.

This biography is about a journey through life which should have ended on several occasions, e.g.

In writing a frontispiece it seems to me similar to reading the last chapter before reading the book. When the writing is completed and you come to consider the frontispiece, the original idea of writing for heritage purposes has been overtaken by the revelation of what was happening to our country during the life of the biographer.

The war to end all wars was partly successful, the Second World War helped to reduce the horror of war, minor wars in Cambodia, Korea, Vietnam, The Falklands and The Gulf have indicated a move away from national war primarily because of 'the bomb' and war has been replaced with world wide terrorism. Two types of Communism appeared post war: industrial in Russia and agricultural in China, and they have changed in the past five years. The Middle East inclusive Libya and small territories in the Americas who could not sustain a war, are taking advantage of the 'deterrent' period via terrorism and the breakup of industrial communism in Russia has permitted terrorist skirmishes in parts of Europe.

The greatest empire in history has disappeared. Law and order is no more, and it is struggling for observance in the U.K.

Punishment of crime is absent. The aggressor receives sympathetic consideration over against the victim. Africa is ignored. The nations that should intervene stand on the periphery - 'the bomb' . . .

It is arguable that there is more suffering now in the 20th century than ever before, inclusive of war. And all in my lifetime.

Chapter One

IN THE COUNTY of Ross and Cromarty and lying to the north of the Cromarty Firth is the market town of Dingwall. Approaching Dingwall from the south through Beauly to Conin Bridge and the village of Maryburgh which is situated on the outskirts of Brahn Castle, you enter Dingwall passing Pitglassy Farm and the Ferntosh Distillery House which was made a listed building in the early 1990's. Today the ruins of the distillery and the outhouses are all that remain and the house is shared by Local Authority Departments. In 1917 the distillery was active and on the malting day there was a grand smell from the distillery when the lids were lifted.

Far away in Europe there was a war raging in France and Mesopotamia and the bugle which had summoned men to war in 1914 was at last heard in America. On the 10th of June, in the year of our Lord 1917, a son was born in Ferintosh Distillery House to Mr and Mrs George Fox. Mrs Georgina Fox *(nee Cameron)* was residing with her parents while George Fox was serving with the Black Watch in Mesopotamia. It was on the 3rd of February, 1918, when I was baptised in Castle Street Church, George Dudley Andrew.

Perhaps 1917, which was to become the penultimate year of The Great War was also the year which signalled the end of the affluent early years of the 20th century. Responsible people realised that manpower had been drastically reduced by war, killed and maimed. Promises of small holdings and cattle were mentioned, but never completely implemented.

The children born between 1914 and 1918 were commonly referred to as 'War Babies' but for what reason, I do not know. Unknown to them and to all concerned, they were a generation born to witness a complete change in every walk of life during the 20th century.

I suppose that my early days could be referred to as being 'idyllic'. Certainly from 1921 when I was considered to be old enough to attend school, from that time forward my memories of my grandparents home at the distillery and at Maryburgh and the Tally Sou on the Brahn Estate where my parents lived, they are happy memories.

The area of ground from the distillery going towards the Town was open space and inland there was a quarry where the tinkers used to camp when they came to Dingwall. The tinkers are not to be confused with travelling people. The tinkers performed all sorts of jobs and repairing the metal receptacles, buckets, basins, etc., and the making of clothes pegs were a great asset at that time. One of my early memories is of the tinkers coming to my grandmother's back door with their 'Tin' for hot water and in nearly every instance they would go away with tea or soup. I obviously heard the household talking about this or I would not have remembered why they came. It was also in the early 20's when electricity was installed in the Distillery House. A memory that has remained very clear was the serving of porridge which grandmother had prepared on the previous evening, and simmered all night. I distinctly remember that the milk had to be in a different bowl. An aunt attempted to change my practise but grandmother told her, quietly, to let me have the milk in a separate bowl. There was a 'bus' which was a vehicle drawn by horses. I believe there were two horses and the passengers sat facing each other, from either side of the bus which may have been named a trap. This bus stopped just outside the house, but I do not remember having travelled on that bus.

We must have moved to Sutherland between 1917 and 1919 because my sister, Helen was born there, (Ardgy) but it is the Tally Sou that I remember clearly after the distillery and that was a lovely place with lots of open ground. It was there that we kept mixed poultry and there was space to play. My first 'sermon' was preached there on a Sunday evening. Wearing one of my father's collars in the approved 'dog collar' fashion, I stood on a box or perhaps a chair and I wish I could remember what the sermon was about. On reflection I must have been copying the minister and no doubt at that age I would be quite serious.

Toy replica soldiers were favourites of mine. They came in long cardboard boxes and I remember playing with them by myself. I have no clear recollection of any other children living at Tally Sou although we may have had visitors from time to time. There were several threats to steal the baby (Helen) while we lived at Tally Sou and of course Tommy was born there in 1921.

My father had been recuperating from war wounds and working with the Forestry Department at Brahn Castle while we lived at Tally Sou, but when Tommy was born we moved to a cottage in Maryburgh and I suppose that was on account of accommodation and convenience to shopping and school. Maryburgh was my first school and the teacher was Miss Campbell.

She lived in a cottage on the main street and continued to live there for many years because in 1944 I took Pat to see the distillery and made enquiries to locate Miss Campbell. I was most surprised when she opened the door of her cottage and as she looked at me she said, "Oh you all look the same in uniform". I replied that my name was

2

Fox to which she immediately said, "Dudley".

Maryburgh school was only two classrooms when I attended and on a recent visit I saw that the school still occupied the same site but had been enlarged by various extensions. There was one occasion when I was frightened by someone with a gun. It must have been a shotgun and perhaps one of the estate people was taking it home. Miss Campbell came to my rescue and all was well. Just past the school, on the way to Dingwall, there was a gate into a field and when I was walking the short distance to the distillery with flowers for my granny, a horse came galloping towards me. A young woman got hold of me and pushed me into the gateway as the horse, a runaway, galloped past. Shortly afterwards my father came along on his bicycle and saw that I was all right.

There is one more memorable occasion before I leave Maryburgh. I mentioned the tinkers earlier. I had strayed from the house while relatives were visiting and when I was missed, my cousins set out to find me. It was Helen Ross who found me near the river and quite rightly began to scold me for wandering away. Sitting on the bridge was a bearded man and he spoke up and said to Helen, "It's all right, nothing was going to happen to Mrs Cameron's grandson". I heard that story retold many times. Mrs Cameron was a highly respected lady and no doubt had filled his 'tin' more than once. There is a saying in scripture about casting your bread on the water. Scots are reputed to do so when the tide is coming in.

It is good that we cannot see in to the future. The 'idyllic' was fast coming to an end and my family were about to embark on a journey into the future which had we known, we would have avoided.

My father was a mining engineer and before the war was working in Cowdenbeath in the coal mines. His stay and re-cuperation in the Highlands had restored him to good health and he obviously had decided to return to mining. We left Maryburgh and arrived in Fife. Firstly to Cairnyhill and then into Cowdenbeath. It was dreadful change.

I entered Fulford School and the remaining memory of my stay there was the antipathy towards Roman Catholic pupils in the nearby Roman Catholic School. There was much in the way of fist fights and the question of hitting back. I had seen nothing of this before arriving at Cowdenbeath.

A baby brother, Norman, was born at Cowdenbeath and lived for seven months.

There was unrest in the mines and difficulties arose between the mine owners and the miners. I knew nothing about any of this at my age, but I knew that we were living in different conditions from the north, and while I did not know what it was at the time, there was squalor and poverty. Poverty that was about to escalate. The death of the baby must have created problems for my mother and we went back to Distillery House for a short spell. My father had carried on by himself in the meantime. There was a cinema in Cowdenbeath and it was the first one that I had ever heard of. It was one penny for admission in the afternoon and there was a film on with Jackie Coogan as the star.

I took an empty jam jar to the shop and received a penny. I went in and have never forgotten how Coogan wore his cap with the front down over his ear. Even as a small boy I must have looked around Cowdenbeath, looked at the shops, watched the men gambling at 'pitch and toss' on the open ground in front of the sawmill, playing at quoit throwing and always swearing. The way of life was indecent, behavioural practise before women and children was dreadful. The import of all of this must have dawned on me at a later age, but the eye had seen and the ear had heard and the result was indelible. It should never be forgotten that young children learn at a different age and for me the comparison between my first five years and what was witnessed in Cowdenbeath scarred me for life.

1924 and we moved to another coal field, but what a difference. My father's health had deteriorated and he was now employed on the surface in the Lady Victoria Pit, Midlothian. We had a small terraced house at No. 15, Gowkshill and I attended Arniston Primary School. This would also be the first primary school for Helen. In 1925 a baby was born, Sheila, and we were now a family of four children, mother and father. The economic situation was bad, although at that time I doubt if children vaguely understood.

Gowkshill consisted of a terraced row of houses, some 30 in number, in wide open country and next to Turnbull's Farm. It had advantages. There was much to do about the farm and there was, throughout the year, many tasks of casual and seasonal work for all of us young children and of course, the womenfolk. As children one of the joys was to walk beside the ploughman as he ploughed the drill with two magnificent Clydesdales harnessed to the plough. It occurs to me now that we must have been company for him too.

In those days during wet and mucky periods, the ploughmen would fasten a jute bag round each leg from knee to ankle and another sack across and round his shoulders. One of the main advantages was after the harvest was gathered in. The steam engine, a colossal machine, would arrive at the farm, presumably on contract, towing behind the engine drivers caravan. The machine had a large fly wheel at the side and to this was fastened a wide webbing belt which was placed on with a twist and then on to the threshing equipment. When the threshing was completed and the straw stacked there was enormous heaps of soft chaff and everyone in the row, (pronounced raw), would bring their tick, (forerunner of the mattress cover) and stuff it with chaff. It was some time before the 'mattress' flattened out in to reasonable dimensions but it was always comfortable.

At the haymaking, the youngest boy could be of use and the old quiet horse would have its collar on and fastened to the rope which hauled the grab with hay up to the people making the stook.

Then the horse would walk back lowering the grab at the same time. There was also the carrying of the oatmeal water out to the people in the hayfield, a delicious drink.

Towards the end of the year there was the tattie howking and whole families took part in this employment. As well as lifting the tatties they were carried to the side of the field where 'tattie pits' were made with the earth of the field and sealed in with straw. Payment was nearly always 2/6d for a day and that was considered good pay in the early 20s.

In the winter, I think it was 1925, there was quite a lot of snow and as you walked up the road you were walking in a tunnel with snow high on either side.

On one occasion the Grieve's daughter, Greta Simpson and myself were the only pupils to walk to Arniston School. When we got there, Miss Lumsden saw us and told us to go into the classroom where there was a huge coal fire burning. There was a peculiar order by the headmaster, who shall remain nameless, that no one was allowed to enter the classroom until the bell was tolled. We were in and the others who saw us in the room naturally came in out of the cold. Mr Mac came in and we were caught! We were told to line up and he began to punish with the 'tawse', (a leather strap used on the hands). Greta and I lined up with the others but Miss Lumsden, who was nearby, came over and told the man that we were there with her permission. I like to think that we would not have told him about her.

1926 and the General Strike. Scotland was at a standstill. The Rev. John Hall is at present resident in Kelso (1990's) and he was the minister in Gorebridge in 1926. He has told me that he was impressed with the 'spirit' of the people. He particularly remembers that when the strike was over, people had to pay one and a half weeks rent to make up for the rent that was not paid during the strike! There was also the question of being fed at school. The situation was chronic and beggars description. Poverty stared the mining areas in the face and but for the school feeding what a dire position the country would have been in. The troops had been called out and stood within the locked gates of the pits. I saw them standing with fixed bayonets and looking out at us, but they were never called to use force against the public. I believe my father mentioned at the time that it was just as well, because most of the soldiers were from mining communities themselves and that is one order that might never have been complied with.

It was the practise on the Saturday to issue rations for the weekend to school children. Tommy was not yet attending school and so I took him with me to receive the ration of two slices of white bread, a Scotch mince pie, and an oxo cube. There was one duty that had to be performed in the mines. The control of rising water. Without the huge turbine pumps kept in constant action there would have been no mines to return to, and therefore pumpmen had to be permitted to descend the pits and keep the pumps operative. My father was one of them and they were kept on relief duty until the end of the strike. While this was taking place we were allocated a house in Newtongrange and we moved there sometime in 1926–27.

For fuel I teamed up with an Irish boy and we used to spend the day in the woods with an axe and a small saw, cutting up the fallen or dead wood and in the evening the men-folk would come with 'trek carts' and carry the wood home.

The poverty was particularly illustrated in one manner by children going to school barefooted. On occasion when the weather was cold, many boys came to school wearing their mother's shoes.

I do not know what the strike achieved but I do know that if a miner could take home £1.10 shillings, clear offtakes, he considered himself in the money. Towards the end of the 20's there may have been slight improvement and this continued into the 30's. I remember one occasion when my father came in with a week's wages of £1.00 and handed it to my mother. Coal and rent had been taken at the same time.

From the age of 10 I started to work. My first job was selling morning rolls for Charley Smith the Pole. Charlie was always referred to as the 'Pole' having come from Poland to live in Scotland. His bakehouse was at the foot of Newtongrange in Roman's Buildings and I had to be up at 5.30am to get down in time for the early deliveries in the village. It was very early, but the bakehouse was lovely and warm, the rolls were fresh and hot and while waiting for them to be ready, the brown sugar tasted good. On Saturday, Charlie would make pastries and pies and at three in the afternoon I would go out with a large basketful, to sell them in the village. My commission was three half-pence in the shilling.

I decided to increase my income by challenging for a 'bundle' of evening newspapers at the Railway Station. These consisted of a pink and a green and having grabbed a bundle, you took them to the newsagent and he would check the bundle and you were off. To the Miners Institute, the pubs, and where you could expect to see men waiting to learn the final scores or results of the days sporting events. Another three half-pennies in the shilling, it must have been the going rate. Now I was employed but not fully. The fruitmen used to come out from Edinburgh in their model 'T' Fords and go round the village shouting the quality of their produce. I was watching one man and he spent his time jumping in and out of his vehicle as he went from place to place. When a woman shouted an order to him he had to make it up and take it to her. I approached him and suggested that while he sold the fruit I would drive the car down the 'backs'. The back streets in Newtongrange were on an incline from the Colliery Railway down to the Main Street. 'Driving' was simply a releasing of the hand-brake and freewheeling, correcting the steering as you went.

The man agreed and I was on for 6d, the pay I would have received for humping 4 shillings worth of goods round in a basket. So, for Saturday afternoon, I sat and freewheeled. There was an additional benefit. As I got to know the man he taught me to drive. I must have been about 12 years of age and driving a Model 'T' in 1929-30 gave me something to talk about in the school debating society. Debating Society: at this moment in time such a title in the days that I am now writing about seems incongruous.

You will have noticed that the emphasis has been on making a living and very little said about education. But there was a man who came on the scene, a school teacher, a real teacher, Mr Wm. George Scott. A man who was to play a vital part in my life although I was not aware of it at the time.

He introduced the Debating Society and no doubt had to explain to us what that meant. He also took an interest in us and started to teach various subjects leading to the qualifying exams. They, but for him, could have been the end of me. No way was I prepared for such an important exam. Education until then had been an interruption of my 'work'. If it had not been compulsory I doubt if I would have been there at all. Perhaps that is too severe a statement against others at that time but Bill Scott was my great benefactor.

I did not pass the qualifying exam. This meant I was to be barred with all the other failures from a secondary education. Why, I shall never know, but Bill Scott said what amounted to, "No, not him, he goes forward". I did. Mr Scott's attitude was always 'forward'. "Never be one of the crowd, think, get out in front." Many years later during the Maria Hertog riots in Singapore when I was responsible for the rank and file within my own department, those words came back to me as they had done throughout the war. School teachers should be more aware of their influence on boys, especially when they, the teachers, are held in high regard.

End of day school. Now full-time work and nightschool.

Chapter Two

THE SECONDARY education did not last for long. My father's health broke yet again and procedure was instigated in accordance with the regulations of that time. Briefly, I was to leave school, being the oldest of the family and take up work. Subject to the condition that I would attend night school and complete all certificate examinations. And so, at 13 and a half, my formal schooling ended. I was given a job on the Pit Head of the Lady Victoria, coupling hutches after they had passed through the tumblers. I started on the Monday and was home on the Wednesday with a bashed finger. I learned not to stand on the wrong side of the hutches. I think my mother was more hurt than I was.

At 14 years of age I was then permitted to go 'doon the pit'. There was more money down below and down I went. It must have been about then I decided this was not for me. But I carried on for a few more years and got all the certificates that had been denied me at school. Late but it had been shown to me by Bill Scott just what education meant and oh, how right he was.

The lack of that early education was to cause me a rough passage in view of what I tackled later on, first in the Army and then at London University Entrance to the Colonial Service and finally at New College, Edinburgh. But I got there Bill and you lived to see it. Mr Scott accompanied by Mrs Scott attended my Ordination and Induction at Ballantrae, Ayrshire, in 1972. Mrs Scott had been one of the teachers at Newbattle School, *(nee Miss Gibb)*.

In 1976 Bill took part in my Installation to the Chair of Lodge Musjid-i-Suleman. I was the first man who had not served in Iran to become Master of that Lodge. You can see that Bill had a tremendous influence on my life and we were friends from the time he met me as a pupil until he died in 1990, when Pat and I attended his funeral at Edinburgh. But now I must continue with my mining experiences until I left to join the army. This had been my objective since childhood.

Lingerwood/Vogrie Collieries

MY VARIOUS JOBS 'doon the pit' were: 'on the air control doors', no.1. Heading haulage engine driver, haulage foot of no. 1 heading, haulage engine Taylor's and haulage for same contractor. Perhaps a brief description of these jobs may be of interest for it is my understanding that with the decline in the coal mining industry, these tasks will not be understood by readers in the years to come.

The air control doors were simply a pair of wooden doors fitted across the haulage way to ensure that the air proceeded in a clockwise way throughout the mine and were fitted at a point where there was a junction. The boy who was first employed on this task had to open the door when either the 'full rake' came down from the coal face or, when the empty 'rake' was being sent up to the coal face. If the door job appears to be a simple task, I think the second job of driving the haulage engine was a very responsible one and on looking back I am surprised that a teenage boy was allowed to perform the duties of engine driver.

I can report that the boy, whoever he was would be given the job to do, it was not 'advertised' in any way. All things even, it was a simple job for an intelligent person, but who ever heard of all things being even in an underground mine? The operation of the engine was controlled by a bell system. One to stop and two to start. There was one emergency signal 'bell six'. When that happened you stopped the engine as quickly as you could. I remember the brake system was far from good, two large pieces of a type of belting on either side of the drive wheel. To apply the brake, you had to release a steel shaft and to give extra weight in a hurry to stop you jumped up and threw your legs round the shaft. (I wonder what I weighed at 15 years of age?).

The haulage was an endless steel rope which was placed on the drive wheel of the engine by a few rounds of the rope. The rope would then proceed via the 'back balance' pulley, round, and then up towards the top of the heading where it went round another pulley and so back to the engine house.

The emergency signal of 'bell six' was strictly adhered to by all people underground. It could have been given for a lot of reasons and danger to whoever gave the signal was a first priority for consideration. Until the source of the signal was found the engine would not be restarted.

When the reason for the 'six' had been established and attended to, the person who had made the signal would then give the cancellation and the signal to start the engine again, (six followed by two). My next job was on the haulage and I was allowed to take this job by Hector Wilson who was the Haulage Contractor. This simply meant that I was stationed at the foot of the dook (incline) to clip the empties on to the rope and send them up to the coal face where they would be taken off by the man at the top of the dook.

As the full 'rakes' came down from the coal face, we would then send them down to the main haulage after securing them with a 'jock clip' which we fastened to the rear of the last hutch in the rake. This job lasted for a short period until the opportunity to perform a similar job, but better paid by the Contractor who was working 'Taylor's Face' came available.

This job had advantages which were not available on the haulage. By working for the coal face men, it meant that you were kept very busy chasing hutches, i.e. on the lookout for empties when your own supply was being used up and this enabled the face men to reach their 'darg' (target) of 10 hutches a shift. When the empties were in short supply for various reasons, the Contractor could not get the coal out and income was jeopardised. It paid to be a 'good haulage man'. The perks came usually on the back shift or when you got the opportunity to go out on the night shift. This would sometimes happen no doubt to make up the tonnage which might have been dropped during the week. On such occasions the Contractor would let us fill a hutch and we would receive a few extra shillings next pay-day. A shilling went a long way in 1933.

The method of getting the coal out and away from the coal face was by first a 'tail rope' which the miners would have pulled down when they took the empties to the 'face'. This was necessary because the haulage rope would not be close to the actual 'face'. When the rakes were ready in the Laigh Side and on the top side (lower and high sides of the coal face) there would be a series of signals to the haulageman and the hutches would be pulled up to the 'Monkey' which was situated on the haulage way.

'*The Monkey*' – This was a very important piece of equipment where inclines, some steep and even when just a slight incline was involved, where the transfer of hutches from one road to another was necessary. The 'Monkey' was shaped like a bar of steel with a shaped curve at the top of the bar which was very thick in dimension. The bar would have a hole bored through so that the 'Monkey' could be placed in the middle of the haulage-way and supported on a bolt which passed through the monkey allowing it to swing forward as the axles of the hutches struck the head of the 'monkey 'on their forward journey.

The 'monkey' was itself fixed in a very secure position and when the hutches were released to rest on the 'monkey', they were held

11

there until the haulageman could clip them on to the rope and send them away. It will be seen that the hutches could not run back because the 'monkey' was so situated to allow passage in one direction only. In addition to assisting the movement of hutches from the coal face on to the haulageways, they were also used on the main haulage ways, such as the main dook in the Lingerwood, for safety in preventing hutches from hurtling backwards if they became detached from the clip or coupling on the upward journey.

The Black Watch – During this period there was a lot of interruptions at work and to be out of work for strikes or whatever was going on at that time simply meant, no income. I was longing to get away to the army and now decided to act. It was on a Monday morning and as I went to the door my father asked me to take the dog for a walk. I said I would as soon as I came in and out I went to see Matt Graham. I needed my bus fare to get to the Edinburgh Recruiting Office and Matt was to be my 'bank'. I re-paid the shilling in the course of time.

The Recruiting Office performance will last in my memory until I am no more. The office was located in Cockburn Street, Edinburgh and the Recruiting Sergeant was of the 1914 waxed moustache type. As I entered he came towards me, dressed in a blue uniform, swagger stick under his arm and the moustache was sticking out at both ends, just like 'Old Bill' on the 1914 posters. The following dialogue went something like this:

> *Recruiting Sergeant:* "What do you want?."
> *Me:* "To join the Army."
> *R.S.:* "How old are you?."
> *Me:* "16".
> *R.S.:* "Get out of here and walk round the building."
> **(Scene 2)**
> *Recruiting Sergeant:* "What do you want?"
> *Me:* "To join the Army."
> *R.S.:* "How old are you?"
> *Me:* "18."
> *R.S.:* "That's better". Documents produced and signed where indicated.

I was then handed a Rail Warrant and money and I was on my way to Perth. I reported in at the Guard Room of the Black Watch Depot and discovered that I was now Private Fox, 2754411.

There were two other recruits and we were taken and issued with a knife, fork and spoon and a mug. From there we were directed to the dining room and as we set off in that direction we were suddenly interrupted by a small man who seemed to be having a seizure of some kind. He was shouting and waving his arms and it then dawned on us that we were the cause. When he came closer, it was now dusk, we could see that he was in uniform and had stripes on his arm. He glared at us and then gave a lecture on how we were to treat the square at all times. We were to stand up straight, hold our heads up and march across the square not . . . saunter. He also made derogatory remarks about our parentage, quite untrue.

I was in the Army! An awful lot seemed to happen in the next few weeks. As recruits we were in a barrack room somewhere above the Sergeant's mess and the Piper's room. There were soldiers in the room, with at least ten weeks seniority. We were suitably impressed. In the morning following our arrival, we had to appear at the side of the Drill Square while the parade was formed up.

No doubt, remembering the 'lecture' of how to cross the Square, I stood very stiff with my hands at my side and my fingers pointing *straight* down. The R.S.M. came along and had a look at us and reaching down, he took my hands and turned the fingers up in the approved military fashion. I had received my first lesson. We were taken and issued with kit and measured for kilts and the usual routine of preparing recruits to be soldiers and leaving Civy Street far behind. There was one immediate perk. There was a shoot on somewhere and the new recruits were to be beaters. It was good fun and we were supplied with sandwiches and bottled beer. I lost out on the beer, I hated it then and I still do. I was keen to let my aunt see me in the uniform of the Black Watch. She lived at Glenfarg some ten miles away.

One of the soldiers offered to loan me his uniform for the day and put me wise to how I must behave and what not to do when wearing the kilt.

I duly arrived at Blindwells, Glenfarg and knocked on the door. My aunt opened the door, took one look and gasped. When she recovered, I was taken in and as far as I can remember had a very good tea with the family. I got that visit in just in time. There would be no more Black Watch visits.

On the Monday morning a Sergeant came for me and said that the Colonel wanted me in his office. I went with him and as he started to march me in to the C.O.'s office he was told by the Colonel to take it easy, "That's only a boy you have there". I now learned that my father, one time Black Watch you will remember, had been up to see the Colonel and the result was that I was to be given a Rail Warrant and sent home. The Colonels final words were, "And when you ARE 18, I will be glad to have you here".

Stirling Castle

I LEFT PERTH and had made up my mind that I was not going home. I got off the train at Stirling and walked up to Stirling Castle to the Recruiting Office. I obviously thought that there would be one there and it also occurred to me to change my name. The records will show that there was a Champion Motor Cyclist at that time and so I borrowed his name, Stanley Wood.

After reporting in I was taken up to the Recruits room which was away at the top of the Castle. It was a formidable room and the feature that was strange to me was the windows. There were four sash frames, one behind the other, facing east I believe. Nothing much happened there for the following week and then one day a Sergeant came up to me and said that he knew my proper name. I have not mentioned earlier that I had been learning to play the pipes and while waiting I had been practising on the chanter.

Well, this Sergeant had come to make a deal, if I would agree to become a Piper he would see that I got in to the Regiment, otherwise I was out. I did not want to be in his Regiment and I did not like the bargain. I like to look back on the occasion as one where I have never liked being threatened or told what I couldn't do. Anyway, I was out and set off for home. I wonder what would have happened if I had gone to the Orderly Room for another Rail Warrant? As it was, part of the threat had been that if I left I would have to walk. I set off to walk and I seem to remember that I got a lift part of the way. I must have done because I was at the Waverley Station in the evening.

I was very fortunate on that occasion for a benefactor must have seen that I was very hungry and I was viewing the trains for Newtongrange, but how was I to get past the ticket collector?

The man asked me where I was going. I told him and added that I did not have the fare. As it happened it was late and there were no further trains that night to Newtongrange. I stayed the night in Edinburgh and on the Sunday morning I was taken home to 102 by this complete stranger, an Englishman. Divine providence? I have often wondered about him.

Meantime my mother was away looking for me in the north. My father was at work and I did not particularly want to meet him indoors. At an appropriate time I went to meet him as he came home from work, better in the open, more room for movement. I saw him in the distance, walking with his friend, Geordie MacLaren.

As I approached they both looked at me and then Geordie said goodnight to my father and walked on. Now what? Newtongrange, again. Nothing, absolutely nothing. I have never got over that meeting where I expected all sort of trouble. Instead, "You've come home boy, you will be hungry" and with that he placed his hand on my shoulder and I never ever heard another word from him about going away. He sent a telegram to my mother to come home and that was that. Looking back I am keenly aware that I must have caused concern at home and yet I also remember that I said I would go to the army. Anyway, it is history now.

I was accepted back and when I went to see my previous employer he said "Aye, start right away Geordie". My father was always referred to as Geordie, and it did not seem to matter that I might have a name of my own.

While the Contractor's name was Taylor, my immediate overseer was a man who was a human dynamo. Small of stature, not much over five feet, he was all go and what a worker. He was also a Jekyll and Hyde character. At work his continuous shout was for . . . "hutches". From time to time there would be a shortage of hutches for one reason or another and when there were no hutches there was no production of coal and then there was no income. Jocky Bowers was his name and when he was angry about slow delivery of hutches or, when hutches came off the rails, which they invariably did, necessitating the help of his miners to put them back on the 'road', the air was blue with language, nearly all adjectives with an occasional verb.

But to meet Jocky away from the work was quite another experience. He was quiet and gentle and considerate for the men who worked for him. That is how I remember him. It is with regret that I remember being told that he was killed by a runaway hutch! Aye, said he, "start right away". I went back to the Lingerwood and down to the haulage/tailrope once more. But I had held the nettle, I had walked across that square and the Colonel was waiting to welcome me back! Mining was now away from the General Strike situation and the early 20's poverty was behind us. But money was difficult to earn even by 'face men' and they were the best paid. Eight shillings for an eight hour shift producing ten tons of coal, loaded by shovel into the ubiquitous hutches and all the safety work that had to be carried out as the coal was extracted by pick and shovel. Haulagemen were lucky to get 5/6d a shift.

Vogrie, Gorebridge.

IN THE COURSE of time I heard that it was possible to earn between eight and nine shillings a shift at Vogrie. Vogrie was about two to three miles from Newtongrange, a very shallow pit and referred to as a 'tatty pit'.

But they were paying good money. I went up and saw one of the Leading Miners and got a job, drawing for him. But I had to keep the news from my father, he would not have allowed it. However, he found out, as he was bound to do and with a few choice words I was left to get on with it but without his blessing.

Drawing – This was the expression used for pulling or pushing hutches where there was no Haulage. At Vogrie there was next to nothing in the way of mechanical aids. Whereas at Lingerwood the Hutches were made of steel, at Vogrie they were made of wood and much smaller. The Coal Seam was very low and the roads leading in to and from the Coal Face were correspondingly low, allowing just enough room for the Tubs(as opposed to Hutch) to pass, the Drawer always bent double. It was agony and a perpetual sore in the middle of the Back which the wooden supporting Beams managed to knock on every shift. There were no crossings at the junctions with the rails on which the Tubs ran, only steel plates. You soon learned to judge and Slew your Tub so that you moved from one set of rails to the other via the steel plate. On arrival at the top of the Dook, (it was a steep one), the man there would place the hook of a steel rope in the tow bar and after a shout, push the full tub over the dook which resulted in an empty Tub being hauled up on the other end of the rope. There was a Main and Tail Engine to assist the Rake over the next incline and then the Bottom Road Drawers would take the Tubs out to the bottom from where they were winched up the shaft. The eight to nine shillings were earned. Getting to and from Vogrie had meant getting some form of transport and if my memory is right in this instance it was the 'Sammy' of my initial Gowkeshill days who came to my assistance.

Sammy presented me with a 'bike' and assured me that it 'was all right'. There were no mudguards, only one brake and it was on the slow stopping side. What I was being presented with was a frame, two wheels, one brake and pedals with chain. No lamp holder – and that was to be my costly error. But I paid Sammy the 2/6d that he was asking for the 'bicycle'. After that he and his brother and myself travelled to Vogrie and on the way home it was a joy, from Vogrie to Newtongrange it is almost freewheel all the way! I believe that on occasion we were given to singing as we returned from the back shift which would be somewhere in the region of 10 p.m.

The singing was not appreciated and on one particular evening the police were waiting at the Greenhall turning where you tried to slow down. I must have been more successful than either Sammy or Willie at stopping for I was caught and charged with 'riding a bicycle without a lamp'. The others had got clear away. What would my father say or *do* now? In due course the Summons arrived and I was called to appear at the Sheriff Court in Edinburgh. My father came with me. The plea was 'guilty'. The fine was *ten shillings*. My father paid it and again, *not a word from him!* Looking back I think he had a lot to teach and I was slow to learn.

Territorials/R.A. Coastel Battery

AT ABOUT THIS time I had been allowed by my father to join the Territorial Army and was now a gunner with the Coastal Battery who were stationed at Easter Road Barracks. Sammy and Willie were also gunners (the coast was safe!). The big advantage of being in the Terriers was that we got quite a few weekends away at Inch Keith Island for training and we were paid! It was for us a holiday. And then there was a summer camp where we went to a castle, which sadly is no more, Tynemouth Castle. Again we were paid. Life was beginning to look up, holidays and pay. I had been trained as a loading number which was either 3 or 5 and those coastal gun shells were heavy. I was not quite 18 and when the competitions were on. I was given the job of looking after the Battery Commanders Kit. That was again to prove beneficial. I had been a Private in the Black Watch and now I was Gunner in the Royal Artillery and I was about to make my final move in to the army. It is of interest to recall that the R.A. never bothered about the fact that I had been issued with a Regimental Number – the regular army made me keep the Black Watch number when I enlisted in August of 1935. There was one important occasion in either 1934 or 1935. The Duke and Duchess of York came to Edinburgh and our Territorial Unit was chosen to line the route in Lothian Road. My position was just above the entrance to the King's Stable road on the left hand side. I do not think we had rifles and there would not be any salute. We were not to know that on the day we were paying our respects to the future King and Queen.

And now that I am about to leave coal mining I want to refer to two separate incidents which left me with a great impression of the type of man that is the real miner.

Indeed, on the second occasion I am of the belief that it was the moment when I switched from being a boy to the status of becoming a man. I do believe there is such a moment in the lives of all of us, male and female.

The first occasion was at the Lingerwood Pit. A group of us had been what is termed in Mining language as 'Lying on', doing extra work when the others had gone home. We were all Haulagemen from No.1 and Carrington and presumably had been clearing a backlog of Hutches, When we reached the bottom of the Big Dook the Main Haulage was still running while the Bogies which conveyed the men to the Pit Bottom Level had stopped running until the beginning of the next Shift. Normally this would mean walking up the Bogie Road and it was quite a long and tiring walk, up a steep gradient all the way.

It was suggested that we should jump up on to the clip pulling the full Hutches and ride to the upper level. I was the youngest and I was to go first. We were already standing on a steep slope.

A man whose name I shall always remember, Walter McVites, (Wattie) stood up a bit from where I was and waited his turn for the next Hutch to arrive after I had passed. The Hutch came up and I must have looked at it and jumped placing both hands on the top of the Hutch BUT my feet slipped off the Clip Shaft and were being dragged under the Hutch. Wattie moved, his hand caught me by the collar and dragged me clear. He was a tall man, powerfully built and I owe him a great debt from that day. During the War I was very sorry to learn that Wattie had been interned in this country because he was a Lithuanian. I never met him again – I shall never forget him.

The second occasion was at the Vogrie Pit. I was drawing to Sandy Ramage and it was on the Back Shift. During the afternoon as I was taking the Tubs out to the Heading I heard this continual creaking of the timber supports and I mentioned it to Sandy when I returned with the Empty. No doubt there was a conversation and Sandy would more than likely have had his pipe going. Some time later, I had just returned to the Face with an empty, there was a loud noise and suddenly the timber supports began to give way. We were standing just in front of what was quite a low Coal Seam at the top of the road and looking towards the empty space which is called by Miners, the 'Boss'. (I think a brief explanation of this meaning will help the reader to understand better what I am about to write).

As the coal Face is advanced when the coal has been mined it is necessary to create Pillars. This task is a specialised one and nearly always carried out by the Night Shift 'Brushers'. The Pillars are erected at each side of the road wherein the rails are laid and packed tight to the roof.

Behind the Pillars a large space is left and it is into this space that the roof falls as the Face is taken forward. I do not know if this is a very good description but it will help to understand what Sandy and I were witnessing.

The noise increased and suddenly there were large slabs of stone, as big as a ceiling, crashing down in to the open space and as the stone continued to fall we huddled back against the Coal Face and waited. After a little while we were able to see that where the stone had fallen on the left of the Seam there was an opening leading in to the Airway. The original Road had gone and we were completely hemmed in except for that opening. Sandy spoke, "Right son, let's see how I am going to get you out of here" and we moved over to the opening. I was not very large nor for that matter was Sandy. I managed with his help to wriggle through and then turned round to help Sandy through the opening. We walked, crouching, down the airway and eventually met other men coming towards us. I do not know what happened after that but for me it was the signal to go and to go now. I never saw Sandy again and when I did go to Gorebridge when I was home on Leave, to look for him I was directed to a member of his family who was living at Arniston. I learned from her that Sandy had lived to a good age and had died at home. Today there is no sign of Vogrie but that memory will live with me. Before going in to the Army I must relate about my trip to Inverness on my Elswick Bicycle, sandwiches in the Carrier Bag and 6d in my pocket.

Newtongrange to Inverness – By Bicycle

I HAVE ALREADY mentioned that holidays from the Pits were in effect Idle Time, there was no such thing as 'Holiday Pay'.

I had this notion to go and visit my Grandmother who was then living at Ballifeary Road in Inverness. There was no question of travelling by Train or Bus, there simply was no money. I set off on the Friday evening from Newtongrange for Glenfarg where Aunty Katie was living at Blindwells. Blindwells is inland a few miles and on the top of a hill from Glenfarg. Travelling North you can leave Blindwells and in a short way down the road turn left, pass the Bein Inn, and away to Perth. I must have been between 16 and 17 years of age at the time and I was fit. Having spent the night at Aunty Kates, I set off early on the Saturday morning and made for Inverness where I arrived in the evening.

On the way I had met in with two other cyclists and as we pedalled along the rain came on, We each had yellow cycle capes and sou'westers and so we kept going. On arrival at Inverness I first called in at 61 and then took my two companions up to Bal na Gaig where the MacFarquhars had the Farm, they were allowed to use the Barn overnight and I returned to 61.

It was a memorable holiday. I enjoyed the Farm and Cousin Willie's company and during my stay The Royal Scot's Greys came to the Bught and put on a Musical Ride. Years later I had cause to remember that display. Willie unfortunately was killed at the beginning of the War. There were two Aunts at the Farm, Aunty Katy and Aunty Annie. Annie was the one I had most to do with and I remember her giving me TWO SHILLINGS to go and see the Musical Ride. It was a full week during which I heard from my Father asking if I was sure I could get home in one day? I did.

10th, June, 1935.

THAT WAS A great day, the long awaited 18th year and arrangements had to be made to leave home and enlist. My Father had never accepted that it was a good idea and there were some unhappy moments before I left. However, in the end, after I had been away for some time and with the idea that I would not be welcome back, I heard from my Father that he was looking forward to seeing me.

If enlisting in to the Black Watch had been a form of Comedy and my acceptance in to the Territorial Army appeared to be very casual the enlistment in to the Royal Corps of Signals was to be a much more serious event.

I left Newtongrange and reported to the recruiting office at Cockburn Street. The Staff were completely changed and there was a great deal more in the way of paper work. I had decided not to return to the Black Watch after learning how much better conditions and rates of pay were in the Royal Corps of Signals. I had been informed that education was part of the training and that you had an option of Trade, e.g. Wireless Operator which could be used when you left the Army. I was most interested in becoming a Wireless Operator and the uniform had its own appeal.

After completing the formalities in the Recruiting Office which had included a Medical Examination and eye test I was given a jolt; I would not be proceeding to the Royal Signals Depot at Catterick Camp until the following Saturday, one week away. I was probably without money at the time and had left home thinking I was on my way so no need for return. What was I to do now.? The benefit I have earlier referred to in my Territorial Service came to my rescue now. The Battery Commander of the Coastal R.A., whose Kit had been made my responsibility during the Competition period at Tynemouth

Castle, lived out at Newington, No. 12 I remember, and so I decided to go out and see him and seek his advice. I walked from Cockburn Street to Newington and found the house, but there was no response to the door bell. I waited and must have walked round for some time and then returned to the house. Still nobody in and it was now dark. I sheltered at the foot of the garden and waited. Eventually Major Bill Sivewright arrived and I made my presence known.

To say that he was surprised would, I think, be to put it mildly and yet I can not remember any untoward expression of any kind.

There would have been a discussion and I am sure that I would have said as quickly as possible that I had joined the Army in the Royal Corps of Signals. Whatever took place Bill took me in to the House and allowed me to stay there until I set off for Catterick Camp on the following Saturday. That was one of the kindest acts that ever came my way. It was a lovely large house and I was to learn that there were servants in the house but had obviously been off for the weekend. They too made me welcome.

The Sivewright family were in the Printing Business which I believe was located just off the High Street below the Tron Kirk.

I happened to go in to Patrick Thomsons for Lunch while attending New College one day and in walked Bill! I made my presence known once again and we had a long chat. Much water had passed beneath the Bridge since the first occasion but it was still the same river.

I left Edinburgh on the Saturday which I believe was the 10th., of August, it is the day that my records state I had enlisted and travelled to Darlington where I changed to a Train for Richmond and then by Bus to the Depot at Catterick Camp. On arrival I reported to the Guard Room and from there was taken to the reception Barrack Room for new arrivals. This room was under the charge of a man with long service and who went under the unlikely name of 'Hitler'. His first words, (about the only ones that I remember him uttering) were, "In the Army on a Saturday you are either in bed or out of Barracks". A strange statement but the point was taken. I had arrived and discovered that I was one of twenty two new arrivals. I also realised that there was a great difference from Perth. We were shown where the Dining Hall was and told to stay in Barracks. There would be an N.C.O. coming to collect us on the Monday morning and until then we were to stay PUT. We stayed.

Sunday was a great day and started off with bacon and egg. There was a Dinner Time and in the afternoon we went for Tea, fresh butter, fruit cake, in addition to the bread. It was quite an experience for me and I don't think that I was alone in my appreciation.

Monday came and we were all ready but I can say now that we

were not prepared for what was about to happen. We were 'marched' to the School building and entered a large Class Room where we were told to occupy a desk, one to a desk.

A Senior man entered and introduced himself as a Warrant Officer from the Army Education Department. We were to spend the rest of the day answering examination questions. I wish I could relate the re-action to this situation but I fear that it is lost in the realms of history. There was English, Arithmetic, Geography, Essay writing and General Intelligence, I think that was all and the Warrant Officer invigilated the lot.

If ever I had occasion to be grateful to my School Master, Bill Scott, it was then. You will remember how he had taken us in hand and how later I had been encouraged to attend Night-School and sit all the normal papers. This now, was in fact to be a re-run.

The result was uncanny, and for obvious reasons, I never forgot the name of Alec Cowan, a recruit from Glasgow. Out of the twenty two new arrivals only TWO were retained in the Royal Corps of Signals, the others were posted away to other units. Those retained were, Alec Cowan and Dudley Fox, both Scots, the others were all English. The Royal Corps of Signals Depot Catterick Camp with all the initial requirements attended to, Health, Education, and the despatch of all civilian clothing we were now Signalmen not Privates and we were moved to another Barrack Room which was under the Charge of a Corporal who had seen service on the North West Frontier of India. It is of interest to note that this was 1935 and that the Royal Corps of Signals had been formed as a Corps from the Royal Engineers in 1922. The Motto of the R.C. of S. is 'THROUGH'. A wonderful word at all times where communication is involved, especially when the lives of Units in action are dependent on support and the Commanders in the Field wish to know how the Battle is proceeding. In retrospect I understand more fully now why they were so careful in the selection of recruits. The Corporal was quiet and helpful, a mature soldier.

We were 'Taken' around under the guidance of this N.C.O. and issued with all sorts of kit and uniform. I don't think much of it fitted very well except the boots of which there were two pairs.

The Shirts and underwear came in sets of three, "One on, one in the wash and one on the kit shelf'. We were then taken to the Tailor and measured and the Tunics and the Breeches were brought in to due form. The main issue to recruits in the first instance was their 'Canvas' and Forage Cap with Cap Badge. The recruit spent quite some time waiting to be placed in a training squad during which time all fatigues, (Domestic duties) were carried out by the Recruits.

Spud bashing was the privilege of the men on 'Jankers', (Punishment) but if the unit was a well behaved one and therefore no 'Janker Wallahs', the recruits performed this essential task.

As I have said, all civilian clothing had been sent 'Home' or wherever they decided home was and the only clothing we had was Canvas which consisted of a Jacket and Trousers. Today's equivalent would be the ubiquitous Denim, which would have been an improvement. So, with this brown 'Canvas' jacket fastened with brass buttons which were held on by a leather boot-lace threaded through tho brass rings that were on the inside, brown 'Canvas' slacks and Army issue boots topped off with the Forage Cap, it was too late to change your mind about 'Joining' – You were in.

Hopefully, the Tailors would succeed in moulding the uniform to suit the body it was meant for, as it turned out, we need not have worried, the army is just as keen as the individual that they should look smart.

In the course of a few weeks sufficient recruits had arrived and been received and we were formed in to No. 5 Intake or, as the Order put it , we were now N0.5 'SQUAD' and our Instructor for the next 14 weeks was to be one of the very best and smartest N.C.O.'s I have ever known, Sergeant Spierpoint. He had also served on the North West Frontier and must have had a very good record for promotion in the R.C.S. was slow; to make Corporal in 12 years was the normal rate and our Sergeant had just 12 years.

Before moving to our Squad Room there was one last amusing incident when Alec Cowan and I were on the Parade Ground one morning waiting to be allotted fatigues. We were standing at the top end of the Square near to the Company Offices when this 'Old Type Soldier' N.C.O., came along and inspected us as to turnout.

We were in trouble, "Why had we not Shaved?".

I omitted to say that when we were issued with kit, the Safety Razor was smothered in vaseline, wrapped in some kind of protective type paper. As I was not yet shaving, the razor was as it had been on the day of issue. We were ordered to leave the Parade Ground and reappear in FIVE MINUTES properly shaved! We left at the double all the way to the Barrack Room. I said to Cowan, "There is no way that I can shave and be back in five minutes, my razor is covered in grease." "So is mine", replied Alec," but never mind, come on, we will be back in time, he wont know the difference", and with that we ran all the way back and stood to attention. Along comes the N.C.O., looked at us and remarked, "That's Better". Lesson N0.1 had been learned, obey do not explain.

It was years later while walking along the street in Cairo that I met

Alec, we had gone our different ways after the Depot training, he was a Sergeant and I was then, Lieutenant. We must have continued to learn.

The Depot – Catterick Camp

THE INITIAL Drill Training began and from that moment I loved it.

After life with my Father, Army Discipline was, 'A piece of Cake'. We were on Parade from 6 a.m. every day except Sunday.

Sunday would be Church Parade. I should say that 6 a.m. was Reveille and 10 p.m. was lights out. In between every hour was accounted for. The training was mainly Drill with P.T. once a day;. then we had weapon training as progress was made, and the first thing we were taught about a rifle was, that we were always to look upon it as our best friend! Then all parts were explained, how it was to be cleaned and finally, how to aim. The last exercise was taken very seriously. The Instructor had a small piece of equipment which was simply a piece of steel wire with a round metal plate approximately 2 inches across. In the middle of the plate which was fashioned as a Target, there was a small hole. The recruit would be on the ground in the firing position opposite the Instructor. The Instructor would then put the 'Target' to his eye and the recruit would aim at the Target.

This lesson was to teach him how to align the tip of the Foresight in the centre of the 'U' of the Backsight and level with the shoulders of the Backsight.

Although Live Ammunition had not been issued to recruits at this stage, the safety procedure was strictly adhered to and it was 'Drummed' in that a weapon was never to be pointed towards another soldier at any time. In the case of training therefore, it was made certain that there was not 'One up the Spout'! The inspection of Arms and Bayonet Fighting are the only other times when the rifle is deliberately pointed towards another soldier during training.

As the weeks passed we became more proficient especially at Drill and we were then taught Map Reading and how to use a Compass.

Education continued on certain evenings and I remember that a Chaplain attended and used to ask us questions on different subjects. On one occasion he asked me why it was necessary to polish Brass buttons so often, "Why, do you have this Shining Parade every evening?". I have no recollection what I said in reply but in fact I realise now that it was essential that every type of civilian entering the Army would have to be taught what was required and the Depot Training is where we would have to learn at the evening Shining Parade, especially the 'Spit & Polish' on the leather work. I do not remember hearing much about religion at those evening classes.

All the Drill Instructors had been through the Course conducted by the Guards and they were smart. Although the Royal Corps of Signals are a Specialist Unit they took their Drill seriously as in fact they did all other duties in addition to their main purpose which was to supply Communication systems for the whole of the Army. So every Wednesday and Saturday morning the Regimental Band was on Parade and it was absolutely grand to march to the Music and of course there are certain movements such as General Salute which have to be taught and practised.

Here again I must relate an incident that took place while the Band was on Parade, I was about to take my first 'Command'. It happened like this. Sgt. Speirpoint was walking behind the Squad and as we were approaching the area where the Band was playing, he gave a command which was not heard by the front half of the Squad. Consequently, the front half continued while the rear half did a right turn away from the Band. "Fox ! take charge and bring them round". I have said how I loved the drill and I had become keen about efficiency on parade. I brought them round and in the meantime the Sgt. brought the rear Half back and we were once more a squad.

There was a sequel to this incident which reared its head again at the end of our Depot Training. As I have said, I had been re-allocated my Black Watch Regimental Number, (2754411) and although I had never placed one foot on the Drill Square at Perth it was held that I was good on the Square at Catterick because of my earlier EXPERIENCE! In addition to the many parts of our recruit training I was also in the Boxing Team representing No.5 Squad and took part in a number of bouts in the 'Blood Tub' which was at the bottom of the Depot on the left hand side.

For me it was a miserable place. The roof was low, the boxing ring was raised well above floor level and the cigarette smoke simply hung like a cloud immediately above the ring, breathing was difficult. Those of us who were in the team took it seriously and would get out of bed just after 5 a.m. and go training round the triangle which was on the road running past the Depot, and round in a loop back to the Barracks. After leaving the Depot the only other time I took part in boxing was on Board the S.S. Rawalpindi en route to Hong Kong. There was encouragement to continue invariably from people who had never taken part in any sport.

The twelfth week of training arrived and now we knew we were on our way, we were permitted to 'Put up our Dogs'. This meant that we could now wear our collar badges on either side of our collar and we could go out at the weekend on a Pass which reminded us that we had to be back inside Barracks by 2359 hrs. (There was no midnight in the language of those days).

Depot Training ended after Fourteen Weeks and we were posted to the company of our choice for Training in the particular Trade e.g. Operator Signals – or Mounted Wing for Linesmen – or 'Don' Company for Despatch Riders. Operators went to 'Eddie' Company.

'F' Company was the Boys Company and in addition there was The School of Signals which catered for members of Army Units and special Training.

At the end of the Depot Training there was the Passing Out Parade and the Commandant with others would attend the demonstration of Drill which was conducted by our own Drill Instructor, in our case of course, Sgt. Spierpoint. The Parade was held on the Bottom Square. I shall always remember that Parade.

There was a presentation of the Commandants Whip to the smartest man on parade. Johnny Graham was the recipient and a grand chap he was. Quiet and thorough. I was informed that my service with the Black Watch *eliminated me from consideration.* But I did enjoy the Depot and now we were on our way to learn more about communications, of all sorts.

1935-36 Eddie Company

On leaving the Depot, life changed completely. We were no longer Recruits, at least, not in our own eyes. With a few exceptions, Military Life as one would imagine it to be, happened in small doses; early morning Roll Call, Company Parades, Guard Mounting and then on the Wednesday afternoon there was compulsory sport.

At the time I was in Catterick Camp there was a project in force called "The Big Dig" and on the Thursday afternoon I believe everybody, of all ranks, had to report to the area for the purpose of clearing the surface of stones. Of Fatigues, I have no memory.

With the exception of what I have mentioned above the rest of our time was spent in the Lecture rooms, the technical rooms where we were taught the elementary principles of electricity and magnetism and thereafter how to trace circuits. There was the primary and secondary circuits of the telephone; the complex circuits of the Simplex and Duplex Board. These we were taught to trace using different coloured pencils and then explain their working. The early morning was nearly always given to learning Morse Code and practising the rhythm of the Key. This was not easy and many men failed in the long run to be competent operators although they knew the Morse Code.

There was also out-door Training with Wireless Sets, the No.1 set was the basic and with it we were taught all about Frequencies and Tuning. We also learned that the speed of sound and the speed of electricity was important to understand in connection with Radio Broadcasting. (Electricity: 186,000 miles per second; Sound: 720 miles per second). The test question was if a man was standing within earshot and you spoke in to a Microphone, who would hear you first, the man in the room or the person receiving on the Wireless Set? The other means of communication was by Aldis Lamp, Heliograph and Flag (Morse not Semaphore). I believe that I have got this right and as Training progressed we were taken out on to the Moors for exercises. I have no recollection of any major manoeuvres with other units at Catterick but we did have very extensive practice with all the various types of communication available at that time.

There was also the message pad and here there was important training required for although I am sure as Trainees we did not appreciate the need for the recipient to know where the message was going after he had received it, i.e. by other means of communication, it was in fact one of the most important parts of the Training. The number of carbons required, the pencil to be sharpened at both ends and more than one to be instantly available. I doubt very much if we recruits realised that the day would come when we would be on duty in Signal Offices at all levels of Command. It was never emphasised in this Basic Training and I expect that our minds would be concerned with the Field Work.

But this basic Training worked as I was to know within the next five years. In addition to our Training as Operators Signals, Sport was of the essence and we were encouraged to take part in every kind that you can mention. Cross country running was a great favourite and if you could not run very fast it really did not matter.

The thing to do was to complete the Course as quickly as you could; some of us were quick and some displayed stamina; I could run for ages. Rugby was Royal Signals Strength. Army Units seemed to specialise and Rugby was our's. During our Training at Eddie Company it was the custom to share the Guard Duty with Don Company, The Mounted Wing being on the bottom side of the Depot and quite some way from where we were located. My lasting memory of those 'Guards' is that when they were paraded for inspection there was always an extra man on Parade. The inspection was then carried out by the Duty Officer and the Regimental Duty N.C.O's. When it was decided which of the Guard was the best turned out and smartest man on parade he was called out by number and told to "Fall out". It was a great Order to receive, it meant that the chosen man was now

'The Commandant's Orderly' and as such he did not do sentry duty, slept in his own bed ALL NIGHT and, carried out message duty, if required, on a Bicycle. Out of eight Guard Mounting Parades I was Commandants Orderly Five times. Not quite sure what happened on the other three occasions. It was now 1936 and the day of reckoning had arrived. The Pillow Fighting when we had caused a certain amount of Trivial boisterous damage which was paid for by surrendering our Half Day and scrubbing the Mess Hall floor, on our knees, from end to end.

I remember the Company Sergeant Major very well. the Squad were on Parade, in two lines. The C.S.M. gave the order; "All those responsible for the damage in the Barrack Room, take one step out of the ranks!". The whole of the Front Rank stepped forward – the Rear Rank took one step to the Rear. There was a moments silence.(C.S.M.) "Mutiny is it – right, you lot will not be seen walking anywhere, at any time, for the next week, at all times you will move at the Double and when not on Fatigues you will stay in the Barrack Room". (That was when we had to scrub the Mess Hall Floor). But we survived and it brings back happy memories.

There was one incident – a man, much taller than me, six foot something, I remember his name, but let it go. He reported us for something or other and I told him what he was. I ended up with a Black Eye and carried the scar for some time. I just could not reach him!! The Day of reckoning – Exams – Practical Tests, reading the Sounder, the flag messages, the Heliograph, Tuning the No.1 Set and the Theory. Those of us who passed were now 'OPERATOR SIGNALS B.111'. And we got extra Pay, that had been my incentive for joining the R.C. of S.

Talking of Pay; my family were better off with me being in the Army. They did not have to feed or clothe me, nor supply accommodation with heating or lighting and from the day I joined until I was Commissioned there was an allotment paid to my Mother every week. And I have to state that was the same for many of my soldier brethren.

Next we were Posted to various Divisions and I went to the 3rd Div. Signals at Bulford. It was a Mounted Unit and very Dull. We spent nearly all our time cleaning stables and horses or going on Grazing Picquet. And there was Stable Guard, but no Commandants Orderly.

There was the National Crisis in 1936 when the Prince of Wales let it be known that he wished to marry the American Woman, Wallis Simpson. History contains the details of this sorry episode and time was to prove that in so far as the Crown was concerned, Divine

Providence was at work.

When not on duty with the horses we spent some time at the week-ends going to garrison Dances and attending sporting fixtures at Boscombe Downs. There was little done in the short time I was there in the way of Training. The most outstanding event that comes to mind was when a number of horses belonging to the Royal Artillery had thrown their Riders out in the country and came running in to our stables. The Senior types in our Unit were quick to seize the opportunity of putting one over the Gunners. I could not ride in those days nor indeed could many others of my time. We were selected to Mount while the horses were held and then we were led to the Gunners Stables where the horses were handed over without a word. It was obvious to all that the riders were recruits without any riding experience.

Over-seas Postings – That did cause a thrill and we were soon at the Notice Board looking anxiously for our name and the country to where we were posted. Most of the Unit were destined for India and that was received with many groans, India was a Five Year Station. I found my own name and was greatly surprised to see that I had been posted to a 'Choice Station', Hong Kong Signal Company. I seem to remember that there was only some thirty two people at Hong Kong before we arrived. I was to learn much at Hong Kong and to obtain experience which stood me in good stead in the near future. The standard of Royal Corps of Signals men was high and noticeably many of the Operators were Ex Boys from 'F' Company, I shall refer to the nature of duties we were to be called upon to perform but first I must give an account of the preparations and journey from Southampton to Hong Kong.

On the Posting Orders there were instructions of what we had to do; Inoculations, Check up on Vaccination, drawing over-seas kit (tropical)and arranging to go on Embarkation Leave which was quite liberal. We were busy and, for me, an important time. My Father had let me know that I would be welcome at home. I travelled to Newton Grange and my Father expressed his surprise at the Notes I had with me for study. It was not the type of Army he had known. I thoroughly enjoyed my Leave and then returned to Bulford to join the Draft and proceed to Board the Ship. That was the greatest surprise of all. No stuffy cramped Trooper with Hammocks for a bed – we were embarked on a P.&O. Liner, in Second Class Cabins – S.S. Rawalpindi (Now of Historical Heroism during the War). We were on our way. Much in the way of Deck Sport and my final appearance in a Boxing Ring. There was a bigger fight on the horizon.

The beginning of the Voyage to join the Hong Kong Signal

Company, with the exception of a serious family intervention towards the end of 1938, was also the unknown beginning of my departure from the Status Quo and movement into the ranks of responsibility. I am unable to explain how it happened, I am now, and I am quite sure that I was then, surprised that from my earlier background which bordered on deprivation and late development in education, I should have been singled out for advancement in the Army. I certainly never applied personally for advancement although I did take a great pride in the Army and in all that I was called upon to do.

S.S. Rawalpindi moved away from Southampton and we made our way towards the Mediterranean en route to Hong Kong.

The memory of that voyage is a lasting memory and what a change from my earlier way of life. Being a civilian Liner the food was of a high quality and much more than we, as Soldiers, were used to receive. It was of course, beyond anything that I had ever known as a child. We had next to nothing to do as Military Personnel and spent most of the time engaged in sport, Deck competitions, Boxing Matches, and making up concert parties in the evening, it certainly was a new way of life. I remember that the 2nd Class Deckspace was separated by a ships rail across the Deck and there were evenings when we could sit near or lean on the Rail and watch the 1st. Class passengers dancing. I also remember that although the Rail was across the Deck, the people on the 1st Class side were friendly.

We called in at Gibraltar and then at Marseilles and here I have a report to make in this year 1990 in view of the current situation with the modern Football Fans not only in England and Scotland, but World-wide. "Disgraceful", and "It never happened like that in my time", and so on.

True, the present day interpretation of Sport and Sportsmanship has altered; the absence of noise at a cricket match or when a place kick is being taken at Rugby has gone. But there was another side to Football even in 1936 and later.

At Marseilles it was decided to select a ships team and we were to play a match against a French Army Team. We collected the kit required and went ashore to the ground. On coming out of the Dressing Room we were to receive a shock. All the way round the Ground, standing on the Touchline, were ARMED FRENCH TROOPS, Fixed Bayonets, one soldier facing inwards, one facing outwards, all the way round. I was playing in the Outside Right position as it was called in those days, I have never forgotten that experience. I do not remember the score but I do remember the troops were wearing Berets, Green I believe with a Plume.

Nowadays they have steel fences – everywhere; but this is 1990!

Disgraceful – It Never happened – It did!!!

Next Port of Call – Port Said

MARSEILLES HAD proved to be an interesting Port and it was generally understood to be a Communist Stronghold and now we were under way to Port Said. The Mediterranean can be very rough as I was to learn at first hand on another occasion but on this first voyage I remember it as smooth, warm and sunny. When we arrived at Port Said we tied up alongside the main wharf and could almost walk straight in to a huge Departmental Store. There was the usual offer of all sorts of haberdashery and Egyptian leather goods. In addition there was the 'Bum Boats' selling their wares from the sea-side of the Rawalpindi and passing them up to the prospective purchasers in a basket which was attached to a rope. Then we had the 'Golly Golly Man' who came aboard and entertained us with his magic, his main act being to produce live day old chickens from the passenger children's clothing. This was an act that persisted for years afterwards and was witnessed by my own family in the '50s when we were travelling on Leave from Singapore.

It was uncanny the number of young people at Port Said that claimed their name was McKay or, McTavish indeed the full range of Macs. The answer given by the troops on board was that the Scots Guards had been as far as Egypt on 'Foreign Service'. There was an underlying reason for this dubious answer but it gave amusement for the time being. There was another act of entertainment which I have not seen performed any where else.

Young men would call for attention and claim that they were going to dive under the ship and come up on the other side. This was accepted and as they dived, passengers would hasten to the opposite side of the Ship and sure enough, the young men came up on that side. There was no question of them having swam round the stern or the bows, they did dive under the Ship.

Their reward was coins thrown by the passengers in to baskets or rowing boats manned by the Diver's friends.

While we were at Port Said an Italian Troopship arrived from the Suez end of the Canal most likely from Abbasinia and they were given a noisy welcome from those on board the Rawalpindi. I doubt if they understood any of the Banter or the call that "They were going the wrong way", a British call between our Troop-ships when they met in Port in similar circumstances. What I do remember is that they seemed to be packed on the deck, not much room for them to move about and they were accompanied by Camels and other livestock. It was probable that they were not on their way to Italy, but along the Coast to Libya. Soon we left to enter the Canal and steam slowly down to Suez, a distance of some 99 miles. Our next stop was to be Aden and I was reminded of the Pipe Tune, 'The Barren Rocks of Aden'. When I was learning to play that Tune I never thought that I would actually see the place. As we approached it did look very Barren and there were fuelling points scattered round the Port to accommodate Shipping.

I must point out that travelling on a Civilian Liner we had all the privileges of the Civilian Passengers when it came to going ashore and this was made easy by the Ship's Agents who came alongside with there Launches and ferried us to the Dock-side. I have many photographs in an Album of this first call at Aden and of course the Camel is predominant in all of them. Aden is, or was, a fascinating place during the period when it was under the British Crown. To see anything resembling *green* was cause for comment, it seemed that there was nothing but sand and again sand. I did not eat or drink anything ashore and perhaps we had been warned not to risk 'Gippy Tummy'. We bought film for the camera,(I had a small Box Type which I had received for saving Daily Express consecutive serial numbers.) I have a photograph of 'Hell's Gates' in the album which I was fortunate to take as we were passing in the vicinity at Sunset, in the Red Sea.

From Aden we set sail for Karachi and it was during this crossing that I took part in my last appearance in the Boxing Ring. It must have impressed many people for I was to hear it referred to several times after we arrived at Hong Kong but it is not a 'Sport' I have any time for, It had been part of our Depot Training and that was that.

Again in Karachi and later at Bombay I have several Photographs in an album. My memories of both places is that they were much the same, crowded in the streets and dirty but, in the open spaces, for example, at Bombay, they were lovely and picturesque. Nothing of any importance took place and we spent our time ashore sightseeing. It occurs to me that we would not have been able to afford to enter any of the places offering food or drink or entertainment.

We arrived at Colombo, Ceylon after calling in at Bombay and that was a completely different experience. The memory that comes back to me is the extraordinary situation regarding their cars and the absence of women. The cars were all tourer type with the hoods folded back and the cloth covers on the seats were spotless white. There was ample room in the back seat for three people to sit side by side and then two in the front.

Women – Girls, not that we were looking for any, there were none to be seen on the street or in the shops, anywhere. It was very odd and their absence focused the realisation that they were missing. The situation changed dramatically during the next twenty years when Ceylon was the first country to have a woman Prime Minister! Next Penang, of which I remember very little, I think it was one of those in and out calls as we were due to stay at Singapore for one or two days. Destiny is peculiar, Penang was going to play a very important part in my life just Twelve years later. But for now we just sailed on. Singapore was to play a major part in my life- I will come to that.

Singapore

Magnificent! We were made welcome by resident Army units; football matches were arranged and R.C. of S. Personnel came to see us. Perhaps, with hindsight, it was the Ship they came to see! In addition to the sporting activities we were as usual given shore leave and we went all over the Town, It was easy to do because the Ship was tied up along side and it is a very short walk from the Docks in to the City.

There was one very interesting and in a way, amusing scene for all of us. As we walked in to the City we passed a number of Traffic Policemen on Point duty. Nothing funny or extraordinary about that except, they did not control the traffic with *their arms!* Instead they had what looked like a Bamboo plaited branch fixed across their shoulders and all they did was turn from side to side. As I write this account I realise that the place of duty must have been a simple Cross Roads. You can imagine the confusion at junctions and slip roads if that system was in operation today.

We were sorry to leave Singapore. It was, without question, the most interesting Port of call since leaving Southampton and we had seen quite a bit during the Ship's stay in Port. At last we were on our way to our destination, Hong Kong, and preparation for landing was soon in hand. As we were a small Draft the details were not as many as they would have been on a Trooper and we were now anxiously waiting for our first sighting of Hong Kong.

The approach to Hong Kong Harbour from the China Sea is on the Port Side and the Ship glides in between Lyemun Point and the Mainland. There is steady progress for quite a way and eventually the Ship arrives off Kowloon where she is manoeuvred alongside the Jetty. There was no landing of civilian craft on the Hong Kong Island itself. That is, Liner Craft. The Royal Naval Dockyard was adjacent to Wanchai and had Naval Barracks at Stonecutters, a small island, just past the Liner Jetties. The Star Ferries operated from the promontory of Kowloon towards Hong Kong less than a mile across, but the Landing Jetties for the Ocean Liners protruded from the side of Kowloon in regulated spacing.

At last we were Docked and as it turned out, the landing Jetties (Or Landing Stage may be a better description) was to our advantage for the Barracks were in Kowloon at Nathan Road. Whitfield Barracks contained a small Garrison; There was a small Military Hospital and to the North of R.C. of S the Kumoan Rifles – the Hong Kong and Singapore Royal Artillery and supporting arms were billeted. R.C. of S. had just two blocks of barracks, which held everything, accommodation, Mess Rooms, Sergeants Mess, Stores, Armoury, NAAFI, Dhoby and Ablutions.

We must have been, at that time, the smallest Unit in Hong Kong. We were shortly to take on International Duties.

Before leaving the description of what was in Whitfield Barracks I must mention the Isolation Hospital. This Isolation Hospital catered for all troops on the Kowloon side and may have taken patients from the Island. Discipline!!! There was an order that no one in the hospital could leave the precincts of the Hospital without proper authority nor; could any person visit the Patients without a Pass. The hospital was cut off from the rest of the Barracks, not with a six foot fence, nor a high wooden railing, in fact nothing above ground level at all. The boundary was marked out on the ground by a wide white painted line, perhaps six inches in width, all round the Hospital Building. I have seen men talking to each other from either side of the line but to my knowledge, that line was never crossed illegally.

And now I must explain what was at Whitfield Barracks for The Royal Corps of Signals. Having described the two Blocks where we had our being when not engaged in Sport or on Duty I now move to West Point which was at the top end of the 'Garrison' and where there was a Massive Transmitter. The area also contained lecture rooms and the Office and workshop of the Foreman of Signals who was referred to as "C.Q.M.S. Foreman of Signals", and our man was "Yorkie". Our West Point has no connection with that other place. Adjacent to our accommodation we had a Tennis Court and most of the men played, indeed some learned to play there and became very proficient in local tournaments. The other Sports that H.K. Signals were renowned for were Hockey and Water Polo. It was quite remarkable that our Water Polo Team were top year after year and some of our men used to go to Macau, the Portuguese settlement, for the Annual Tournament of Hockey. As I have said, we were a small detachment and carried no unnecessary manpower. There were three Despatch Riders, a Line

Section and the remainder were made up of Operator Signals, Technicians and admin. personnel. We were all concerned with our respective duties, mainly on Hong Kong Island. The D.R.'s and Linesmen were in daily touch with Lyemun Point and of course where-ever they might be needed, but that was their main area.

The Army Headquarters was located on what was named, "Seven and Sixpenny Hill". To get there we had to cross the harbour and walk from the Star Ferry terminal along to the Y.W.C.A. and then up a slight incline until we reached the Signal Office in the Main Building. The 24 hours was broken in to 'Reliefs' and when going on night duty or returning to Kowloon, if there was no Star Ferry, we used what was called a "Walla Walla Boat".

I must mention the Y.M.C.A. in Kowloon. That was where the Water Polo Matches took place and it was also the place where most of us learned to swim, including myself. That describes the area in which we had to work and play. Next the work.

Chapter Three

A S YOU ARE aware our new arrival meant that the Unit was faced with a draft of recruit operator signals, with very little practise of operating and completely ignorant of what was expected at Hong Kong. There was one N.C.O. there and although I have refrained from mentioning names I have no hesitation in referring to L/Cpl. George Cox. Looking back to those days it seems incredible and yet he succeeded in shaping us in to a useful and efficient unit.

We spent quite a number of hours at West Point practising Key work and learning a very practical rhythm. What had been accepted in the U.K. was now a different matter. Operating and receiving was bedevilled in those days with what was referred to as 'Xs', (Atmospherics). Although the Transmitters were on Crystal Controlled Frequencies there were occasions when the signal would practically disappear or be so faint that it was not truly recognisable. It was then that experience counted and the operators at Hong Kong, when we arrived, were in a different league. George Cox was among the Elite.

With practise and procedural training we soon fell in to varying categories and although we were all competent Operators, some were more competent than others. The day came when we were allotted to Relief Duty and of course the training continued.

Being in a Relief meant the same as being in a Team and we had different duties to perform. It was here at Hong Kong that I was to gain experience, (Unknown how important at the time) in the handling of Communication Traffic and the preparation of communications for transmission to the United Kingdom or to Northern China. The official designation of the Duty was, Counter Clerk, but it was quite some time before I realised how important that position was in the Team. The 'Plum' duty was to 'Work Aldershot' and clear all Traffic.

Our Communication network was all means in Hong Kong and Kowloon. There was the telephone switchboard (Military), DRLS, (Despatch Rider Letter Service) and of course, Our Line Maintenance section attended to all Military routes. The Wireless Communication was World Wide and the established Net was HONG KONG – ALDERSHOT with Delhi – Egyptforce – in between. Then there was HONG KONG – SHANGHAI – TIENTSIN and there was a Sounder

Line from TIENTSIN to PEKING. This became most important in 1937–38 when the Japanese invaded the North and Civilian Communications were interrupted. It was then that we became responsible for Civilian Messages to the North and I do not remember for how long that state of affairs lasted.

I have always thought how peculiar that period of our National History appears to have been forgotten! British Troops were involved at Jessfield Park in Shanghai. I remember that two of the Units were The Royal Ulster Rifles and the Loyals. There would have been others. Also, I remember the Japanese troops appearing at the Border of the New Settlements. There was a high Barbed Wire Fence, (Dannant Wire) I believe. I do not remember being impressed by their appearance and I have a recollection that they were scrounging for Chocolate.

I do not remember that the incident caused much of a stir but it was at the same time as the Hitler Scare in 1938 and perhaps that accounts for it having been transferred to the 'Back Page' of Military Matters! I must add a remark here, based on 20 – 20 Hindsight; Perhaps our Peers would have done well to rethink their attitude to the 'Little Yellow Man'? It will be seen that we were a very useful unit in what was at that time a Civilian Climate. What was not appreciated by any of us in 1938, was the tremendous and valuable experience arising from the Duty performed at Hong Kong.

The situation at Shanghai and the Scare in the United Kingdom in 1938 must have been responsible for a sudden change in Hong Kong Signals. A Mobile Unit was formed and the initial Cadre was moved to the C.B.S. (Central British School?). It also became known that further drafts of R.C. of S. were on the way to Hong Kong. The C.B.S. was on Nathan Road just opposite the Whitfield Barracks.

Earlier I mentioned that there were two occasions when I was recalled for Family reasons. First it was to leave school and assist to maintain the Family, attending Night-School to complete my education. Now comes the second call. Totally unknown by me my Mother had been forced to seek help soon after my Father's death which was the result of War Wounds, a combination of shrapnel and Gas. My allotment at the time would not have been much help and in those days there was no such thing as D.H.S.S. The eldest son, (me) was in the Army and it was decided by the Authorities' that I should be released and return to the family, at the same time being placed on the Army Reserve. (A second discharge and with a qualification). I was not to know, could not in my wildest dreams have guessed, that because of this interruption in my chosen Career, my life was being saved. And perhaps I may be forgiven when I say that on reflection, I have a strong Faith in Divine Providence. I was duly summoned to the Office, handed my embarkation papers, and proceeded to embark on the SS 'Lancashire'. This was a Troop Ship and a six week dreadful experience. SS 'Rawalpindi' was a beautiful memory.

But now, Back to Civy Street, by Command! It was a long journey broken only by the stops at Singapore, Colombo, Bombay, Aden, Port Said, Malta and Gibralter. Yes, these were all subject to Great Britain and much better crontrolled than in 1990.

There were two outstanding occasions during my short tour of duty in Hong Kong, one of which was representing the Royal Corps of Signals on the Coronation Parade held on the Island in honour of the Coronation of Their Majesties King George VI and Queen Elizabeth. The Representatives of the Unit were; Sgt. Morgan, Cpl. Lancaster and Sgmn. Dudley Fox. I am particularly proud of that memory and of the smartness of the turnout which was inspected by the C.O. and Officers before we left for Hong Kong. There were Representatives from other British Units as well as Foreign Forces who must have come to the Island to take part in this important parade. The Shipping in the Harbour helped to make it a most colourful occasion being 'Dressed overall' and outlined at night by small lights following the contours of the various ships.

The other occasion was in connection with Flying. I do not know why but an invitation was given to us from the R.A.F. to report to Kai Tak and gain flying experience. It was voluntary and only three of us from Hong Kong Signals turned up on the appointed day.

It is a memorable occasion and there was a most amusing incident when we were being briefed by the Pilot what to do if we should have to bale out. The Aeroplane was a Dual Control Biplane and to reach the Front Cockpit you had to start by placing the left foot in the aperture, (I believe it was the *left* foot). We were also fitted with parachutes upon which we would be seated when in the cockpit. The fitting of the parachutes was demonstrated in detail and how to use the Rip Cord after we had left the aircraft. Also, if we landed in the Sea, we were shown the 'Quick Release' plate at the front of the body. This plate had the four straps from over the shoulders and from the crutch secured rather like the present day car seat belts.

When the briefing was completed each of us in turn had to repeat what we would do if we had to use the parachute and if we landed in the sea. There is a saying in the Services "That time spent on reconnaissance is never wasted"; the same can be said for briefing. One of our Trio had donned his parachute as per instruction but when it came to toppling out of the aeroplane his next move would have been interesting. Instead of the count of ten and then pulling the Rip

Cord which was at the left side of the body, he demonstrated how he would twist the plate and strike it with his hand thus releasing the Harness of the parachute from his body, and this was before he had reached the Sea! My turn came and we took off. It was the first time that I had ever been in an aeroplane and after we had passed over the 'Peak' and gained altitude the Pilot started to show what the machine could do. We Looped the Loop, did all sort of aerobatics and then dived to Sea Level aiming at the Sampans as they sailed along. It was exciting and I loved the experience.

I never knew why we were given this opportunity but it was not very far in to the future while serving with 7th. Armoured Division in the early days of the War that I replied to a call for volunteers to train as Pilots in the R.A.F. More of this later and in sequence. Upon arrival in the United Kingdom we were taken to Catterick Camp, that is, a number of time served men and myself, and there we were handed discharge papers and a warrant for rail fare to our home stations. I was now on the Reserve List of the Army, subject to recall in time of war.

I was welcomed home by my Mother and it soon became clear to me that she was having a very difficult time. The year was 1938 and had been a very trying year for the Nation facing the threats from Hitler's Germany.

My sister was employed in Eskbank with live in accommodation; My brother Tommy was employed as a labourer (17 years of age); and the youngest of the family still at school. My first priority was to find a job and this I set about doing by approaching the Head Electrician at the Lothian Coal Company, (The Lady Victoria Mine). The man's name was Rutherford and in reply to my asking for a job he said there was no vacancies at present but I could leave my name and address. I thanked him and he started to take down particulars of my experience and training. When I said that my name was Fox, he asked if my Fathers name was George Fox? I said yes. "Right", he said, "Start tomorrow". I became an assistant electrician and worked with a first class man named Joe White.

Joe played a major part in our family as it turned out. The next move on my part was to get Tommy out of labouring. He came in one day after working at Butlerfield where he had been digging by hand for some repair near the Bridge. He was soaked and bedraggled and our Mother broke down in tears. I told him that he was no longer going to be a labourer and arranged for him to see the Head Electrician at the Pit. Tommy got a job as an apprentice and soon he was on his way to becoming an electrician.

Years later in Singapore, a Chief Engineer of the Ben Line described Tommy as one of the best tradesmen he had ever known.

Joe White and Jimmy Kerr were the tradesmen who taught Tommy in the first place and later he was to learn much about his trade in the Royal Navy. After the war he worked on several ships of the Ben Line.

In a further attempt to improve income, I approached the Head G.P.O. telephone exchange in Rose Street, Edinburgh, and applied for a part time job explaining that I had been in the Royal Corps of Signals and had worked on Army Exchanges. I got a job.

Just as we were settling down, 1939 became more ominous – War? My memory of this period is one of hustle and bustle. Letters from the War Office concerning my recent return from Hong Kong arriving with other letters from Record Office in connection with my discharge and transfer to the Army Reserve and then my recall to the Colours. It must have been confusion confounded. However, the situation at home in 102 had been resolved and the economic position had greatly improved. Tommy and I were both employed as electricians at the Lady Victoria and Tommy was also in the Pipe Band as Leading Kettle Drummer, and very smart too, in his uniform and on the drums! As I have said, I also had my part time job as a telephone operator in Edinburgh at Rose Street.

It must have been in the middle of 1939 that I was ordered to report to Bulford Camp for training and as I remember, it was a very happy occasion. We were billited in Bell Tents, 16 men to a tent and as we were all trained men we seemed to have a lot of spare time on our hands. I became friendly with a Reservist named Beswick and as I had never had a driving test he took it upon himself to show me how to handle Army Transport. I did know how to drive, thanks to my earlier experience with the Fruit Lorries but 8 cwts and 3 tonners were something else.

I was duly passed out by Beswick and if I remember correctly, my final test was to get up to 50 miles an hour and then change down through the Gears, double-de-clutching and keeping it smooth. An Order appeared on the Notice Board that all men due for a driving test should report to the Transport Officer at the Transport Pool. I joined the others and passed my test somewhere near Boscombe Aerodrome. Beswick was pleased. So was I. At the end of this period we were sent home but this time we had been fitted out with kit which was just as well for we had hardly arrived at our homes when we were ordered to return. This must have been sometime in August for by the 3rd of September we were on board a ship standing by on the Clyde, a medium sized passenger vessel with a French name, "Mont Calm".

On the Sunday morning as we stood by the rail of the ship, we heard the declaration of war by the Prime Minister. We sailed for a destination unknown. It was a beautiful day. I remember that we sailed down the Clyde and it was particularly lovely on the Helensburgh side. I remember the man I was speaking to at the time was named Ransome.

We had travelled by train from the Bulford area, probably via London to the dockside and then embarked straight away. There was no hanging about and as we sailed. We joined up with other ships and made up one of the first convoys of the War.

My last memory on leaving home is that when I had said goodbye to my mother, Tommy, who was due to play in the Band, came with me to Edinburgh Waverley to get the train, and we had high tea in Woolworths.

That really was the end of an era, we were never to be the same again. Before the convoy reached the Mediterranean the Navy sank a German submarine.

Once more good fortune came my way thanks to knowing a little about electrical maintenance. The ship was a civilian passenger ship and although operated by the French, the engineers and electricians were British (this is to the best of my memory). In the course of conversation with the Head Electrician he asked me if I was prepared to inspect all the electric motors operating the equipment on board; e.g. cranes, fans, winches and so on. As the maintenance was of a simple order, i.e. examining the brushes on the rotors and where the carbons showed sign of wear, changing the same. I was kept busy on this all the way to our destination which turned out to be Port Said. The 'Good Fortune' was that I dined with the engineers in their mess and for the life of me I do not know to this day why I was never called upon to do duty (Military) during the voyage. Unless it was because the ship was a passenger vessel. There certainly was detailed lookouts on the bridge and at other vantage points, but I was not called upon to perform that or any other duty.

Egypt

It has been said on more than one occasion that we won the war because we made less mistakes than the Germans. Our arrival in Egypt was met with utter confusion. Nobody wanted us. We were kept waiting for some time and then we were ordered to board a train for Cairo. On reaching Cairo we were taken to Abbassia, the local garrison, and thus to the Royal Signals Barracks which were adjacent to the Heliopolis airfield. And still no one was pleased to see us!

On the morning following our arrival, Ransome, whom I mentioned earlier when we were leaving Glasgow, was with me in the barrack room and the window was open. Apparently he had served in Egypt before his discharge and transfer to the Army Reserve. The Regimental Sergeant Major was talking with a Sergeant as they passed the open window and remarked, "I do not know why this lot have turned up here, you will remember Ransome, he is with them . . ." and so it went on for a few days more.

They soon found work for us to do. Our Trades or grades were of no interest, the order of the day was to fill sandbags and we were in the right place for sand. All the offices were to be protected and I believe that the barrack rooms were also partly protected, ie. sand-bag walls built to a height approximately 4 feet high. When this fatigue was eventually completed, we were detailed to other mundane duties and I found myself in charge of the recreation rooms with the ugliest native I have ever seen who was responsible for keeping them clean.

Posted to 7th Armoured Division.

I am not certain at this point in time but I believe that the Royal Signals Barracks in Abbassia were divided into two and the men manning Abbassia Signals Office were in one half and the other half was allocated to the 7th Armoured Division Signals.

Later there was reference to 6th L. of C. Signals and men from that formation would have been employed in other Base Areas.

I was posted to a 'relief' consisting of one N.C.O. and two operators and a driver/mechanic. We were given a No. 3 type wireless vehicle which was huge by 1939 standards and the equipment was very powerful.

We moved out from Abbassia and proceeded to Mersa Matruh from where we moved as required by 7th.. Armd. Div. Our duty was to act as the link between the 7th and H.Q. Cairo. The N.C.O. was Sid Greenwood, a Reservist who had seen service on the Indian Frontier and was good at his job. I was not in his league but learned quite a bit from him.

As I have said, we were not expected when we arrived but some one must have done their homework smartly when the paperwork or whatever information did come through, because the posting and allocation of the various tradesmen worked out very well in accordance with individual ability. The men who had come from India were first class and of course they had served their full time as members of Royal Signals. While on the other hand, as I have shown, I had just began to get into my stride at Hong Kong where, again, men of long service were outstanding. I am glad to say that it began to 'Rub Off' and even I became a bit more efficient as time went past.

Those early days in the Western Desert were peculiar. We moved about West of Matruh; The R.A.F. at Bagush consisted of Gloucester Bi-planes and I think there were a few Blenheims, certainly not many aircraft at all. We, as a detachment spent a short period of service with 4th Indian Division and then back to the 7th. By having a Large Signals Vehicle it was possible for two to sleep inside but we must have decided against that because I remember we had a tent pitched just outside the steps of the vehicle.

The days were hot but the nights could be very cold. I managed to get hold of two or three wooden cases in which the petrol cans arrived and converted them in to a bed which I placed in the lee of the vehicle. Thus, with clothes on and top coats as 'blankets' sleep was possible.

The war began to take shape and General Wavell was in command of Western Desert Force. I doubt if we, the rank and file, had any idea of how little equipment we had as an army. Artillery was scarce on the ground – Bren Guns were few in the infantry battalions – air cover was really NIL. The basic ration was corned beef and biscuits (I remember there was an occasion when a large tin of army biscuits arrived and indented on the lid was the ubiqitous ARROW and dated 1918).

Communication by despatch rider had to be altered in the desert.

Motorcycles were hopeless and causing a lot of injuries. They were replaced with Morris 8 cwt.trucks. Sand tyres were introduced but I am not certain when this happened. At the declaration of war there had been three infantry battalions at Matruh. Such was the state in 1939–40.

On one occasion our equipment failed and a relief set was sent up to us. It proved to be a *tank* complete with driver. I looked inside and was interested to note the type of controls and steering. It seemed also a good idea to know how to drive the tank (just in case), and the driver obligingly explained what had to be done. Fortunately, we never had to make use of this knowledge. It was my turn one night to share sentry duty and I am referring to the occasion for one specific reason. In the early hours of the morning I was on duty and armed with a rifle. As I looked out from the rear of the vehicle I thought I saw a movement and concentrated my attention on the area where this movement had taken place. Yes, there it was again and this time I distinctly saw a head move. I brought my rifle up and remained ready. Should I challenge, I continued to watch but there was no further movement in my direction. When my relief appeared I told him what had happened and together we went forward to investigate. It turned out to be a clump of stone and sand. It was a lesson that I did not forget. If you think that you see a movement in the near darkness and concentrate on it, you can lull yourself in to believing that it is actually moving.

One afternoon the three ton lorry came to our position North of Matruh to take us down to the shore for swimming and I went with the others, glad of the break. On the way back the conversation turned to football. Various teams were mentioned and their merits discussed according to the bias of the speaker. Imagine my surprise when I heard the village team mentioned from the part of scotland where I had come from. But it was the next part of the statement that caught my particular attention. The speaker went on to say, "Don't mention that in front of 'Jock . . .' That evening I went across to the 7th Signals Mess Tent and asked for the name that had been mentioned. A man came out and I recognised him at once. He was from Midlothian where I had lived part of my time as a schoolboy, his aunt was a prominent member of the local society. He had been reported as killed in a road accident some years before the war! There had been other stories at the time and perhaps the 'killed' had proved convenient. His Army NAME was certainly not his true name. Strange how such things come to light, even in War – and in the desert.

I suppose by this time I was bored with what we were doing or rather, with what we were not doing, and the news reached us that the army had received a call from the R.A.F. for volunteers to train as pilots. I applied for a transfer and in due course I was told to return to Abbassia and report for a medical examination in connection with my application to transfer to the R.A.F. I went for the medical and was pleased to be passed fit. (looking back I wonder what they would say today to such a Medical). I was subsequently called before the Adjutant at the Signals Barracks and asked about the transfer. It was quite a brief interview.

The Adjutant's name was Peter Lunnon. I was told in a few sentences that I had been overseas and gained experience which was valuable to the Corps. I was not going to the R.A.F. The following day I appeared on orders promoted to be an N.C.O. and to act as an instructor.

It was not long after that when I found myself promoted yet again and this time I was to be Superintendent of the Abbassia Signals Office, which was quite a small office and not nearly as important as the Hong Kong Signals Office had been (perhaps someone had done some more homework?). My next move was to H.Q. British Troops in Egypt and placed on a relief (B) for the receipt of communications and re-direction to the various units in the desert and Canal area, in fact all units in the Middle East. Within a short period of time and to my surprise I was promoted to Sergeant and became Superintendent of the B.T.E. Signals Office in the Semarimis Hotel which stood adjacent to the Kas er nil bridge. I was then in my 22nd year and the early training and mixing with senior men was standing me in good stead.

It was decided that all units had to be proficient in weapon training and this included technical units as well as the Infantry. Consequently, N.C.O.'s had to be sent for training and on return from the course at Gaza, colleagues of mine told me how stiff the course was.

I asked to go on the course because I was interested in shooting and had scored quite high during our initial training. I was permitted to go and reported to Gaza to take the course. It was a long Course and we dealt with every type of weapon in use with the Infantry at that time.

The result was incredible. We, members on the course, were sitting in a bus preparatory to going on a scheme when the results of the first part of the course were suddenly brought over by one of the instructors and read out to us. Top of the course in all weapons, (not an Infantry N.C.O.) 95% plus – Sgt. Fox.

I recall this in sincere humility, I had taken a great interest it is true, but this was beyond my expectation. In due time we completed the second part of the course and during this period a South African sergeant had asked me if I could strip a Bren mechanism by feel. I could not. He showed me how to do it hands behind my back and explained the delicate trigger mechanism and its replacement. I also practised the T.O.E.T's and managed to correct the gas failure fault in six seconds.

At that course there were N.C.O.'s from all over the Commonwealth; Australian – New Zealand – South African – Rhodesian – British and all were as keen as mustard.

The results of the second part were declared; 95% minus – Sgt. Fox. There was one item that was literally thrown in at the end of the course and when you consider that it was after all meant to be for Infantry N.C.O.'s, it makes sense. They would all be conversant with "Section Leading". I was not. I took part but this prevented me from coming away from that course with distinction, the first non-infantry soldier to achieve it. The Diploma stating this is in my study at the moment as I write this biography. But I had learned much from, once again, first-class men.

I returned to the unit and took over weapon training, which was held in the early morning, before going on duty in the Signal Office. And there was to be a follow up.

I was told to report to the C.R.E.'s office with a junior officer for instruction? It was a fascinating experience. We were told to write down different formulae in connection with certain explosives. We were then told how they should be used.

The use of salt water aided by a bayonet was described in the destruction of communication cables. There was to be a vehicle equipped for desert use, sun compass, and other specialist equipment and we were to act independently within a unit which was to be named at a later date. I had that little leather book with the formulaes until the 31st of January, 1969, when it, with all our household goods in the Redruth Depository, went up in flames. I was never called upon to perform this special duty and I have often wondered about it, what it might have been. I was certainly qualified to perform whatever might have been required – and, probably would have been scared stiff.

I returned to my duties at B.T.E. and then it appeared that someone must have been keeping an eye on me. I was sent for and reported to the office at the top of the H.Q. building. I was marched in and found myself in front of an elderly officer whom I did not know. After a few questions he asked me if I would accept training for a Commission.

I have no recollection of how I reacted. I know that I would never have applied for a Commission. I loved the Army and in a way I had began to make my way and show proficiency in what I was called upon to do. But I had no illusions about my academic background. That had been a struggle. And yet, here once again, I was being singled out for promotion. And in a way, I had never given much thought to being promoted, the people I knew, were much better educated and had a different school background compared to mine. Anyway, I accepted and in the course of time I often regretted my rash step. I suffered much 'Midnight Oil' and the theory was difficult – very difficult. However, I did end up with an AY rating. A for Practical and Y for theory, but the memory of the training haunts me, even now. (A.B.C. – Practical X.Y.Z. – Theory).

Middle East O.C.T.U.

While it was true that I had never given any thought to being commissioned, (people in that world were far removed from mine), I must admit that I was ambitious and had no intention of remaining in the 'crowd' as my schoolmaster had referred to the rank and file of this world. Perhaps this is what had become obvious to my superiors. I reported to the Officer Cadet Training Unit at Maadi which was just outside Cairo and, after registering and being allocated to a tent, I made my way there and arranged my equipment after which I made my way to the mess. In due course, orders appeared on the Order Board and a new way of Military Life had began. As we were coming in so the Senior Cadets were preparing for their Final Dinner before putting their 'Pips' up.

They were a mixed lot and I remember there was one man who, according to the Mess gossip, was going to be known in future by a hyphenated name! I am not going to try and go through all the items that were in the curriculum for the Cadets, the main one which soon stood out was, that if they could break the man they would. And on reflection, why not? After all in the course of time there would be soldiers who would depend upon the character of the officer.

Basic training fell into two parts, drill and technical lectures.

The first was, for me, a pleasure and I delighted in the exercise but the technical lectures were quite another thing, and it was not long before I was working late into the night, reading and studying, yes, and struggling.

At the end of the initial introduction, we were then sent to the Sydney Smith Barracks at Accre, north of Haifa in Palestine, where we had to go through a period of infantry training.

I was much happier there and the life was very demanding. We did not have much time to ourselves and often we would be out in the dark on exercises until the early hours of the morning. I referred to what might break us. This took various forms and what may appear to be a simple method was the order to get down in the mud as 'we were under fire'. At three o'clock in the morning, knowing that you are going to be on parade in a few hours, wearing that same equipment, and being inspected by Officers and N.C.O.'s who were happy to 'take your name' for dirty equipment could be, and probably was in some cases, the straw that broke the camel's back. However, in spite of this, we came to be proficient, those who fell by the wayside disappeared without fuss, (R.T.U – Returned to Unit), and those of us who were left actually came to appreciate, (I think LIKE would be too strong a word), the instructors and our drill was of a very high standard.

The Drill Square in the British Army is where discipline is instilled and the reflex action to orders honed to a fine point.

Saturday morning was the high point for me and it was not long before I was selected as 'Marker' for my platoon. The band was on parade every Saturday morning and the Commandant was there to take the salute. It was in a way 'Perfection Day', everything had to be at its best. Turnout, neatness, smartness, high shine on the boots, not a speck of dust or sign of dullness anywhere. The Regimental Sergeant Major, (Guards) would call for 'Markers' and we would go through the drill movements and march out in to the middle of the Square, from there we would move out to the allotted position and then stand at ease. To get any of this procedure wrong, in front of the whole O.C.T.U. WHO WERE WAITING TO COME ON PARADE, was to die a little. (It rarely happened).

When the main parade was formed and inspection completed, the Cadets who were acting as Platoon and Company Commanders took up position and prepared for the March Past. They gave the Orders for 'Eyes Right' and when past the saluting base, 'Eyes Front' and the dressing of every platoon was, as a rule, perfect in line and file. I enjoyed my time as Cadet Company Commander and this is the happiest memory I have of Saturday morning at Accre.

There was an incident on one of our final exercises which I have often wondered about. Our Company Commander, Major Ibbitson, who was liked by all, was out with us on a particular scheme and during the exercise he called me to go forward with him and observe the preparations of the 'Enemy' who were to attack across open ground. As I watched, lying beside the O.C. I happened to say to him that if this was the real thing. I would not be lying there watching them prepare to attack. From where we were watching it was clear that the 'Unit' preparing their advance were sheltering behind a rise in the ground and their 'O' Group had shown movement to the right of the position. The O.C. rose up and looking at me said, "Let us go back and join the Company". We did and when we got there he told them of my remark and stressed that it was on my own initiative I had made it. He said a great deal more and it appeared that the enemy would have been in a bad way. He had asked me what I would have done and the answer had been easy. I never have waited for someone else to take advantage. What causes me to wonder is that it was a simple observation to make. Perhaps I should have stuck more closely to simplicity.

Forced March. The Evelyn Waugh 13 and ½ miles. I cannot remember the correct title for this final trial which took place before we left Accre. We were taken by lorries over the Syrian Border, 13 and a ½ miles from the barracks, and then we had to march, flat out and expected to reach the barracks in approximately 3 to 3 and a ½ hours. I remember the test very clearly. I was elected by the Platoon to lead them and what happened to some of them will not be forgotten.

The choice of Leader was voluntary and up to the members of the Platoon. In each Company at O.C.T.U. there were two Platoons and obviously there was going to be competition between them. Each Cadet carried a rifle and full kit, i.e. Webbing small pack and large pack, but no steel helmet nor great coat, that is to the best of my memory. The Platoon Commanders did not carry a rifle. When we reached the start point one of the Instructors, a Major in our case, was there to see us on our way.

There were umpires located along the route but we never saw them and they were able to make notes and report to the Company Office. When everyone had adjusted their equipment and felt that they were ready, we set off for Sydney Smith Barracks. We knew from what the previous Cadets had told us that this forced march was a severe trial and many Cadets ended up in the Medical Inspection room or even in hospital.

It was a hot day and for the first few miles all seemed to be going well. We observed the rule of resting 10 minutes in the hour and it was then that problems began to appear. The common ones being blisters.

One Cadet, who had been a newspaper reporter in London before the war, had blood coming out through the lace holes of his boots. He was also one of the best types of man you could hope to meet. I remember him now even as I write.

We set off again and then the pace began to tell. Our Platoon was made up of British, New Zealanders, Australians, South Africans and Rhodesians. As some of the Cadets began to wilt, I took the rifle and detailed two of the tougher Cadets to fall in at the rear with the struggling Cadet, i.e. struggling to keep going. (If a man fell out this was acceptable but the Platoon lost 300 points for every man that did not complete the march.) The situation deteriorated and I had to use persuasive language to keep them going. There was quite a lot of readjusting to be done before we sighted the barracks and we were straggling just a bit. I was now carrying three rifles! However, it was my intention that just before we reached the finishing line we would halt, take stock and MARCH over that line. I noticed that our Company Commander who had been standing near the line, moved away as we were in our straggling formation and did not return. The Platoon also observed this move and muttered their dissent. We did march over the line and in formation and then on into the Barracks where we halted, turned to our left and stood for inspection.

From the inspection we then proceeded to the assault course which started on the beach. In spite of their exhaustion, not one Cadet failed to present himself at the start point. We began the assault by climbing up from the beach, not a very high cliff face, and the Bren guns opened up, operated by senior N.C.O.'s, once clear at the top we made for a ramp and on reaching the platform at the top we then had to jump outwards over Dannant Wire on to the sand, proceed to 'Tunnels' of barbed wire and crawl through, reach two iron rails, jump up and haul yourself over an artificial drop, run towards a high wall where we had to anoint each other to reach the top, drop on the other side and then we were faced with the open air swimming pool, full of water.

The objective was to get up on the side nearest the sea, (Mediterranean) and run along the narrow top of the length of the pool, you had an option, if you were going to fall, you could fall in to the pool complete with rifle and kit or, fall quite a bit on to the beach and remain dry and perhaps, uninjured. At the end of the swimming pool you jumped down, ran forward to a 25 yard firing range and aimed five rounds at a target. I believe most of us hit the target and then it was all over.

I had to attend to those who were needing medical attention and then I went looking for the Company Commander. When I found him he took me on one side and then we walked for a bit. I have no recollection what was actually said but I know that it was something like "I hope I never do that when what they need is encouragement".

After the passing out parade we returned to our parent branches of the O.C.T.U., i.e. The Technical Services Cadets did, the Infantry Cadets were posted to battalions. I duly arrived back at Maadi near Cairo.

It was not long before I realised that the advanced training of the Royal Signals O.C.T.U. had too many Shibboleths for me and one of my greatest fears is failure! I had worked hard and overcame the initiation period; I had been happy at the infantry O.C.T.U., that had been practical and how to fight, I suppose that was my basic nature based upon my need to survive the earlier demands placed there at an early age. Anyway I saw the Commandant of the O.C.T.U. and feared the worst. I don't know that I was thinking too much about divine providence at the time. From time to time people from all walks of life speak of divine intervention – divine providence and the Muslims believe in fate as, of course, do others who profess the Christian faith. I, personally, believe in divine providence, the almighty creator has a role for us to fulfil. It just had to be in my case. Why should anyone have taken the bother to keep me on as a potential officer? And yet, they did.

The Commandant was kindness beyond belief. I was offered an option and promptly asked for a posting to train as a pilot. It was not allowed. I was asked to think it over and I remember an officer coming with me and we walked and talked about what was best for me. My record was referred to and my practical ability in the past as a senior N.C.O. In due course a compromise was reached. Was I prepared to go before a W.O.S.B. (War Office Selection Board) and let them decide where I should go? I agreed.

I reported to the W.O.S.B. and was allocated to a squad of potential officers. The tests started and we were armed with what looked like half a telegraph pole. This pole had to be with us at all times and when you consider the conditions that the tests subjected us to, that pole became either a friend or a handicap. The exercises continued and then we had I.Q. tests – essay writing – and finally the psychologist. (I have met with one more since then – and that was when I was a candidate for the Ministry).

I have no idea what the Army man said or thought but I remember seeing, written across the top of his papers, "Aggressive = Infantry and then further writing. I left the W.O.S.B. which incidentally, I enjoyed. It had been once again practical and the tests had been on tactical and strategical methods. I was posted to the London Scottish for a brief spell and during my time with them it transpired that the 10th Bn. of the Royal Berkshires were having difficulty over the position of a trained Signals Officer. The Brigade was in special Training for the invasion of Sicily, (168 Bde – 56th. London Division). I was ordered to attend for interview with the Commanding Officer of the 10th. Bn., Lt. Col. Ian Baird, DSO. (at that time but there was to be further decorations) and after that interview I was instructed to return to the Infantry O.C.T.U. where the necessary procedure would be carried out in connection with my commission. It was done and, (ironically) I was Gazetted Lieutenant because of my length of Service. Why I was not thrown to the wolves I will never know.

There is one point that I should bring out now before it is overlooked. Many years later, 1960, I was employed as Head of a Department with an Engineering Firm in Cornwall. I received a letter, a letter which made me feel very humble, and there have been other incidents which have had the same effect. The letter was from the Officer who had been responsible for my being at O.C.T.U.. He was now out of the Army and finding difficulty in securing employment.

He had heard where I was from an old friend. Could I HELP HIM! I did all that I could and actually had a meeting with the Chairman of the Company but there was nothing suitable. (The moving finger writes . . . and?).

Commissioned.

Why I had to come all the way back to Geneva in the Suez Canal Zone for the purpose of receiving my Commission has never been clear to me. I do not remember exactly what happened but I was eager to be on my way and yet there was no hurry on the part of the Administrative Staff.

And now I am Lieutenant G.D.A. Fox, (30018) the old regimental number, 2754411 is in the past as at midnight and the world has changed; or has it? I went about the task of fitting myself out with Officer uniform, shoes, boots and, most important of all, a trench coat. At the same time I was trying to find out how to get to my new unit.

Looking back it seemed to be every man for himself. I had been used to receiving instructions of posting and where to report etc., but whether I did get a movement order or not, I clearly remember making my own way from Geneva to Alexandria in search of a ship to catch up with the 10th Bn. By this time the invasion of Sicily was under way and the war was going on without me.

At the time we were all concerned about being in the war and thanks to my interrupted stay(s) at O.C.T.U. I had been out of contact for a few months. I now know since the end of the war that for every man at the front and in contact with the enemy there are seven men in the rear supporting the frontline requirements.

I have also learned that thousands of troops engaged in the war never saw the enemy in action. But at the time when I was trying to get to the 10th. none of that registered and I was remembering the C.O.'s need for an experienced Signals Officer.

I eventually found myself in a draft bound for Sicily and in due course landed at Syracuse. There was nothing exciting on arrival and we were billeted in a tented reception area where there seemed to be organised chaos. I was quite surprised to find everything so quiet and when I went to the mess tent I received a further surprise in meeting a soldier whom I had not seen since being in the same class at school. We spoke for some time but he was very quiet and said that he could not remember me. I remembered him, especially the hard times of the strike when some children had come to school, as we said, in their barefeet. Alec. had been one of them.

While looking around and wondering how to get out and on to the Bn., I noticed that while the civilian population looked to be in pretty poor shape, the priests and nuns were of ample proportions. There was one incident where two hefty Sappers of the Royal Engineers assisted a young woman with a baby to give the baby a drink of water. The water supply must have been out of order and one of the Sappers loosened his water bottle and after cleaning his hands, placed his fingers over the baby's face so that a little water found its way to the infants lips. (these dreadful soldiers!).

It was while walking through the town and looking for an office where I might get some information about the location of the 10th. Bn. that I suddenly saw an officer wearing the Royal Berkshires Cap Badge. I shall always remember his name, it was Jackie Chrighton. It seemed no time at all until I had collected my kit and we were on our way to Battalion Headquarters. The Battalion had moved to Lingua Glossa, a small village situated on the eastern side of Mount Etna, a volcano which was and is very much alive. The 10th were resting and training after the battle at Primasole Bridge.

I was made welcome by the Colonel and introduced to the Officers who were in the building which was being used as a mess. It turned out that there was another Officer very similar to myself in appearance and the C.O. decided that we were not to sit at the table together. He said that he found it difficult to tell one from the other. In the event however, we were all billeted in local houses and Mr. C. and myself were in the same billet.

It was clear that time was of the essence and we were about to move again. The 10th. were one of the Battalions making up 168 Brigade of the 56th. London Division in the 10th Corps of the 8th. Army. The Corps had been placed under the Command of the American 5th Army who were about to proceed into Italy and thereafter move up the west coast.

I met the Signal Platoon Sergeant on the following morning and went down to meet the members of the platoon who had assembled at the Signal Office in a house on the edge of the village. The first man I met was a member of the Royal Corps of Signals, Bishop by name. He was the senior operator of the Brigade Link Set.

Having met with all the personnel of the platoon I arranged with the Sgt. for all Signal Equipment to be brought out including the Despatch Riders machines and the 15 cwt Truck. These were all distributed on and around the village green which was also at the entrance to the village.

I had no idea how efficient the operators were nor what standard of training they had received. I had heard enough to make me feel that there was little or no confidence in the sets. Thus, the first part of the training was to see that all equipment was cleaned and lubricated where this was necessary. The transport vehicles of the platoon was the responsibility of the driver/despatch riders; the cable and the sets with ancillary equipment were my main interest and it was essential that the small 18 and 38 Sets were calibrated.

Chapter Four

It is firmly held by many in the services and probably in the civilian population that training – reconnaissance and experience are of great value. It was certainly all of this in the 10th when we started to check over the sets at Lingua Glossa. The main company sets were trans/receivers and it was imperative that the transmitter and the receiver of the set had to be on 'NET'. The smaller set, the 38, was mainly for platoon communication, over a short distance, with the company set. Therefore, in theory, all company sets would be on 'NET' with Battalion H.Q. and communication would be possible right up to the forward platoon in contact with the enemy.

When we attempted to calibrate the 18 sets, it was soon obvious that all was far from well. Although we were very close together, we were not able to speak to each other, that is, not all sets.

When I checked each set in turn, (there are usually 5 in a Bn.) I discovered discrepancies, slight, between the transmitter and the receiver of the set. With slight adjustment of the 'Netting' control it was possible to bring all sets in to communication.

But it was essential to know what the discrepancy was on each set, if any. We carried on practising this operation and then spread out over a distance. I am not certain but it occurred to me that the operators became more alert and acted as if they had more confidence in the set.

I kept a note of the serial numbers of each set and the company to which the set would be allocated. One of the greatest difficulties was in ensuring that the operator would not be changed, (subject to casualties). The wireless communication was a top priority and then we had telephone cable, (D8). This was the standard cable in use but there was another type which I had heard of from a friend and I managed to get hold of a supply. It was called 'Assault Cable' and because of its smaller gauge it was possible to get approx. 1 mile of this type on to a D8 reel.

We kept on training and checking and trying out ideas which were not to be found in any text book.

The laying and reeling in of telephone cable for use by infantry commanders presented many problems, There was first of all your own support vehicles ranging from trucks, lorries, carriers, tanks and then there was the enemy shellfire, mortars, and patrols. The Latter presented quite a problem.

The enemies method was simple; capture a signaller for information, cut the cable, take cover and wait for the signaller to come along to repair the damage. The answer was obvious; two men went out, one armed with an automatic weapon and at a distance behind the repair-man.

Field crossings and gateways were a particular hazard and required the cable to go deep. Then comes the reeling in. When possible we used the despatch rider's motor bike! It was while we were training that the idea was 'tossed' in, "Why not use the rear wheel of a motor cycle?". All that was needed was a D8 frame, a good pair of gloves (as used for laying barbed wire) and a motor cycle. Always providing that there was time to reel in, (there were occasions when we left the line out for the relieving troops coming on behind).

It was necessary to take a telephone and go out and release the cable where it had been made secure. When this had been done; connect the telephone and ring through to the persons at the 'motor cycle' end that the cable was now ready to be reeled in.

We did not have to do this very often but I remember introducing it to the School of Signals (Inf.) section when I went there on a refresher course some time later.

The rest period at Lingua Glossa was far too good to last. Just up the hill from where we were billeted there was the most luscious black grapes and I certainly enjoyed them. I had also taken the opportunity to go back with one of my colleagues and see the area where our 'B' Company had been ambushed. The company Commander had been taken prisoner while attempting to supervise the withdrawal of what was left of his company. Four officers and 47 other ranks were killed. Quite a lot was learned from that battle but to my knowledge the circumstances did not repeat themselves again.

It was a Sunday afternoon and we had finished lunch when the telephone sounded in my room. It was the Brigade H.Q. and the message was short and to the point. The 10th. were to move out at once to Messina and there to embark for Salerno. The message was given to the Adjutant and in no time at all we were on our way to Messina.

The main landings had taken place and there had been quite a number of casualties. We received hearsay reports of what the Americans had failed to do and the usual rumours were flying, but in the event we reached the beaches of Salerno after some organised chaos at Messina. We had embarked and then we were dis-embarked. Units that had been going to Salerno were ordered to report to another embarkation to return to the United Kingdom!!! I remember sitting with the C.O. and the Adjutant at the side of the road while waiting for fresh orders. As we sat there I saw a small fire start under a three tonner which was carrying ammunition.

I jumped in to the cabin and drove the vehicle away from the fire.There was some leg pulling and the incident was promptly forgotten.We eventually embarked in landing craft and made our way to Salerno wondering what lay ahead. We went through the drill of landing on the beaches and the Navy had dropped their, I think they called it a 'Kedge Anchor' this was to enable them to pull the vessel back in to the sea once we were ashore. We hastened up the sloping beach and I remember that there was a building facing where we were coming ashore. The main road leading to Naples was at the top of the beach and on the other side of the road there was an orchard.

Salerno: We approached the orchard and arranged for a meal.

During this time the battalion would be sorting itself out and the Company Commanders would be attending to the many unusual duties that this unique situation warranted. I do not remember that I had very much to do at this stage and most likely would be answering to calls for various kinds of minor assistance.

We moved out and marched towards Naples. On the way we must have put up at a collecting point south of Pompei for I clearly remember being able to pay a visit to the ruins of Pompei and walking round the original streets wherein you could see the wheel marks of the vehicles of that period. There was evidence of cultured and refined living conditions, especially bathing conditions and under floor heating.

After that visit we must have moved quickly and we reached the Palace at Casseila where there was a Headquarters of British and American Personnel. One night there and we were on our way.

It has to be remembered that we were 168 Bde., 56th. London Division of the British Army (10th. Corps. 8th. Army) to assist the Americans! We moved in to a Forming Up area prior to our first battle in Italy.

Pignataro: Having crossed the Volturno and moved on to Pignataro, it seems odd when looking back and realising that the Battalion was, in a manner of speaking, stripping for action. The area where we were was in the vicinity of the village and we reached it by way of what I would describe a 'jeep' track. One Company, 'D' Company relieved units of the Coldstream Guards, (The Bn. had come temporarily under command of the 201 Guards Bde.) 'C' Company also went forward and occupied a small ridge. H.Q. Company occupied a house and set up a signals office where the Adjutant, Intelligence Officer and C.O.

were close by. It is of interest to note that some bright spark organised a public lavatory, not too far from the 'Office', by placing a builders ladder at a convenient height on supports at either end of a deep trench. It was a very public lavatory but the spaces between the rungs formed ideal seating The real point of that ladder was that it became a most important tool. With 'D' Company forward and on a hill a brand new set of circumstances faced the Signals Platoon. From now on it became obvious that most of the fighting was going to be on the hills and in the mountains. The Carrier Platoon were also going to be affected by this in the immediate future. It was the evacuation of casualties and the supply problems to 'D' Company that exercised the minds of all concerned with this priority need of the troops in forward positions.

The communications link with Brigade by radio was supplied by a 21 set which was very heavy and required to be powered by heavy batteries. It was also a most important set because of its 'Flick Frequency' which meant that it could be netted on to the gunners in support of the Battalion. I have a hazy idea that this was my own introduction agreed to by our 'F.O.O.' (Forward Observation Officer for his guns). I never had the opportunity to discuss with other Bn. Signals Officers or, if I had, it never occurred to me to raise the question. The ladder. It was the Platoon Sergeant, Sergeant Burnett, who came up with the idea that the ladder could be used to carry the 21 Set; the Batteries on the top of the ladder and the set slung underneath. The rungs at the end of the ladder to be removed so that the Carriers could take the weight on their shoulders leaving their hands free. That is exactly what happened and a number of men from the Armoured Carriers Platoon were attached to us for the purpose of transporting the 21 Set leaving the operators free to attend to transmissions as required.

There was one incident that took place at Pignataro with one of the 'villagers' just before we moved out. A concealed door was found in a cottage and when one of the men went in to investigate he found a complete German uniform.

The man whom we had seen about the place, no trace. There were two further incidents that stayed in my memory; The man carrying the Bren Gun Magazines was found to have left so many rounds per magazine out to lighten the weight! I would like to think that he was still around at Damiano later on. The other incident was the blowing up of a jeep by a mine on the area adjacent to the track leading in to Pignataro. In spite of the activity and movement by many people no one had gone on that particular spot until just before we moved out. I heard that one of the people in the jeep had been killed.

We moved off in darkness towards Rocchetta walking up a country lane with high banks on either side. In to those banks the local people had opened up what is best described as 'sloping downwards tunnels' wherein it was said they kept their vino and other wines. I was to appreciate one of such tunnels in the approach to Calabritto in the near future.

As we moved up the lane, men had been left as markers to direct us past openings and keep the rear troops on the right way. The marker then fell in at the rear of the column ensuring that no one got lost. In the dark this was absolutely essential and there was one brief spell when we were faced with an opening but no marker. I decided to walk up a little way and see if there was anyone in the vicinity. Not very far along there was a sudden burst of machine gun fire and it seemed to me that this was not the way. I returned to the column and continued in the direction we had been following. Fortunately at the next opening there was a marker, all was well.

We continued through the night without any further problem and reached the top just after daylight. The Battalion was forming up for the attack on the start line and the troops were in good spirit. As we had neared the top someone complained that we were marching too fast. There was a swift retort, "Marching too . . . fast, we are flying too . . . low." At the top of the approach lane it was obvious that the Sappers had been busy with their mine detectors and a number of Teller mines were lying at the side of the track. I was standing nearby when I saw a soldier walk towards the mines carrying his rifle in front of him and as he approached the mines it was obvious he was going to 'poke' them. I gave a shout and he nearly fell over, it was quite incredible, what was in that mans mind?

The Bde. did not take long to clear the area and movement forward was fairly quick. In fact from here via Zuni – Teano – Gloriani and on to Roccamonfina, the Germans were pushed back and offered weak resistance. The outflanking action of Teano proved to be more difficult owing to the fact that a German machine gun post had not been eliminated as planned for the night before. There were casualties and the Company Commander of 'D' Company was wounded early on in the attack. Command was taken over by Lt. David West.

As I approached, the Carrier Platoon Commander had gone up on a piece of high ground to 'take a look'. For some reason or other he was wearing coloured gauntlets. He must have been conspicuous for there was a sudden burst of the German machine gun and the bullets spattered the tree near to where he was standing. We were warned and proceeded cautiously.

Just in front of where we were at that moment 'D' Company had taken up their position and we heard that the Company Commander had been wounded. Moving on round by the hedge we could see that the doctor with some stretcher bearers was at the top of the field which appeared to be bounded by a wall. Unfortunately, it was not a very high wall nor was it continuous in height. As we looked we could see that a soldier had been hit and was down on the ground. The German gunners must have seen him go down and were spraying the area with bullets. I saw the doctor move forward and then run out and pull the wounded man to safety.

Making for Battalion Headquarters I passed the end of a track leading away from our position and huddled together in the lee of a grassy bank were three soldiers of another Battalion. I had a word with them and encouraged them to get on to their unit which I believe they did. A little further on and I found H.Q. and Col. Baird and his signaller,Lansome, just behind a ridge. Lansome was a grand type of man and one who had continuously refused promotion. I believe that he did accept promotion later. Anyway, Lansome was leaning over his 18 Set and I remember that he was wearing his Great-Coat. At the top of the right shoulder of his coat there was a hole and on close examination it turned out that a bullet had gone right through the material and Lansome knew nothing about it, had felt nothing at all.

A report was made to the C.O. that a number of Germans were in the hollow to the right of Bn. H.Q., the gunner Officer gave radio bearings and almost immediately the 25 pounders were on target.

Shortly after that a number of German prisoners came down past our position and one of them with his arm in a sling, might have been an officer, asked if he could see our automatic artillery (25 pounders were not automatic).

The Battle came to an end and the enemy retreated. 'C' Company went forward and occupied the village of Gloriani and at this point there seemed to be no reason why the 10th should not push on to take the Corps Objective – Roccamonfina.

Roccamonfina was planned to be occupied on the 30th October. Messages were passing to and from Brigade and the C.O. was told that it was unlikely that supplies could get through to the Bn. until the Teano – Roccamonfina road was open. We were in open country at the time and had forgotten all about roads. Everything was being carried by special carrying squads.

We moved forward and on the way witnessed an act of barbaric cruelty. An Italian had been tortured and apparently the people concerned had removed his teeth with a jack-knife. The body had been left just inside the mouth of a cave. By evening of that day we reached a chapel situated in a wood.

I remember that there were no pews or chairs inside but it was an ideal shelter and I was able to put the Bde. Set just outside the door. It was from this location that the answer of the C.O. to Brigade was sent in reply to the statement that there would be difficulty in sending supplies. I was told to signal, "There are plenty of chestnuts in the woods, we can live on those". The woods were full of chestnuts and had been the main topic of conversation since we arrived at the Chapel. We moved out first thing in the morning and went across country towards Roccomonfina.

There was no obstruction and 'C' Company had gone on ahead so there was no likelihood of meeting the enemy. As we approached there was evidence that the enemy had left the area in a hurry. There were large trees on either side of the track and tied round them there were white slabs of explosives ready for detonation. We walked on and entered Roccomonfina arriving on the date as planned. (With hindsight, I have wondered if the 10th, thanks to their quick advance across country, caught everyone out, including our own planners? e.g. "Unlikely that supplies would reach the Bn. until the Teano – Roccomonfina road was open" , and then from the enemy point of view; they had blown up houses to block the road from Teano, and had also cratered that road.) But, there we were, on the dot and there was no fighting to take Roccomonfina.

There was, and still may be a monastery at Roccomonfina. We decided to share with the monks and they agreed. Roccomonfina was to play a major roll in the days that lay ahead. The following is an abstract from the 'History of the fighting 10th'.

Roccomonfina: Roccomonfina was a focal point of considerable importance which later became the Road-Head for months of bitter fighting in the Monte Camino area, and its capture so early by the Royal Berkshires caused surprise and delight to the Corps Commander.

As in Sicily, so here the Battalion set out on foot across rough country, leaving their vehicles miles behind, and in three days they had fought and advanced over eight miles in to the hills. The success of this operation was very largely due to the high standard of training of Platoon and Section Commanders who led their men with skill and determination through the most difficult of country and carried the pursuit many miles in to the hills.

Looking back I remember much that happened both in Roccomonfina when we were drying out equipment and ourselves, (I wore my Trench Coat at one period, day and night) and in the battles which we took part in at Mt. Croce – Vezzara – San Clemente – Mieli – 'Bare Arse' (A hill that had no protection by way of Trench) – La Murata. For me, all of this was leading up to Calabritto where 'C' Company in particular was heavily engaged in close contact fighting, aided by supplementary patrols from 'D' Company and in the initial takeover, two platoons of the London Scottish had to remain in Calabritto to assist 'C' Company. Both 'A' and 'B' Companies were heavily engaged over on Mieli and 'Bare Arse' and it had become obvious that the Germans were desperate to reach the high ground on 'Bare Arse'.

Communications with 'C' Company at this vital stage were Nil. They had arrived in Calabritto just as the German counter attack took place and the 18 Set never came on the air.

Ironically, there was no line out to them for prior to their move forward, the linesmen would have no idea where to go. I say ironically because it was for this Battle that I had taken the opportunity to obtain assault cable from a friendly Royal Signals Officer. During the afternoon I had taken my men from where Bn. H.Q. was and laid the assault cable all the way down to the rear of the Chapel at the entry to Calabritto which in fact became Bn. H.Q. for the whole of the Calabritto battle.

We had taken great care to place the cable deep in the ditch which ran down on the left hand side of the road we were following, and succeeded in keeping the cable below road level. I remember that as we neared the bottom of the track we met the sappers coming towards us – they were using their mine detectors.

The cable laying was a success and the C.O. was able to speak to Brigade almost as soon as he reached his forward position. There was much favourable comment at the time.

Thanks to the Brigade Signals Officer an additional 21 Set was brought forward and assisted by The Scots Greys the set was taken in to 'C' Company in one of their tanks. This was quite an operation because the track leading in to Calabritto lay close to the German lines. Thanks to this combined operation Lt. Donald Jones, commanding 'C' Company was able to hold the position and to call for 'more ammunition' (Maj. David Foster, 'C' Company Commander was acting as 2nd in Command of the Bn.). The Battle of Calabritto had been won by the 10th and now there was to be further planning for a major offensive on Camino. The Bn. Companies returned to Mt. Croce and H.Q. Company returned to Roccomonfina where there was a complete overhaul of equipment and issue of clothing. The Companies came in by turn and soon the Bn. was ready for the next battle.

It was at about this time that it became obvious that one Senior Company Commander did not recognise the difference between the responsibilities of a signaller and a rifleman.

My aim was to ensure that our means of communication, all types, was operative and that if any of the platoon had ran in to problems, now was the time to sort them out. I had said to my Platoon Sergeant that Signal Personnel were not available for sentry duty. He had passed my instruction on to the Company Sergeant Major who was responsible for allocating guard duties.

However, I had reported to the Medical Officer saying that I was feeling under the weather and he promptly sent me to the Field Hospital quite near to Roccomonfina. That was quite an experience. I was treated for exhaustion and put to bed on a stretcher supported on boxes. I must have been tired. I fell asleep and did not waken for the best part of 24 hours. I do not remember exactly how long I was asleep but I do remember the orderly referring to the long period. I got out almost immediately and returned to the Battalion.

There, I was met by this irate Company Commander demanding to know why signallers were not to do sentry duty. I tried to explain the necessity and importance of the platoon to see to the equipment and the absolute priority for communications to be in good order for the safety of the Battalion.

I believe that he must have taken it up with the C.O. and after that I heard no more from the Major. It was also at this time that the training at Linguaglossa re 'Netting' and the details in my notebook paid off. 'A' Company had gone forward and the Bn. were in a holding position. The line had been static for days and hardly any enemy activity. Suddenly, 'A' Company were off the air. Prior to moving up to the present position I had contacted Brigade about 18 set batteries and after a deal of persuasion I had managed to get a few.

Bob Turner, one of the despatch riders who was temporarily 'Grounded' because of the hills, came with me, armed with a Tommy gun, (I shall explain) and we made our way to 'A' Company's position where I met Major Robson in his trench H.Q. He was glad to see me and after I had replaced the battery and retuned the 18 Set, he was through to Sunray (Code for Commander). My own Code name was 'Pronto' and I attempted to live up to it.

That Tommy gun: It was only this year, 13th May 1990, that Bob Turner whom I met at the 50th Anniversary of the Battalion told me how he had a Tommy gun. (They were not infantry issue). He had come across a dead Italian earlier in our advance and as he had no further use for it, Bob had relieved him of the weapon.

News reached us that the 'Big offensive' was about to begin. The civilians with live stock had been evacuated from the area. There was much complaining. I remember having to chase a few away who were attempting to filter back, and the war went on.

Camino: There was tremendous activity in the Calabritto area, making dumps for rations and ammunition and advance parties of the 46th Division, (emblem was an Oak Tree), moved in and went on reconnaissance guided by men of the 10th. The Battalion were relieved by the 16th Durham Light Infantry and moved back to a rest area leaving a small party who were to guide the leading Companies in the coming attack.

The 10th Corps attack was described as a great success. The 46th attack was continued by the 56th following through and up in to the hills and as the attack progressed The Guards Brigade and 168 Brigade were called upon to maintain the impetus.

The final positions occupied by the Battalion were the villages of Formelli and Camino with the London Scottish on Rocca Devandro. The advance had come to a standstill along the line of the river Garigliano. It was now the 15th of December and minds were on Christmas. I was to return to the Garigliano in January but I was not to know that my infantry war was over.

The whole Battalion was transported to a rest area far behind the lines for the first long rest in a safe area since they landed; the name of the rest area was Casanova.

I have to mention here that when we had been preparing to leave the hills I was among the last to leave with a number of signallers and men from the Carrier Platoon.

It was dark and the weather favourable and as we waited the troops began to sing, quietly, just in front of where I was standing. Not Barrack room ditties but favourite songs. They made a splendid sound and it was then that the Christmas party idea took form. There was further good fortune when we got to Casanova for in the Signals Platoon Billet there was a piano!

Casanova was a return to civilised living. Hot baths, new clothing from the skin out, boots and equipment. Short leave for those who wanted it and preparations for Christmas. I got the 'artists' together and we started to rehearse for the concert.

One of the men turned out to be a poet and wrote a poem about the Africa Star. This is the medal that was to be awarded to those who had taken part in the Desert Campaign. At the time of Casanova no one had seen the Medal.

We had a pianist and all went well. The opening commenced with every one of the party on stage singing a song and one character had decided to introduce his own contribution.

The Officers were all in the front row and as he stepped forward, he undid his tunic and threw a cockrel among them inviting them to share it among themselves. The concert was a success and the Colonel expressed his delight at the proceedings.

Just before Christmas Day there was an incident with the Americans in Naples that I shall never forget. It happened in this way.

Beer for the troops had to be severely rationed and it was said that there might be a bottle and a half each. An officer from 'C' Company and myself decided to go to Naples and see if we could improve on the ration. In the event we could not find additional beer anywhere, but we did find a quantity of "Laquer el Christi", (Tears of Christ – I think this is the spelling and translation).

Later in the day we were returning to Casanova and it was early evening as we drove out of the city. The vehicle in which I was travelling broke down and the driver/mechanic could not get it to go. The other vehicle had gone on to Casanova and I went in to an American Police Post to see if I could get assistance from them.

As I entered the post I saw a number of American servicemen round a games table and throwing dice. I stood there for a few minutes, totally ignored, when a door opened and a large individual who turned out to be the officer on duty, came in to the room. When I explained why I was there he asked me to show him on the map where the Battalion was resting. I did.

"Hi Guys, look at this, if we help this officer to get to his battalion we can write home and tell the folks we were at the front for Christmas." I tried to explain that we were a long way behind the lines but it was hopeless, and if you could have seen how they behaved on the way to Casanova, it was unbelievable. The distant flashes in the sky, miles away, had them ooh and ahhing.

There was an anti-climax. When we reached Casanova my Platoon Sergeant came out and he took charge of the other ranks while I took the officer to our mess. I heard later that they had been offered a beer! The stay at Casanova was thoroughly enjoyed and as I have said, officers and men were able to take a few days leave at different areas.

Meantime the Battalion was being brought up to strength and preparing to go back in to action. In January, the 56th moved back to the Garigliano and relieved the 46th. I remember that we seemed to be on the lower ground from where we had been prior to going back to Casanova. The company commanders 'O' Group was called to go forward and I was with them. But that was to be my last duty with the 10th. I was very surprised to be told by the Adjutant, Rupert Hedger, that the Colonel wanted to see me right away.

I was even more surprised when I heard that an Army Order had been published stating that where personnel had been on active service for a given period they were to be repatriated to the United Kingdom. It appeared that I was the only officer in the 10th to which this order applied.

It was queer, and I remember standing with Colonel Baird in a room of a building near to where the Battalion was forming up for their next attack. It is with pride that I remember that last meeting with the Colonel. He had asked for me to be his Signal Officer and his final words to me were that I had given him good communications with the Companies, the best. Colonel Baird was a highly respected and loved C.O. I was only one of the many who strived to give him the best. I collected my kit and made my way to Nola which lies at the foot of Mt. Vesuvias and near to the harbour at Naples. It was a collecting point and there I met other personnel, nearly all regulars, who were being repatriated under the Army Order. It was then that I was appointed to command 146 Scots Guards, the R.S.M. being Mr Wessel. We were waiting for a ship and a new type of adventure. I still remember Nola as an extraordinary experience, one moment at war – the next on the way home. And this is how we travelled.

Orders were issued to embark on the "Hai Lee" at Naples dock and this we did without any bother at all. It turned out that as we were quite a large number, we had the ship practically to ourselves and there was another factor that gave us quite a kick.

The "Hai Lee" was considered to be capable of doing 18 Knots and therefore it was decided that she could travel, un-escorted, from Naples to Philipville in North Africa. Whether or not she could there was nothing that we could say about that and in due course we set out for Philipville. The crossing was uneventful and all to short. The Captain was a Dane and the food was something that none of us had seen for a long time. (I shall have to return to the "Hai Lee" when I reach the 1949 part of this story but in January 1944 I had not the slightest idea how we should meet again, or where!)

Philipville: On arrival there was quite a lot of activity at the port and I have vague recollections of R.A.S.C. officers attending to our disembarkation and directing us to a tented area near the docks.

My next encounter was with a Brigadier who had the London Scottish uniform on and when I reported to his office I was asked why I was "improperly dressed". I have never forgotten that incident and at the time I had not the slightest idea what he was talking about. Apparently the 'Africa Star' had been issued to all those who were eligible and I was not wearing the Ribbon. I wish I could remember all that was said at the time but I don't and when I did say that I had never seen it he issued orders to someone that I was to be given sufficient Ribbon for the Unit that I was now responsible for; it was done.

I do remember what happened when I got back to our camp. The C.Q.M. Sgt. put it round his neck in the form of a neck-tie and various remarks were made by the troops. I decided that it would be prudent that all men should have it on their tunics by morning, after all, we wanted a lot of things out of this area if we were to get away and the Brigadier could be a good friend.

There was one hitch before we got away – it concerned the exchange of money and all that I can remember now is, that when the Quartermaster came to issue the various amounts to the troops there was a shortage. It was eventually sorted out. My orders were to embark in a lorry convoy and proceed overland to Algiers via Setief(?) – Constantine and then report to the Embarkation Officer at Algiers for onward transportation to the U.K. There were one or two odd bods waiting to get out of Philipville and they were attached to us for the journey. I remember that we seemed to climb up in to the hills as we left Philipville and we also saw snow as we twisted and made our way over not such a bad road under local circumstances. We camped towards the end of the day and it was very cold but we were able to light fires.

On the second day we were travelling at an easy pace, true army speed for convoy, when there was a jerk and instinctively we knew that the driver had started to dose. The shout from those in the rear was very loud and the convoy was brought to a halt. In the rear of the lorry there was a Transport Sergeant of the Scots Guards and he took over and the R.A.S.C. driver was glad to get in to the rear of the lorry and I suppose that he went to sleep.

There was nothing eventful after that incident.

Algiers: As we arrived within sight of the town of Algiers it was in the afternoon and the sun was bright. As I remember the occasion, we were descending towards the town which still lay quite some distance from where we first saw it and beyond there was the Mediterranean. As we came down the road there was a sign board informing us that there was an Army Reception Camp within and in we went and reported our arrival.

Two other officers had joined us at Phillipville and Lt. Phillips had become my Second-in-Command of the detachment. We were given a warm welcome and allocated an area of tents for accommodation. Mr Wessel, the R.S.M., with the senior N.C.O.'s proceeded to billet the men and attend to the minimum details necessary for our small encampment until I received further orders about our onward journey. I was also very pleasantly surprised to be given a staff car which as I remember, was a Canadian estate type car, a Ford and I then proceeded in to Algiers and reported to the Army headquarters (embarkation department).

I was to make many calls at this department and it was obvious from my first meeting that they knew nothing about us nor where we came from. In fact, there had been no information forwarded to Algiers or, if there had, then it was mislaid and I never heard about it. I attended to all the details they asked for, strength of detachment, nominal roll by rank, name and number, unit and so on. I made it quite clear that we were there on our way to the United Kingdom under the army order that was calling all regular soldiers with long service overseas. I believe it was referred to as 'Lilap' in the usual army form of abbreviation.

While attending to find a ship we spent quite a lot of time wandering round the town and in the evening we went to the officers club which was a hotel but had been taken over by the services. We were able to get some good food and there was entertainment and music. While there I had a most interesting experience. It will be remembered earlier in this story that I had made an application to join the R.A.F. and was about to depart from Abbassia and proceed to Rhodesia for training as a pilot.

That transfer was stopped by the Adjutant of the day, Captain Peter Lunnon and my first promotion followed almost immediately. Now, here in Algiers, in the Officers Club, I saw this group of Senior Red Tabs sitting at a table and one of them was Lunnon although what rank he held I could not see. Junior officers did not approach general staff with the question, "Remember me?" and so I left well alone.

It was also at that time while dining one evening at the Club, when we left to return to our Camp, we discovered that we no longer had a staff car! It was never found and we were informed by the Military Police that there never would be any trace of even a bolt or nut belonging to that vehicle.

That was quite an eventful night because it transpired that my chaps, the Guardsmen, came in to contact with the Americans in the town and there was quite a 'battle' which the Red Caps had to sort out. On the following morning Mr Wessell reported to me with the charge sheets! The charges had been made out by the Military Police and action was required off the officer in charge of the detachment. I remember this incident quite well because it was in a way ludicrous. What was I supposd to do with about a dozen defaulters in a tented camp on the edge of the desert. Mr Wessell and I discussed the situation and I remember him saying, "Hit their pocket". We went through the usual procedure, Sec 40, "Behaviour prejudicial to good order and military conduct" (252). The men were spaced out at so many paces in line and the R.S.M. read out the charge to which the soldier made his reply. I believe that I delivered a 'fine' of seven days pay in each case and then called a parade of the whole detachment in a large marquee. The gist of what I said was that they were seasoned troops of a famous regiment and from now until we got on board they were to avoid the Americans. It would also have been a delicate matter for them to come in to contact with the Americans knowing of the American 5th Army's poor record in Sicily and at Salerno. I regret to say that as a result of the 'battle' in the town, a Sergeant of the Guards was detained by the Military Police to answer a serious charge.

At last we received news that we were to embark and I was kept busy at 'movements' making the final arrangements. We were to embark on a ship, "The Christian Hugens" I have no doubt that we lost no time in getting aboard that vessel and we were now in the company of many differing types of service people. There was one man, an entertainer, who was in time to become world-famous, Peter Ustinov and he must have been with probably an ENSA group.

There were nursing sisters and many other non-combatants making up the personnel on board and when we were all called together, by the ships C.O., I found myself with a further duty. I am sure it was because we were seen as a guards detachment and mainly regulars, I was detailed to attend to the discipline of the ship's company. I am not sure now just what was entailed and I do not remember that we were called upon to perform any particular duty.

The ship sailed out in to the Outer Roads and there waited to form up in the convoy which was to take us to Liverpool.

The journey home was uneventful and there must have been emotional reaction of various kinds among all on board especially those of us who had been away since September 1939 and now returning in March 1944. I suppose that I must have been aware of my trip out on the "Mont Calm" and my examining the commutators on all the electric motors. A duty that had ensured me of good food in the engineers mess. And now. at 26 years of age, I was returning home as Officer in Charge of a detachment of 146 Scots Guards and to march them in to Pirbright Barracks, pipes playing, and there hand them over to the C.O. But, there's many a slip 'twixt the cup and the lip.'

1944 – Feb. Disembarked from 'Christian Huygens' (Stretcher) by Ambulance to the 'David Lewis Hospital', Liverpool.

Admitted and left lying on the stretcher on the floor, a nurse came and spoke to me while my cap was down over my face. Apparently she did not hear my reply and knocked my cap on to the floor. I found myself looking at a lovely red head. I now know that she did not take to me but that was put right on the 11th of September – I married her.

Why I was in hospital I never found out, but think of what I would have missed if I had gone on to Pirbright Barracks to hand over the 146 Scots Guards to their own command.

This was also the year when the Second Front was opened on the 6th of June. For me it was a peculiar year. After hospital I was sent on leave and then told to report to Richmond where there was a training unit for infantry signallers. This was located at the Marquis of Zetland's estate and the officers were billeted in the house. I remember seeing the most beautiful collection of wild birds eggs laid out in the drawers of a chest of drawers which was in the room allotted to me. There was a Major and three officers at this unit and my arrival amongst them seemed to upset them. I never really found out why the atmosphere was very formal and utterly different to what I had experienced in the field.

During my stay at Richmond my brother Tommy was due to go overseas in the Navy and I applied for leave to see him before he left on duty. This was granted reluctantly. On return to the unit I was told that I was going to Catterick School of Signals on a course. I enjoyed that and was able to see what improvements had taken place in regard to equipment. While there, I was asked about the practical situation in the field and for any advice that I could give, based on my own experience.

On one exercise I prepared a communication plan as the instructor was detailing the plan and as he rose from the position on the ground where we had all been lying as an 'O' Group, I handed it to him. I was surprised at the amount of attention the course gave to this simple matter and I was aware that the other officers and senior N.C.O.'s making up the course had never done this.

After that I was then asked about line laying and I spent time explaining about securing lines when there was likely to be weapon carriers or tanks in the vicinity of their positions. Many a unit had been cut off by tracked vehicles spinning as they came through gateways or even, accidentally turning on the spot where the battalion signallers had laid their cable. There was also the need to consider the follow up troops, whether a supporting unit or even Brigade H.Q. Rather than reel in your own cable, arrange to take over from the people coming up and leave cable down so that they would have immediate communication as soon as the forward troops had linked up from their new positions. (See my report prior to arriving at Calabritto). Teaching the use of the D.R.'s. motorcycle to reel in caused a lot of interest and showed how quickly this could be done when there was need for speed. There was also the lectures I was encouraged to give on the recognition of small arms fire and I hope they proved to be useful.

I left Catterick and went via Richmond to Dover where I was required to form a Signals Platoon for the Sherwood Foresters. 30 men were selected and I drew the necessary G 1098 Equipment and set to work.

The whole Unit was posted from Dover to Maresfield Camp in Sussex and we duly left Dover and arrived at Maresfield at the end of 1944. However, while at Dover, I was granted 10 days leave and went to Scotland where Pat and I were married on the 11th of September, 1944.

Maresfield Camp was the beginning and the end of my soldiering in the U.K. but I was not to know that at the time of my arrival. As well as being Signals Officer I was appointed Assistant Adjutant and most of the time as Adjutant. I also became involved in other aspects of infantry training; e.g. 25 mile route marches and then putting in an attack at the end of the march. It was useful but fortunately I never needed to put it into practice.

Chapter Five

1945

Pat had joined me at Maresfield Camp and we shared a house at Nutley with the Whites. The wife was a good companion for Pat. Once settled in Nutley, which was a small village to the west of Maresfield Camp, Pat joined me there towards the end of 1944. The house was shared and Pat enjoyed the companionship of the lady who had advertised in the local press.

There was a great deal of activity at this Infantry Training Camp and constant posting of reinforcements to France. In addition to weapons training, there was .22 team shooting and I remember that in one Brigade contest the training team won. I scored one short of a possible but there was no objection raised! Pat had shown an interest in shooting and I taught her the basics using an Enfield. She went on to compete with a modified service rifle, .22 and won several events at home and later at Singapore .22 and the Singapore Rifle Club open range.

In early 1945, the Unit received an A.C.I. (Army Council Instruction) the gist of which was that volunteers were required for service in the Far East as Civil Affairs Staff Officers. Application had to be made through the Unit Office and forwarded to the War Office.

There were three applications sent from our Unit, a Major and one other Lieutenant besides myself. In due course we were called to report to an office at Hyde Park Gate, but on different dates. It transpired that some 52 applicants were being interviewed daily but only two out of that number were being accepted as a rule although there may have been more on one day than on another.

In our case the Major was not successful; my colleague and I were. We received orders to report to an address on Wimbledon Common which turned out to have been a Teacher's Training College. I do not remember how many officers attended, quite a number and of all ranks. Red Tabs, Colonels, Field Officers, Wing Commanders and a smattering of junior officers such as ourselves.

The training was intensive and we had the pleasure of being lectured by Sir Reginald Coupland and Dudley Stamp among other experts from the police and financial affairs. I say pleasure because at the first lecture there was no haste displayed to find a seat. For the rest of the time you had to be there early to get near the front.

The training was in three parts, first of all theory, then exams; followed by practical and exams; and then over to the School of Oriental Studies which was located at that time at Sussex Square, (Sault Place?). Our Language was Malay and Professor 'Jock' Sturrock and Miss Lewis were the teachers. There was also an instructor who I believe was named Winsted but I regret that I have forgotten his name. I never actually met him. The language instructors had all been in the Education Department, Malaya.

At the end of the training a Major Thom and myself passed top in practical and were sent on leave pending posting overseas. The first two postings were an officer from bomb disposal and myself and later we met up with eighteen others in a hotel at Buxton.

Pat stayed at home in Scotland with my mother during my absence overseas. This happened on other occasions and while they were inevitable because of the service, these partings hurt.

From Buxton we made our way to Glasgow by train and boarded a ship bound for Bombay. The journey was no holiday. Among the party on board were men who had senior departmental service in pre-war Malaya and as soon as the ship got under way arrangements were made to study the Malay language in particular and further lectures from qualified people in our midst. There was a lawyer who no doubt had been suitably employed elsewhere and among the subjects chosen, he offered to teach shorthand to anyone interested.

The journey to Bombay was enjoyable and on arrival no time was lost in disembarking and joining a train bound for Madras. That was the longest train journey that I have ever experienced. We set off in the early evening, four officers to a carriage, each carriage was self contained, two let down beds and the daytime seats became beds catering for the four occupants. There was also a shower room/toilet. Meals were taken at appointed stops en route and this must have been organised before we arrived, or else this train made a regular trip between Bombay and Madras.

We were two nights and a day on the journey and on arrival at Madras we were then taken out to Palavaram. This was a type of 'camp' but well below military standards. There were derelict huts scattered around and it was very much a question of looking after ourselves. There were a few officers who seemed to be in charge of administration and in spite of the apparent chaos things got done.

I seem to remember that there was the first general election taking place in the United Kingdom and rumour came in that a bomb had been dropped on Japan. It is difficult to record just what happened then, but various types packed their bags and took off for Calcutta.

Our '18' joined the exodus and we duly arrived at Calcutta where we were accommodated in a reasonable hutted camp.

The senior members of our detachment got in touch with the local military authority and in a few days we were split in to two groups of nine. There was some haggling with one type who did not want to fly, but we reported to Dum Dum airport for further orders. On arrival at Dum Dum, we were met with what seemed like casual preparations for our journey in to Burma where we were told we would be landing at Pegu.

The Civil Affairs Staff was under the Command of General Sir Ralph Hone, with Brigadier Pat McKerron and Colonel Paul Regester as his immediate 'Field' commanders. The journey to Pegu was to be in two Halifax aircraft which had been stripped and converted for the journey. What the conversion meant I do not know but there was talk of a 'blister' having been removed from underneath the body of the craft and a temporary 'flooring' placed over the open space, the inside was bare and there was no seating. Personal kit was loaded and we were ready for the off.

We had been formed into two groups of nine and boarded the aircraft accordingly. The pilot of our machine was a New Zealander, short stocky type, and I obtained his permission to sit in what was probably the mid-gunner's seat. Why no one else had tried for that seat I do not know and the significance of the two units being of identical composition escaped me for a long time in to the future.

As we crossed the north east coast line I could see the rivers which appeared to be in flood and then we settled down to the journey. It was some time later that we ran in to what was probably monsoon rain and the cloud was closing in. Suddenly I saw what looked like the top of a mountain right in front of us and the pilot must have seen it at the same moment. From flying sedately on our way, the pilot dropped the Halifax and went down in a tight turn before levelling off. It was probably all over in a few seconds but in my opinion he was a grand pilot.We were told by him that this was the first time he had been in this area and now we had to find Pegu. Navigation or luck, I do not know, but we had arrived over the jungle and then turned north to find Pegu.

There was quite a lot of crashed Japanese aircraft littering the tops of the trees and then we saw a landing ground with a number of RAF planes lined alongside. Our pilot was having a good look and flew round the area during which time there were no signals from the ground and then we went in to land. It was a very good landing as we were to find out. As soon as the wheels were on the ground the pilot had applied the brakes and must have used them studiously because of the area available to him.

The landing strip consisted of steel channels, perforated and linked together and as we neared the end, all too quickly, the pilot managed to broadside the Halifax and we were very close to the trees. Some airmen came running across and assisted with the opening of the door. As we climbed out of the machine there was a lot of chatter and an RAF officer came over and his first words were addressed to the pilot demanding to know "What the h... was going on, this is a fighter LG not meant for Halifax type machines". There was further discussion between the Officer in Charge and our pilot which resulted in the fact that we had to take off again and proceed to the Pegu landing area.

This presented some difficulties and it was necessary for the airmen to assist by man-handling the rear of the aeroplane to get it turned and then we taxied as far back as possible and again the airmen assisted by manoeuvering the aeroplane right back to the edge of the jungle. We took off and missed the trees and finally found the Pegu we were looking for. It was a grand experience.

We had our complete kit which we carried on our backs and this included a light weight folding camp bed with inclusive mosquito net. One night at Pegu was enough. We found a vacated basha with a raised floor and unfolded the camp bed and arranged the mosquito net, very securely, round the bed. Lorry transport was available and we left as soon as we could for Rangoon. Prior to leaving we were told that bombs had been dropped on Hiroshimo and Nagasaki with devastating results and that the Japanese war had ended. It was all too much to take in and probably we considered it to be rumour.

On arrival at Rangoon the unit commanders reported to the appropriate authority and we were issued with embarkation instructions. The ships that were in port had all been prepared for the anticipated landings and this enabled us to get away from Rangoon quite quickly. We then knew that our destination was to be Singapore and we heard of a code word, Shackle, for the first time.

On board the ship there was rumour and counter rumour and in the end the truth was more startling than any of the conjecture given out as rumour. It will not be too difficult to recognise that we at that moment in time, had no idea of what the atomic bomb had done or could do.

Between Rangoon and Singapore there was much done in the way of preparation and when we look back and realise the confusion caused by this complete change from invasion of territory stretching from the Kra Istmus to Singapore and whatever may have been planned for the east coast, the administration was excellent.

Duties had been allocated to our units and it now transpired that there would be 23 officers landing at Singapore from landing craft. We were to climb down scrambling nets from the ship in to the landing craft. We descended the net somewhere near Raffles Point and made our way towards the wharf. As we neared the wharf we passed close to Japanese shipping and the Japanese who were looking over the sterns of the shipping, just gaped at us. If we were confused I wonder how they must have felt.

We scrambled ashore and made our way towards the gate which was No 3., right opposite the Singapore Railway Station. As we came out of the docks the scene around the area was one never to be forgotten. Wherever we looked there were masses of people on the top of all the buildings especially on the right hand side as we approached the station. I have thought about that reception by the people many times over the years. The roof tops must have been of the flat type and at first it seemed as if the people preferred standing there rather than stand at the side of the streets. Of course, until we came ashore, the Japanese were still in charge and driving about in their cars with their particular flags fluttering on the car bonnets. This may have had an effect but what a blessing that while the Japanese had bombed and fought to occupy Singapore with dreadful results to the population, the British return was received almost in carnival conditions.

The surrender of the Japanese was carefully observed and there was doubts in some minds as to whether they would obey their Commanders, or indeed if the local Commanders would believe that the war was over. The entry into Singapore was swift, there was a Royal Navy destroyer standing off near Raffles Point and an Indian Brigade came ashore very quickly, consisting, among others, Gurkha troops. Any lingering doubts in the Japanese minds must have been quickly dispelled.

Our first sight of Prisoners of War was immediately across the road from the railway station. They were British and penned in behind wire fencing. Opposite the POW's and to the right of the railway station there was a building which had been a Customs Office, but which was then being used by the Japanese as a Military Office which may have been a controlling point for the docks. As Colonel Regester and I walked into this office there were Japanese officers coming along the corridor. The Colonel quietly said that we move to one side as we pass them. With hindsight on my part, the Colonel was absolutely right. I was told to go to Tanglin and find out what was happening there.

While I was finding out how to get to Tanglin, a male chinese stepped forward and said he would take me in his car. I accepted the offer and off we went to Tanglin. We soon arrived at a building and as

I got out of the car I noticed steps leading upwards but arranged in flights with flat spaces between the flights.

I was puzzled by the quietness of the area, entirely different from the dock area. When I reached the top of the steps I was met by a man whom I thought was a Japanese. He bent his body forward, hissing all the way down and up again. (I was told later that this was a form of courtesy.) Then he spoke, "To the British Officer, I surrender with all these people who are the civilian population of the area". Behind him, sitting on the floor, backs to the wall and in the gloom, were men and women and probably children. Presumably they were Japanese/Korean nationals. I was taken by surprise but had the presence of mind to tell him to remain there and that he would be held responsible for them.

I never saw him or them again and went on with my earlier quest. On enquiry from my 'Guide' I learned that this 'Tanglin' was the Tanglin Club where all the Tuans met. The Tanglin Club stood opposite the Goodwood Park Hotel. The Tanglin that Colonel Regester had in mind was the military H.Q.'s which was much further up the road in the Alexandria area. There was nothing to report and there was practically no activity in the area at that time.

Our return to the Customs Post took us past the British General Hospital on one side of the road and the Outram Prison on the opposite side. As we went over the crossroads and began to ascend the incline, it became obvious that the car was not going to reach the top. Lining the sides of the road were crowds of people and when our predicament became clear to them, several ran forward and pushed us to the top of the hill. Fortunately it was all downhill from there on and I reported back that I had been unable to contact any Military Personnel but that the Tanglin Club was holding civilians.

That particular incident could provide material for an after dinner speech. As it was, although the Club had been surrendered to me, some seven years later I had to pay $150 to become a member. The days between the 5th and the 12th of September were hectic and for the Senior Staff must have presented tremendous problems. But on the 12th, Lord Louis was on the top steps of the Municipal Building waiting for the Japs to be marched along the road , past the Supreme Court building, and then up the steps of the Municipal Building and in to the Chamber where they had to sign the various documents of surrender. I was not aware of it at the time but, standing on the other side of Lord Louis, in the packed crowd on the verandah, was my brother Tommy. His ship, a converted aircraft carrier, must have been in the vicinity of Singapore. We never met at that time. It was our mother who, on receiving letters from both of us, realised that we were there at the same time.

From September to the end of the year, life was very full and much of what had been planned re personnel never took place. I was asked if I was prepared to assist the Superintendent of Prisons at Outram Road. I agreed. It sounded just like another job and to be asked was a change. I could have been ordered but looking back, I suppose it would have been awkward to post an Officer to such an appointment without training or a knowledge of the type of work. The man who was the Superintendent had been chosen during the planning days and had been engaged in similar work in Palestine before the war.

However, there was to be a sudden change. The man involved apparently had a record from the Palestine days and a cable arrived asking to confirm, of all things, his initials. The outcome of that was that he was immediately recalled to the U.K.

Commander Bayley, Inspector General of Prisons, returned after a visit to the Chief Secretary's Office and told me to "Put up the third Pip". This meant that I was now promoted to Captain and further, that I was now Superintendent of the Prison. (This will give a very clear idea of the confusion and expediency that the Senior Authority was having to deal with). The Course at Wimbledon was paying off although my own special study had been in connection with Police Duties, Law and Finance. (In fact I had in my possession a letter, offering me contract employment as a Cadet Superintendent of Police, from the Colonial Office to take place after demobilisation).

Lord Louis, with General Hone, had asked to see it when they called in at the Outram Prison Office. Apparently it was the first one they had heard of. There was some talk also of my being 'Too young for the job as Superintendent during that visit'. However in the afternoon I was told to put up the Pip.

1946

I continued as Superintendent until my departure for demobilisation during the first quarter of 1946 and it was a very full and demanding experience. During that brief period of time I became responsible for Johore Bharu Prison and was involved in the future planning of Changi which had been left as a wreck by the Internees. The latter was a very brief involvement and I remember being more concerned with the field of fire and placing of light machine guns on the perimeter walls than on anything to do with the inside of the prison.

There were 146 Japanese war criminals pending trial in Outram Road.(Many of them were eventually executed after the civilian authorities resumed government of the colony). Commander Bayley gave me a lot of advice and what to look out for. There were over 1700 inmates and they were of all types, not necessarily the usual criminal type.

Apparently, it was the habit of the usual run of convict to cause trouble at the Christian Festivals. The Commander had alerted me to this habit and he was to be proved right as we approached Christmas, 1945. It was during the afternoon on Christmas Eve when the alarm was given and the report reached me that there was a riot in the Remand prison. Internal action was taken to control the situation and the police and security forces were informed.

It transpired that two chinese males had encouraged a number of men to sharpen the rims of their metal plates for use as weapons. They then proceeded to rouse the people on remand and telling them that there was "Only one white bas.... on duty", get him.

The riot was brought under control and I was able to look up the regulations for dealing with such an occurrence and discovered that the Superintendent had summary powers for dealing with an aggravated offence. It was in or about the 60th section.

The procedure was to establish the cause of the riot, and if the leader or leaders were identified, they were dealt with under the summary regulations. Interpreters were appointed and the charge read out. Witnesses were called and the accused were informed of their right to question the witnesses. Under the circumstances there was no doubt that the two men were guilty as charged.

They were examined by the prison doctor, (who had many years prison experience) and passed fit for punishment. Sentence was 12 strokes with a rattan on each man and punishment to be carried out immediately. From 4.30p.m. on that Christmas Eve until I left for the U.K. in March, there was no further trouble. Whether there was any connection or not with Johore Bharu prison I do not know, but there was an outbreak there on the same afternoon and this was dealt with in accordance with the authorised procedure. I do not know how prison authorities act in normal peacetime conditions, but punishment in these particular cases, summary and immediate, had the desired result. A deterrent (to deter) must always be available but it must not exclude punishment when, as a deterrent, it fails. There was one most important matter in 1945 – Lylie Helen was born on the 16th of October but it was to be about six months later before I saw her.

I left Singapore to be demobilised in the U.K. aboard a liner which had been converted for carrying troops, the 'Monarch of Bermuda'. The trip home was uneventful and after arrival we were subjected to the normal army way of movements until we reached the demob.

centre which in my case was near Oxford, something under Lyme.

If there was not a suit to fit or indeed anything really suitable, your details were taken and you proceeded home in uniform to await the arrival of your demob. suit. Coupons were required for everything and it was absolutely necessary to depend upon the Demobilisation Centres. I did not have to wait too long and I was fortunate that the person taking my details had been very efficient.

Mine arrived when we were resident at Drabbles Road, Matlock; a grey, double breasted suit which fitted me very well. Before that however, I had to report to an office in Nottingham for registration in order to get a civilian job. It was my first contact with socialism - The Labour Party.

I was in uniform and when I went in to the office I was met by a civilian (male) who had presumably spent the war in the civil service. He enquired what I wanted and on learning the nature of my interview advised, "You would have stood a better chance if you had been a Lance Corporal instead of that uniform".

I did make a few enquiries for employment as it was our hope to stay in the U.K. and finally was offered a job as a lift man at the Hydro. That was that.

I had still my offer of employment from the Colonial Office as a Cadet Superintendent of Police in Malaya and Pat and I agreed that I should write and accept the offer. I did and was accepted.

Return to Civilian Life H.M. Overseas Service - Malaya. I left from 50, Caldwell Road, Allerton, Liverpool, 19th July of 1946. Pat and Lylie joined me in January 1947 when I was stationed at Changloon Kedah. Our first Government Quarter was a refurbished Native Land Officer's house at Jitra and so began our family life as civilians. We were the only expatriates in the District with Douglas McCauley, manager on the Jitra Rubber Estate, to the north.

1947 - to December 1948. Kedah: Sheila Trounson was born in Penang on the 22nd of January, 1948.

1949 - January to January 1957. Singapore: Andrew George Dudley was born on the 1st of December, 1953.

1957 - 1964. Cornwall: Katrina Moira was born at Redruth on the 27th September, 1959.

1964 - 1968. Sabah (was North Borneo): District Officer Sandakan until 1965 and then Assistant Secretary Ministry of Finance until November 1968.

November 1968. Selection for Training at new college for the Ministry of the Church of Scotland.

1969 January to October: Temporary employment Bank of Scotland.
1969 - 1971. New College, Edinburgh University.
1971 - 1972. Probationer Assistant Ness Bank, Inverness.
1972, 21st September: Ordained to Ballantrae Parish Church.

It was in May or June of 1946 that Pat and I decided there was nothing in the U.K. for me and that I should accept the offer of employment from the Colonial Office. We had been living in a Bungalow at Drabbles Road in Matlock, which had been rented to us by old friends of Pat, and now we had to return to 50 Caldwell Road, Allerton, Liverpool 19, where Pat was going to stay with Lylie and her mother until I could send for them to join me. We had bought a very good Austen Ten and after a visit to Scotland we decided to sell it and accordingly advertised it locally in Allerton.

I believe that we received the asking price; good cars were at a premium and there was no hope of people getting a new car at the time we were selling. I remember the man came and after seeing the car he asked me to wait until he went home and got the money. Back he came, with a bundle of bank notes, reeking of the smell of fish and chips.

We then attended to the details of medical injections and passport procedure and after several letters from London instructing me to obtain tropical clothing and to embark on the 'Empress of Bermuda' sailing from Liverpool on a date in June, once more I was on my way to Singapore.

It was still travel by troopship methods and I must have shared a cabin with others but of that I have no clear memory. It must have been a very ordinary journey and there were all sorts of people returning to the Far East. I suppose that after the war it was all very tame and we reached Singapore in about three weeks. I was met by an Officer of the Immigration Department in Singapore and taken to a hotel.

I spent a week being briefed and then went to Penang, where I reported to another senior Immigration Officer and spent a few days with him where I received further briefing. This man had been interned by the Japanese and was not too kindly disposed to ex-army officers.

I was posted to Changloon in North Kedah as a Deputy Controller of Immigration and there to take over from a man named Ridley, but whether he was an army officer or not I do not know. We certainly did not take over/hand over and he disappeared as soon as I reached Changloon.

I found myself with a mixed and small unit of two inspectors and some ten outdoor officers, Chinese and Malays. My accommodation consisted of what might have been called an outpost; a 'basha' (hut) on high stilts, a place to sleep, a place to bathe and a toilet, a room to sit and to dine. Kerosine lighting, a mosquito net round the bed, and a Chinese cook who spoke no English.

It was the 16th July, 1946. I remember that clearly because on the 16th of December I passed my first language examination in Malay. Now I could tell the cook that the same thing for dinner, day after day, was very boring.

Changloon was 25 miles from Alar Star and just short of the frontier with Siam (Later to be called Thailand). The Siamese Border Post was at Ban Sadau and between them and us was 'No-man's Land', great scope for illegal immigrants.

The Chinese Inspector who had been on duty when I arrived was returned to the Police Department at Alor Star and I was glad to see the back of him. On arrival at the check post I had mixed with the travelling public to see what the procedure was when examining passports.When my turn came to have my passport checked I went forward and handed it to him. I was not impressed with his behaviour and glad to discover that he was only temporary.

The other Inspector was a gem of a man, Tham Kok Thye. Kok Thye had been a member of Force 136 and had played an important part in that Force during the Japanese occupation. However, he was a very loyal servant of the British and did not go off with Chong Peng when the emergency was declared in 1947. We got to know one another very well and I am sure that I learned much from him about local customs and local people. I will return to our activities in due course.

Jitra – Changloon 1947

Looking back to the night when Pat and the baby, Lylie, arrived at Penang I can still remember the occasion and how nervous I felt, nervous to the point of being ill. We went from the ship to the Metropole Hotel and settled in to the room which I had reserved. Once Lylie was safely in bed, Pat and I went in to the bar and ordered dinner. While we were waiting Pat was about to experience her first encounter with 'creepy crawly' creatures. Chi-Chaks are to be found in practically every residence and hotel, mainly on the ceiling and they travel quite fast from one part to another.

Where we were sitting, there were a few immediately overhead, and when Pat became aware of this, she was far from pleased. I assured her that they rarely fell on anyone and not to worry about them, she would get used to them in time.

You can guess what happened, before we went in to dinner, a Chi-Chak dropped right on to Pat's head. I cannot remember that there was ever a repeat performance during the rest of Pat's stay in the Far East.

We left Penang for Jitra, some 70 miles to the north, crossing by ferry to Province Wellesly, and then by road to Jitra. Pat was to discover that she was the only European woman living at Jitra. Another lady did arrive while we were there but some time after to join her husband who was the Rubber Plantation Manager of the Jitra Estates.

I will describe the 'house' and what Pat had to contend with on her first time away from home and to a country which had been over-run by the Japanese army. Facilities there were none. The house had one bedroom, a dining room, a place where you had a cold shower. There was a separate compartment, a dry toilet, and this was cleared by employees of the sanitary department, usually during the early hours of the morning. There was a short passageway from the rear of the house leading in to a 'kitchen'. This was a wooden construction and there was a fireplace in the middle of the floor with what looked like a series of 'flower pots' arranged round the fire and in the event that you wished to make a roast, this was achieved by placing a four gallon kerosine tin on its side and above the fire.

How long that lasted I do not remember but it was eventually replaced with a Dover stove. Of course it has to be remembered that this was a native house that had been hurriedly converted for our use and on the orders of the Resident Commissioner who refused to allow Pat and Lylie to live any further north because of the 'armed robbers' as they were then called, (Later C.Ts. - Communist Terrorists). We had some interesting times in this little house, and Pat has told me that she quite enjoys the memories and the experiences we had while living there. The thunder storm for example when Pat had to lie across Lylie on the bed to protect her from the crashing noise of the thunder which shook the road and surrounding ground. I had gone to Alor Star and when the storm struck I was making my way back to Jitra.

Trees were being up-rooted and debris littered the road. The rain was lashing and the wipers useless. I had to drive with the door open and eventually got back to find Pat with Lylie as described above.

Then there was the prowling tiger, which was finally shot, across the road from our 'driveway'. The water buffalo came in to the compound at night and frequently shook our 'house' by scratching themselves against the corner posts. (I should have said that the house was built on stilts, about five feet above the ground level). This also meant ticks, which came with the Water Buffalo (Kerbau), which our dog had to suffer and of course the dog, Nigger, had to wear a metal licence disc attached to his collar. He invariably lost it in the long grass and on one occasion Pat asked me to look for it. She was not going to risk meeting snakes in the grass. I assured her that there was no chance of seeing a snake near the house and proceeded down the steps to prove my point. As I reached the bottom of the steps I had to ask Pat to get a brush for me. She did. There was a black cobra lying comfortably in the gutter which ran round the house. Fortunately, Ismail, my despatch rider, was passing at the time and he suspected that there was something wrong.

He left his machine at the main road and came in. It was Ismail who finished off the Cobra and then insisted in getting a shovel to remove the dead snake and the ground where it was lying. He explained that was to ensure that its mate would not come in there looking for it. He took the remains to the other side of the main road and scattered them over the ground. (A lesson learned in dealing with dead snakes.) After a few months at Jitra we were allocated a house in Alor Star which was as different as could be imagined. This house was approached from the main road and stood back for approximately 100 yards. There were four bedrooms and each had its own bathroom, but there was not one bath in the whole house.

Shanghai Jars with Dippers was the order of the day. The Japanese must have removed the baths and up to 1947 the P.W.D. had not been able to produce replacements. More of this later.

Alor Star was the Capitol of Kedah and a few miles to the north west there was the boundary with Perlis. Journeying to the south the main town was Sungei Patani from where you could branch off and proceed towards Grik in north Perak. After Sungei Patani the road continued towards Province Wellesly from where you had to go by ferry to reach Penang.

Penang was approximately 70 miles from Alor Star and usually the European population would go to Penang on a Thursday afternoon for various reasons, but one special reason in 1947 would be to collect tinned butter, it was the only source at that time, and rancid or not, it was appreciated. I believe it was imported from Australia. We were dependant on the cold storage for beef and in general, most provisions that we required, although there was a provision shop in Alor Star with mostly tinned goods. Fruit and vegetables were available but great care had to be taken with the local produce and hygiene was of the highest order. Milk was of the powdered type and the most popular was klim. It will be noted that dealing with infants feeding presented problems and in the case of Lylie at that time, we bought lactogen in bulk. There was either one or two dozen tins to the carton. During the whole of our time in Malaya we never saw fresh milk and it was in Singapore that we registered with the cold storage for fresh milk. This was in 1949.

The European community in Kedah was very small and consisted of Government Officials and rubber planters. In Alor Star there was a mill and the manager of the mill was European. The Resident Commissioner was stationed at Alor Star and the Sultan of Kedah had his Istana on the outskirts of Alor Star. The community got on very well together and of course, whenever there was a ceremonial function, practically everyone would attend. In 1946, the daughter of Sultan Badleisha(?) was married at the Istana and a very happy time was enjoyed by the whole of the community.

There was the Bersanding and the Berlima and the festivities lasted for days. The Kedah Royal Family, who have a most interesting history, were well-liked and had no hesitation in mixing at the Kedah Gymkhana Club or taking part in local sport. Tunku Yacob, brother of the Sultan, was one of the most pleasant men you could hope to meet and was, as I remember, connected with the veterinary department. The Sultan's heir was keen on riding and often appeared at the Club, where he had no hesitation in riding the difficult horses. Charlie Renwick, a close friend of ours, was the veterinary surgeon for Kedah and had much to do with horses being available at the Club. There was an amateur race course connected to the club and within the race course there was a 9-hole golf course.

I shall never forget how I first became directly interested with polo. One evening when I went round to the stables, I saw Charlie on horseback and moving a ball around on the ground with a polo stick. I asked him what he was doing and the conversation turned to the game of polo. I was also learning to ride with instruction from Charlie and Harry Wheeler. At Alor Star we were complete; hospital, gymkhana club, residency, Istana, cinema, work but no church. Dining out was frequent and there was good social contact. At this point in the narrative I feel that I must give an account of the job and what Immigration Control meant based at Changloon.

The staff consisted of one inspector and 10 outdoor officers. I was gazetted as Deputy Controller of Immigration and this must have been for the convenience of the Immigration Ordinance and in order to grant the necessary authority to carry out the duties of document examination and or issue of temporary passes to people living on or near the actual border between Malaya and Siam (Thailand). Tam Kok Thye was the Inspector and knew the Form as did a few of the others.

It was from them that I learned what actually happened at this gazetted point of entry and of the local problems. Coupled with the briefing at Singapore, and slightly more detail at Penang, I was able to commence duty and be guided by the Immigration Laws which I began to study at once.

I had been handed loads of 'bumf' and the terms of my engagement had been made clear to me and what was required during the first tour of duty, i.e. three years. Examination in Immigration Law, Criminal Procedure Code, Penal Code and Laws of Evidence were foremost. There was also Colonial Administration, Government General Orders, Financial Procedure and the Language. The latter was in three standards and if you achieved standard three you were among the elete.

My arrival at Changloon was in mid July and, as Pat did not arrive until early 1947, I was fully occupied through the day and after the barrier was closed and darkness fell, I concentrated my primary efforts in learning to speak Malay.

I had been introduced to the language at the School of Oriental Languages by Professor Jock Sturrock during the staff training at Wimbledon, where we had been training for the invasion of Malaya. The School of Oriental Languages had been located at Sussex Gardens, Sault Place, which as I remember, is quite near Paddington.

Jock was a retired Malayan Education Officer, and had held a senior appointment before the war. He was elderly and very popular and succeeded in cramming us with many useful phrases in the short time we were with him. I shall never forget his parting words to us as we prepared to leave London to embark for overseas. "Gentlemen, be kind to the Malays, they are this world's real gentlemen". Times may have changed since 1945 but at that time it was easy to identify what Jock had meant when I did meet the gentle and courteous people in the towns and especially in the Kampongs.

That early teaching proved to be of great assistance. On the 16th of December 1946, (Pat's Birthday) I passed Standard 1. Then the overall studying began and the spur was the realisation that Government retained the right to reject officers who did not pass all examinations during the cadet period of three years. A few exceptions were made if the officer was seen and known to be keen. The immediate neighbouring state was Perlis and the gazetted point of entry from Siam into Malaya was at the railway station on the frontier at Padang Besar. This was in fact the actual frontier. The Immigration Office was in Malaya but the Station Master's Office was in Siam although on the same platform.

The staff at Padang Besar consisted of an expatriate officer, a Chinese inspector and a number of outdoor officers. The only communication from Malaya to the Padang Besar Kampong was by rail. The railway was the main railway line from Singapore to Bangkok but there were few trains in those days. The roads ended at or close to Kangar and if you wished to reach Padang Besar outside of the train timetable, there was an alternative to walking. The rail jeep. The railway station at Bukit Ketri housed a jeep which was fitted on to railway wheels.

That was the only difference to the normal jeep, the wheels. The vehicle was driven in the usual way although the speed was at a very reduced rate. The person who made this possible should have been given an honour, it made life a lot easier and in due course was to prove of great benefit to me.

The only other way of getting to Padang Besar from Malaya was to walk. I have to add that it was possible to go by road from Changloon to Ban Sadau and then proceed west on what was referred to as a track. I made that journey once after meeting my opposite number in the Siamese Immigration Office at Ban Sadau and can say without fear of contradiction, it was a one off!

From end to end you were for ever placing the road wheels carefully on the ridges and moving forward slowly. Between the ridges there were trenches of varying depths and if the vehicle, (again a jeep) had slipped in to one of those trenches I know we would have had a problem.

There was a jungle path leading from the Padang Besar Station via a Kampong towards Kangar and I made that journey on two occasions, the second time with the head of the Malayan Immigration Department. As I remember it, there was a known compass bearing referred to, but the pathway was quite clear of jungle growth and my surprise at such a senior officer wishing to make that walk was answered as we neared a Kampong where an old Friend of the Director lived.

As we neared the house, I was told that he had not seen this man for some time and that he was not sure if he was still married to the same woman. I was further informed that if in the future, when I would have lived in the country for some years, I was meeting an old friend, it was advisable never to enquire after the health of his wife.

"You see", he said, "You may not be talking about the same person". As the years rolled by I came to understand why.

During 1946-47 there were reports of activity by 'armed bandits' throughout the country and it was suspected that there were groups of them operating on or near the Siamese frontier. This coincided with reports that there was infiltration of illegal immigrants on a large scale and the area where the immigrants were entering was in the direction of Perlis.

In the course of time we discovered that Chinese immigrants were making their way from China via Hong Kong by ship to Bangkok and then by train to a station near Padang Besar. From there on it was by foot and through the jungle towards Perlis. These batches of illegal immigrants were conducted by 'couriers' and if and when they reached Perlis, the rest was easy. The Customs Department were also concerned with smuggling and the veterinary department were most concerned about animal traffic from Siam into Malaya. Because of this the departments joined forces and attempts were made to apprehend the people concerned.

The police at Perlis were also informed of our activities and on occasion took part in our 'night manoeuvres'. There were many nights when we would go out and set up an ambush position for illegal immigrants or smugglers, but I do not remember that our efforts were initially worthwhile. The procedure was eventually changed and I will return to this point.

With animal traffic the situation was quite different. I never heard anything official about cattle coming in from Siam but there was a cattle pound at Padang Besar and there were Pathan Indians operating in the area. These men were known to be expert at their trade. The gossip was that owing to the shortage of beef in Malaya, the 'import' of cattle from Siam was welcomed and care was taken to ensure that the beasts coming in were not diseased. Whatever was the true situation it was certainly not common knowledge.

There was one occasion when I was on a tour of inspection, (after I had been appointed to take over from the previous expatriate - this is another story) with a close friend of mine we happened to come upon a fight between two Siamese and an elderly Pathan near the rest house in Padang Besar. We stopped the Siamese and encouraged them to return to their own side of the border. The Pathan expressed his gratitude and then went about his business. There was a sequel to this incident. Some time later, much later, when I was in Penang with Pat and Lylie shopping, as we passed an Indian shop, the owner came running out in to the street and spoke to me. He knew my name and who I was.

The fight at Padang Besar was referred to and I was thanked once again for 'saving' the Pathan cattleman. He insisted on giving a present and Lylie became the owner of a rag-type doll. I believe that Lylie has that doll still as I write in 1992. I could make a fairly accurate guess at the relationship between the cattleman and the proprietor of the shop and right up until we left Malaya, that family kept in touch with our movements but at no time did they ever attempt bribery.

Chapter 6

But it was uncanny that as the ship called at Penang when we were going on leave or returning from the U.K., flowers were delivered to the cabin. Even when we departed from Singapore on Malayanisation, (pensioned off), representatives came on board with a token farewell gift of a brooch, a simple and inexpensive gift. I never really knew why beyond the fact that we had stopped a fight.

The smuggling of pigs was another story. This activity took place right across Perlis and Kedah. The method was quite simple. Usually it was carried out by boys and the method was to bring two pigs with rope or wire tied to the rear legs, out of Siam and through the jungle where there was ease of access. The pigs walked in front of the boys and were encouraged to keep going.

For some reason or other Sintok, near and east of Changloon, was a favourite centre of the journey from one country into the other.

Chandu was the other favourite for smugglers and the methods employed were ingenious. There was considerable amounts carried on the person and while it was simple to deal with the male and discover the small tin tubes containing the Chandu, the female presented a different problem and it was some time before their particular method was discovered. Thereafter female officers were left to deal with them.

On one occasion at Changloon, I entered the 'office', a basha, on the side of the road and walked past the travellers who were waiting until their documents were endorsed for entry. On the table there was a clean new border pass and on enquiring to whom did it belong, a small Chinese man came forward, wearing long shorts dangling below his knees.

The shorts were filthy and he was not too clean. I referred him to the Customs Officer who shared the 'office' with the Immigration Department and he carried out an examination of the man. He discovered that there was attached to the man's waist and all round his middle, small tin tubes threaded one above the other, all stuffed with Chandu (opium).

The Chinese would-be smuggler was taken to Alor Star and that evening commenced a six month sentence in the local Gaol. All because his border pass was clean. Today smuggling or possession of drugs is punished by death.

In 1947 there was a change in the attitude of Government towards what had been referred to as 'armed bandits'. The illegal immigrant problem was causing concern and there was a new factor.

Clearings were appearing in different parts of the jungle and there appeared to be a military system of accommodation as if surrounding a parade ground. At about this time I was asked, quietly, to become a member of the M.S.S. and to operate under a controller who was an officer of the S.B. The main purpose was to discover any information as to how the illegal immigration was being organised and by whom. Also, to note anything that was unusual in the rubber estates or parts of the jungle where I might be on patrol. We discovered much and by using M.S.S. means of reporting, the risk of 'leaked information' by locals was eliminated.

Briefly, in one simple operation, by making friends with the Siamese officials, we were able to get hold of information showing not only where the illegals were coming from but also the routes that were being used and the 'holding areas' as each batch was passed from one area to the next. The line of illegal entry started in China and was traced all the way into Singapore through Malaya. The situation was serious and a section of armed soldiers was sent to Changloon and positioned at the opposite side of the road and at the barrier. During my time at Changloon there was no serious incident involving the soldiers.

It was during this period that Pat and Lylie had arrived and first we were at Jitra and then to Alor Star. The Resident Commissioner, O.E. Venables had ruled that my family would not live at Changloon. Office space was found for the Immigration Department at the secretariat and all office equipment was transferred from Changloon to the secretariat. I was now resident at Alor Star and the office was in Alor Star while the Gazetted Point was retained at Changloon.

My responsibility had also been increased to take in Perlis and I was now the Deputy Controller of Immigration, Kedah and Perlis. The situation had completely changed since my arrival in 1946 and from mid-July 1947 it had become obvious that the 'armed bandits' were in fact something much more sinister. Early one afternoon as I was passing through Jitra the police stopped me and informed me that the Deputy Controller of Immigration Perlis had been shot at Padang Besar. The bullet had passed through the top of his legs and he was being brought down to the hospital. I reported to K.L. and went up to Padang Besar at once.

Arriving at Bukit Ketri I was able to get the rail jeep and proceed to Padang Besar where I found the staff in a disturbed state. It can be imagined just how they must have been confused over the attempted murder of their Tuan, shooting government officials was a very serious matter.

The Inspector at Padang Besar, Yap Fook Chong, was a very quiet and good type of officer. Tall for a Chinese and well-liked. He gave me an account of what had happened in so far as he understood the position. It was difficult to understand why the officer had been shot but it was obvious that the shooting had been carried out by armed bandits.

As I have explained earlier, the boundary between Malaya and Siam was geographically aligned in such a way that it passed through the middle of the railway station and then down through the Kampong. Whether the bandit was in Siam or Malaya when he fired on the immigration officer was not clear but he had apparently fired from within one of the bashas (nipah roofed wooden hut) as the immigration officer had walked through the Kampong. The cause was never established and at that time it had become known that the bandits were in fact Communist Terrorists although I do not think that this title had become widely used just at the time of the shooting. The immigration officer spent time in hospital and eventually recovered but he was never sent back to Padang Besar. I reported to the Controller of Immigration at Kuala Lumpur and during this conversation by telephone he ordered me to take over at Padang Besar. Having carried out an inspection of the Revenue Records I told him that I was unable to accept responsibility on the grounds that the 'books' were not up to date. The counter instruction was that I was to carry on after sealing the Revenue Records which would be collected by the O.S.P.C from Perlis. (Police Officer Superintending the Area). New records were opened and normal working resumed.

I found Padang Besar most interesting. It was not long after the shooting incident when Fook Chong and I went down in to the Kampong for a coffee at the Chinese Coffee Shop. There was a young Chinese sitting in the shop and at some time I had been introduced to him with the additional information that he had been an officer working with Force 136 during the Jap occupation.

He was then suspected of being a Lieutenant of the 'Green Dragon Gang' but at that time there was no evidence to support this suspicion. There were quite a number of Chinese sitting in the Coffee Shop and I was aware that they were armed. It was obvious that there were bulges in their clothing and in a few cases I could see the butts of revolvers sticking out of their pockets. I have no memory of what was said but the 'Lieut.' knew that I had seen the butts of the revolvers and we had continued our casual conversation. It was during 1949 while I was on leave in the U.K. that I learned the 'Lieut.' was killed during a battle with the Security Forces. Whether he had anything to do with the attempted murder in Padang Besar of the Immigration Officer I never heard.

While I am at this part of my story there is something which would be appropriate to refer to now although it happened sometime later. My constant travelling to and from Padang Besar always raised a question in my own mind. There appeared to be no danger.

While travelling to Padang Besar which was frequent I was always aware of the possibility of ambush. After the declaration of the emergency this was highly possible in any part of Malaya and as the jungle came right up to the edge of the railway track, there was little hope of being able to do anything about protection from ambush. At Changloon, in Kedah, the approach was by road and travelling from Alor Star the whole route was practically bordered by rubber plantations. This would have made it more difficult for the purpose of ambush.

There were many occasions when cars were stopped on the road in different parts of the country and the occupants shot. At Changloon, when I was in my car I always travelled with a Lugar automatic laid on the floor where I could reach it without too much movement. There never was any need to resort to the Lugar.

My intention was that should I be stopped by Communist Terrorists, the ones nearest to me were coming with me, but in the rail jeep that was not possible. The point of this account is that it was a long time afterwards, after I had left Kedah, that the thought came to me. Tham Kok Thye and I went all over the area and never once were we in trouble. The thought, Tham Kok Thye was a much respected officer of the one time Force 136, and many of the Communist Terrorists had been members of that Force during the Jap period. During the emergency, Tham Kok Thye was ordered away from the closeness of the border. I was also ordered well away from the border, but much more happened before that took place. I am left wondering if my 'safety' was because of my close working with Tham Kok Thye.

There was another occasion when I thought I was going to have to use the Lugar. It was during the afternoon when a message was relayed to me by the police that three deserters from the forces had been causing trouble in the villages and were thought to be making for Siam. If they continued north they would have to pass through Changloon. Would I keep a look out for them. There was only one easy way to pass Changloon and I decided to go out and wait quietly to see if they would come that way. The Lugar was in my pocket. In due course I heard people coming towards me and they were speaking in English. Two soldiers and a sailor came up the path and I stepped out and stopped them.

There was a brief period of silence and then the sailor suggested that they should rush me, "There's only one there." I told them to move out towards the main road and do it now. They hesitated and then turned to the road with me behind them.We reached the road and turned down towards the check post. As we walked away there was a movement in the growth beside the road and there stood Kok Thye, dressed in black shirt and slacks, grinning. Perhaps I had been tested by him. It was as well for the trio that they had not attempted to 'rush', they would have suffered.

The climax was also a lesson to me. These three servicemen had come in to Kedah from Perak, a neighbouring state, and I decided to charge them with illegal immigration to the State of Kedah. I felt that I had to do something with them. They were taken before the magistrate at Alor Star, charged and sentenced to six months in the Alor Star prison. The Military Authority must have been informed and they were collected on the following day. I never heard of them again. I had not taken my law exams at that time and it would appear that the magistrate must have been confused with my introduction of National Boundary Laws to military personnel crossing the state boundary within Malaya. However, there was no harm done and I had learned to distinguish between national and state law. The point of this also, Tham Kok Thye was there when needed and without my knowing. Perhaps my 'thought' about 'safety' is accurate.

At this point in writing I want to mention Pat and Lylie. It has to be remembered that Pat was only 24 years of age and had never been out of Great Britain until she came to join me in Malaya at Jitra. From Penang we came straight to Jitra and took up residence in what had been the Native Assistant Land Officer's Quarters. I have described them earlier and yes, there had been structural alterations; mosquito netting of the verandah and in the course of time the installation of a Dover stove, and that was about all.

Although there were a few shops in Jitra, shopping for main supplies had to be made in Alor Star or, a journey of some 80 miles to Penang.Pat and the infant took it all in 'their stride'.

Pat has assured me recently that she has pleasant memories of our little house at Jitra, crashing thunder storms; wandering tigers, poisonous snakes, water buffalo scratching their rumps on the verandah posts, all of this and she made a great success of the whole venture. There was also the transition period of armed bandits becoming Communist Terrorists and I have no recollection that this concerned her at all.

We did eventually move to Alor Star and took up residence in a large house, facing on to the main road. This house had been used as a hospital during the Japanese occupation. The Kedah Gymkhana Club was approximately 200 yards to our right as we faced the road.

There was one outstanding occasion when the Governor General, the late Sir Edward Gent, came visiting in the north of Kedah during 1947. The District Officer, a Malay, laid on a tea party for the Governor and we were invited to attend. I remember that it was a bright sunny afternoon and we were quite a small group of people, no pomp or ceremony. I am sure that His Excellency enjoyed that afternoon, wearing his lounge suit and brown trilby. No fuss, uniform, plumed hat nor guard of honour; seems unreal when compared with todays security requirements all over the world. It was shortly after this visit that Sir Edward was killed in an air crash over England.

Pat and Lylie settled in very quickly at Alor Star and of course Nigger was with us. Breed, looked like a labrador but no doubt he had many strains in his veins. I had found him under a wooden seat in a Kampong near Changloon as a puppy. He was given to me by the owner with the warning to watch that the 'Chinese' did not get him!

Apparently black dogs are a delicacy. The Malays are not too fond of dogs particularly when they are wet. I do not know why, perhaps because wet dogs can make life uncomfortable. However Nigger had one group of people that he did not like, policemen. When we left Kedah we could not take Nigger with us because it was forbidden to move dogs from one state to another in accordance with the Quarantine Laws. We asked around for a 'good home' for Nigger and thus he became the property of the Chief Police Officer. During our stay at Alor Star we became part of the European Community in every sense and during that period every family was connected with Government service.

There was a good relationship all round and there were one or two 'characters' in our midst but none that were unacceptable. Pat and Lylie took part in all social events involving mothers and children and during this period also, Agnes came to live with us and was a companion to Pat. She may have come to us when we were at Jitra but whenever it was it was a good decision, Agnes was a gem. She was a member of a Chinese family in Ipoh and her people were not too happy about her coming to Kedah. Agnes stayed with us until we departed for Singapore.

Later we heard that she was training to be a nurse and then that she was a sister in a Malayan Hospital.

Although a small Community firm friendships were made and Pat became friendly with Mary Renwick who was a nursing sister at the Alor Star Hospital. Indeed we were friendly with Charlie Renwick and Mary (McLean) before they were married, a friendship that lasted until they died; Charlie at 59 years of age and Mary a few years later. This was in the mid-1970s.

Although we were all involved in the run up to the declaration of The Emergency in 1947, life went on without any dramatic happenings and a busy social life was enjoyed at Alor Star centred on the Gymkhana Club. Tennis was played every afternoon and evening until the daylight failed at about 7 p. m.

There was also a riding school and many people learned to ride at that time including myself. It was mainly thanks to Charlie Renwick that the school took shape. Harry Wheeler, of the Customs Department, an accomplished horseman and owner of racehorses, gave advice on the merits of riding.

The riding school was successful and in the course of time a Gymkhana Meeting was arranged and clubs were invited from all over Malaya and Singapore to take part in the Amateur Racing at the Gymkhana Club Kedah. It was at Kedah where I first took part in a race and came in second to Harry Wheeler. The horse was 'Tommy' and had already won a race ridden by Charlie Renwick. There is a very nice photograph of Pat leading 'Tommy' in on that occasion.

I have to confess at this stage that when I was introduced to racing by Harry Wheeler on the first occasion, I became so enthusiastic on the run in that I lost my stirrups and came off! There was another occasion, a few years later when we were living in Singapore, that I agreed to ride a horse for a trainer at a meeting in Alor Star. These meetings had become an annual event during the emergency. The horse that I was riding for them was named 'April Vale' and had served her purpose as a professional racehorse. There was another horse from the same stable named 'Kimberley' and he had been banned from professional racing on account of his temper.

The man riding him on this afternoon in the 2.30 p.m. race was the assistant Secretary of the Singapore Racing Association and did a lot of riding out in the early morning for different trainers. During the race as we approached the home turn Kimberley's saddle slipped and the rider fell under his belly and was log rolled between the front and hind feet. Kimberley panicked and came straight at me with his ears flat back on his head.

'April Vale' moved like a streak and we were heading straight for the crowd on the opposite side of the deep monsoon drain which ran alongside the race track. I remember standing up in the stirrups and hauling her head round to my left. It was not enough; we reached the Monsoon Drain and she took off right in to it, longwise, I was thrown for a long distance. I got my breath back. April Vale had to be destroyed. I had sprained my thumb.

There was a jockey present in the stand and he had seen the whole incident through his binoculars. Now retired and a member of the Racing Association it was most helpful that he had been present and witnessed what was a serious accident. 'Kimberley' was found later that evening having bolted from the racecourse over the paddy fields. The rider was taken to hospital on the Saturday afternoon and did not regain consciousness until the following Thursday. I met with the trainer on my return to Singapore and after a brief conversation never heard another word. However, there was no more attempts to enter barred racehorses at amateur meetings.

Returning to 1947, Pat knew that she was expecting our second baby in early 1948 and naturally there was pleasure and planning for the arrival of the new baby. As the time drew near for the birth, we decided that Pat and Agnes would move to Penang and rooms were booked at the Metropole Hotel approximately six weeks before the anticipated date. Dr Lee had been advising and looking after Pat and she was to be attended by him at the birth. The baby was born on the 22nd of January, 1948, Sheila Trounson Fox.

I saw her during the afternoon and I shall always remember the very large amah at the maternity hospital in Penang saying that this was a very good baby, going to have a very good future. Perhaps I accepted that statement as politeness or even superstition but I now know that it was a correct prophesy. And now I will leave Pat and the babies to their normal routine while I return to my duties and the effects of the emergency.

The Immigration Office was now housed in the secretariat building in Alor Star and I was constantly on the move between Alor Star and Changloon and also in the surrounding area. I was co-operating with customs and police and in the course of our work I was also learning from them. Tham Kok Thye was active and our main concern was immigration from Siam or I suppose, the apprehension of illegal immigrants from China coming in via the Siamese routes.

I must have become aware that we were only touching the edges of illegal immigrants and from information reaching us from the south, it was obvious that many people were getting past the frontier posts. I took, what was to be one of the most important steps of my career, although unknown by me at the time, and wrote a report to the Resident Commissioner of Kedah advising him of what we were finding in the jungle as evidence of military style camps and suggesting that we should be armed to deal with what might come our way.

I was sent for by the resident and when I stood before his desk I saw my report, heavily underlined in red at certain parts. The resident referred to the report and ended by giving me a stern rocket for suggesting shooting at any one. I went back to my office and filed the report. Sometime later, on a Saturday morning, a tall man walked in to the secretariat and said he was looking for Dudley Fox. I told him who I was.

Mr J.S.H. Cunyngham-Brown, OBE.

This gentleman was unknown to me at the time but he was to make an entire difference to my future career. (As I write this part of the biography it has come to my notice that he has just died and there was a write up in the Daily Telegraph about his service to the country.) After due enquiry I discovered the name of his bank and on application to the Manager of the Bank, stating my reason for applying, he kindly forwarded a copy of the 'cutting' from the Daily Telegraph which they had kept in the bank file. I now include the contents of that report in this biography for the reason stated; this was the man, who in my opinion, changed the course of my career and what lay ahead of me in the years that followed.

On that particular Saturday morning he had come to see me and to discuss the territory immediately adjacent to the Frontier with Siam (Thailand). He said that he had heard I knew the area and would be able to answer his enquiries. We had a long discussion at the end of which he asked me if I had made a report of my findings. I explained what had happened when I reported to the resident.

C.B. asked if I had a copy of the report and could he see it. I took the report from the file and handed it to him. He asked that he might take it with him and I agreed. At the time I probably thought that was that.

Sjovald Cunyngham-Brown (1905-1989)

Sjovald Cunyngham-Brown who has died at Georgetown, Penang, aged 83 was a member of the old Malayan Civil Service whose adventures in the 1939-45 war were featured in the nostalgic BBC Television series, Tales from the South China Seas.

After serving as a magistrate in Singapore and as a Controller of Labour in Johore, Cunyngham-Brown was caught up in the "Mad Hatters Tea Party" (As he described it) of the Japanese invasion of Malaya as an officer in the Malayan R.N.V.R. and in the "Grand Guignol of horrors" that followed the fall of Singapore in 1942.

The extraordinary story of the ensuing 3 ½ years was told by Cunyngham-Brown in an autobiographical account, 'Crowded Hour' as well as to Charles Allen for the television cameras.

He related how he ferried refugees to Sumatra in a small naval vessel; made a gallant attempt to sail an outrigger to Ceylon; was captured and sentenced to death. Then came months of solitary confinement followed by the ghastliness of slave labour in the construction of a railway across Sumatra – years in which his greatness of spirit displayed itself in the way he tended the sick and the dying and in his lack of bitterness towards his persecutors. Saved from execution by the dropping of the atomic bomb, Cunyngham-Brown, through the kindness of a fellow member of the MCS, was given the unusual privilege of receiving the surrender of the general commanding the West Coast Regiment of the Japanese Imperial Army in Johore.

Of Shetland-Scottish descent, with a dash of French blood and Viking like in appearance, John Sjovald Hoseason Cunyngham-Brown inherited a yen for travel and adventure that never left him. Born on August 5th 1905, he was educated at Blundell's and read medicine at Birmingham for two years before abandoning his studies to go to sea. He worked his way out to Australia in order to sign on as a deckhand on the square rigger William Mitchell, last of the grain clippers, on what turned out to be its final voyage.

In 1929 he once more sailed out to the 'gin clear seas' of the East – this time as an Eastern Cadet to join the Malayan Civil Service. He began his apprenticeship in Georgetown, Penang, before being posted to India for a three year spell as an assistant emigration Commissioner in the Madras Presidency, where he became fluent in Telegu.

After the war Cunyngham-Brown returned to civil administration, spending three years in Johore as Deputy Resident, followed by a spell as District Officer in Kinta. His last six years with the MCS were spent as President of the Municipal Council in Georgetown, where his genial presence did much to ease the transition to Malayan Independence.

Afterwards he threw in his lot with the country that he had helped to develop, setting up a small export spice business in Penang and continuing to play an enthusiastic role in the affairs of his adopted home for the next two decades – most notably as a local historian as well as acting for 16 years as French Consul.

Cunyngham-Brown's death ends a trading link between the Malayan Archipelago and Britain that goes back to the early days of the East India Company.

He used to describe his enterprise as one of those old perfumed trades where one has to have a bath to get the smell of cloves off one in the evening. It makes me laugh to think that this is where we came in, young men of the East India Company collecting cloves as I am and supervising the export of this precious commodity.

Equally at ease with Cantonese, Malay or Telegu, Cunyngham-

Brown was Georgetown's honorary godfather, a familiar figure to all and loved by many. A man of immense charm and erudition, he was the embodiment of the noblest virtues of the old Colonial Administrator.

He was appointed OBE and a Chevalier of the National Order of Merit of France (End of report in the Daily Telegraph - 25/4/1989)

Cunyngham-Brown had also told me that he was on his way to Hadayai to take up the post of British Consul. It was shortly after that meeting with Cunyngham-Brown that life changed dramatically. It was about teatime one evening when a large American car turned in to the driveway of our house and Pat and I stood on the verandah waiting to see who had arrived. It was the Head of the Immigration Department, Malaya, Mr S.E. King accompanied by the Deputy Controller of Immigration, Penang, Mr Tony Roach, (the gentleman who did not care for ex-army officers) and the Officer Superintending Police Circle from Sungei Patani. S.E. knew Pat and his first request was whether she had any of her scones for tea! This having been attended to S.E. then asked me to unfold a map of the Kedah-Perlis area which I did and placed it over a bamboo screen which stood at the entrance to the dining room and acted as a draft protector.

Not all was revealed but I was told that my report had caused a stir in K.L. and I was now asked how I intended to implement my recommendations. I commenced on the Perlis coast and made my way across the map towards Perak Boundary.

I explained how the Natural Geographical Frontier with Siam was impossible to control and that we needed an artificial frontier – running in a straight line – as far as possible. This could be achieved by gazette notification and moving from Kuala Perlis (may have been Kuala Sanglang) to the railway line, then on to the trig points and following existing features right across the country.

When this was done all personnel moving in the gazetted area would be required to carry identification. When challenged by immigration or police, they would be able to prove that they were bonafide residents from the Kampongs or travelling on a border pass. There would be an age starting point of 12-years-old and the identity card would bear the photograph of the holder.

There was a great deal of detailed discussion and in the event I was ordered to get on with it. Dakota Aircraft was to be employed to assist with the registration and I was allocated $100,000. Two M.C.S. Officers were posted to assist me (and that caused a small fuss), John Watt and Mike Morgan.

It was objected to by an M.C.S. Officer on the grounds that I, as a departmental officer, would be giving orders to an M.C.S officer. It was unusual for departmental officers to be placed in charge, but these were unusual times and I had more experience of the area and spoke a reasonable amount of Malay although I was still studying the language and had a long way to go. John and Mike got on with what they had to do and there were very few occasions when orders had to be given.

I can now pick up my narrative having introduced Cunyngham-Brown and the important part he played. It is obvious from the writing above that he was quite a man.

The physical part of the creation of a new boundary south of the geographical frontier was attended to by Gazette Notifications and camps were set up at Jitra in the north and at Grik in the south. The supervision of these was carried out by John and Mike.

I had quite a task to attend to in arranging for the introduction of Identity Cards and the photographing of all above the age of 12-years living in the Kampongs which were scattered throughout the jungle. I would like to explain that it was not all impenetrable jungle; there were rubber estates and roads of a kind leading towards the Kampongs and where the roads ended, there would be paths well used by the Kampong people.

The first thing was priorities; the people had to be informed about the Identity Cards and the means of communication were limited. There was one important factor, every Kampong had a Pengulu, (village headman) and the police were represented by at least one constable. The other means that had become available was aircraft, the Dakotas.

Pamphlets were printed and dropped all over the area telling the people to contact the Pengulu and what it was we were going to do. There were obviously difficulties which will be hard for the modern person to imagine but it was the only way at the time. The major problem was how to get the photographs taken and, much more to the point, how to get the photographers and sufficient film without the traders pushing the cost sky-high.

I discussed this with Tham Kok Thye and at first I thought it would be easy to carry out a scheme within Kedah and collect all the flm available. My idea was to descend on the shopkeepers in the early hours of the morning to maintain the surprise element. As I look back I shudder at this proposal. I actually had an interview with the Mentri Besar, (Chief Minister) and explained what I hoped to do. He was very patient and it was clear that the idea would have to be dropped. It was.

However, Kok Thye informed me that many of his war time friends were now in business scattered throughout the state. Some of them had been with him in Force 136 and they were not too happy about the Communist Terrorists operating in the area.

This gave me an idea and I asked Kok Thye if he would invite all the shop owners who were connected with photography to come to Alor Star and attend a meeting with me. This was done and we met one afternoon to see what could be done.

The plan was simple but looking back, I think it was audacious. There was the question of the ferry crossing to Penang from Province Wellesley and therefore timing was very important. I explained to the 'gathering' what was required. They were all required to go to Penang on the same day and if possible arrange to be on the same ferry, allowing that this would be difficult because they all needed to have their own transport in Penang it was necessary to ensure that they had all reached Penang before approaching the sources where the film was on sale. The town of Penang is not too wide spread and I believe Kok Thye went along as co-ordinator. Once everyone was on the island they would proceed to pre-arranged shops and at an agreed time they would enter the shop and ask about available film. The scheme was a complete success. Each man bought up all the film that was available and then made his way back to the ferry termial and home to his own area. Penang had no film left and I believe that it was some time before they were able to get sufficient film for the PenangResident to begin registration at Penang. (Years later, 1964). When I arrived in Jesselton (Kinabalu) on a Sunday, I was met by Tom Mackie who took me to the only hotel catering for government officers at that time.

On entering the Bar on the ground floor Tom introduced me to an expatriate who was sitting at a table. On hearing my name he enquired if I had ever served in Kedah.

"Yes", I replied.

"Then you are the man who cleared Penang of Film and held us up for a long time".

I remembered quite well what had transpired after we had purchased the film. The Resident had made a press announcement that Penang was going to introduce the Identity Card system and that they were going to be the first in the country (Malaya). I did not know about this at the time and while I heard about what was likely to happen to me, etc. etc. I never did hear one official word from anyone. And how long Penang had to wait, I have no idea. The man at the table had been in the Resident's office in Penang, probably an M.C.S. officer.

Thanks to the Chinese business men, photographers were chosen and appointed to specified areas. The administration and the price of the photographs was attended to, 50 cents for two copies and temporary staff were employed to prepare and issue the I.C.'s. There was quite a lot to do and the main difficulty was the illiteracy of the people.

The filing of the counterfoils of the cards was a major headache and I remember an officer of the Postal Department spending time with me and describing a system for the quick sorting of counterfoils. I knew nothing of Holleriths in those days but looking back I am sure that what my friend was dealing with was a close relative of 'Hollerith'.

The plan appeared to depend on a large oblong card with holes punched all the way round. Long steel pins were required to be placed through the holes at a particular letter and at that point all cards with a complete circle could be lifted out. The others would only be 'half circled' at that point. That was basically the idea and I do not remember if it ever entered in to the system. Immigration, training of the volunteers, completion of the camps, educating the people in the Kampongs to the new emergency regulations, continued and my time in Kedah was drawing to a close in the latter part of 1948, although I was unaware of that at the time.

During all of this preparation for dealing with the Communist Terrorists (C.T.'s), not only in Kedah and Perlis, but throughout the country, Pat and the children were getting on with life at home and all of the expatriate women were kept busy with their families. I believe I am correct when I say that all of the children were primary school age or infants. The secondary school age children would be at home in the U.K. or in Australia or New Zealand. It was strongly recommended in those days not to keep British children in the Tropics after their 8th birthday.

As we neared Christmas, people were busy making preparations for parties and sending invitations to the single men and women to come to Christmas dinner on the day. I remember that we had a houseful; the Renwicks, Gutteridge, Foss, to name some of them and it was a very happy time.

The telephone rang! I had been posted to Singapore as an Assistant Controller of Immigration and had to report there on the 1st of January, 1949. One week to pack up and travel from the north of Kedah to Singapore by train.

Lylie, three years of age and Sheila not quite one. Pat should write at this point she was not amused. My replacement arrived with his wife and in order that they would not get in Pat's way, I took them to a race meeting in Penang! What with P.W.D. assistance, the Amahs, friends looking in to say goodbye, it was the best thing I could do . . . looking back I can only remember a confused situation and a great deal of hustle and bustle. It is to Pat's credit and to my shame that I did not take a more active part instead of going off to the race meeting at Penang. I have no memory of the couple who came to take over except that at a later date I heard that he had not been accepted in to the department and we never met again. There was the incident of the bath arriving from the P.W.D. I have mentioned earlier that although there were four bathrooms in the house there was no bath. Cold showers were the order of the day and hot water would have had to come from the kitchen.

And there we were, a group of us on the verandah, when in came the P.W.D. men with the new bath. As far as I remember, Pat, politely told them to put it under the verandah.

On the night of the 30th December, 1948, we travelled by train from Prai which was the railway station on the mainland opposite Penang and arrived at Kuala Lumpur in the morning of the 31st. We stayed in the Kuala Lumpur Station Hotel, a fine building right on the station and the rooms were air-conditioned. We stayed in with Lylie and Sheila and enjoyed the comfort of the hotel. In the evening, we boarded the train for Singapore and arrived at Singapore on the 1st, of January 1949. We were met by Harry Noble and Tan Kai Cher and taken direct to a Division 2 house, No.7 Goodwood Hill.

Incredible. Christmas Dinner at Alor Star and then posting to a new station and on the spot on New Year's Day. Malaya was behind us, mixed feelings, I had my first trophy won by 'Tommy', ridden by Charlie Renwick and 'Lead In' by Pat. I came second on 'Tommy' at the same meeting but I cannot remember what the prize, if any, was.

Much was about to happen and we were going to be in Singapore until 1957. The major event took place in 1953 when Andrew was born. We did not know that 1957 was to be our final year when we arrived in 1949. However, the return of Lee Kwan Yew from Cambridge, The CRY for Independence, The 'School' Riots, the 1950 Riot (Maria Hertog), the time to go had come, sooner than the Colonial Office had anticipated, and we had all played our part in training local officers to take over our jobs and so end our careers in the Colonies.

Today, as I write, I am glad that it ended in the way that it did. The Dutch and the Americans did not leave with the same rapport from Indonesia or the Phillipines.(In fact, I believe the Americans are still 'leaving'!). Once more, into Singapore.

The first time I entered Singapore was in 1937 and of all the sights that we saw on that occasion, my remaining memory is of the Traffic Duty Policeman standing on a dais which looked like an up-turned wooden barrel, cut to approximately ⅓ of its height. The policeman had a bamboo 'arm' strapped across his back and when he desired the traffic to move he simply turned through an angle of ninety degrees. That was 55 years ago. The changes today in 1992 could not have been envisaged in 1937. Indeed, on arrival in January, 1949, the changes were well advanced.

My second arrival at Singapore in 1945 was as a member of 23 Civil Affairs Staff Officers. It was not intended that we should arrive as a 'spearhead' to re-occupy Singapore and to be among the first to enter while the Japanese were still in 'office' with their flags flying on their cars and above the Municipal Building. But, that is what happened. The atomic bomb had been dropped on Hiroshima and Nagasaka.

The effect was devastating, the confusion among the armed forces was widespread and it was feared that the Japanese in south east Asia would not obey their High Command to cease hostilities. But they did. In 1945 we were all thankful for the 'bomb'.

It was during the succeeding years that the world questioned the use of the 'bomb' and many points of view have been stated. War is war with all the horrors that mankind can conceive and it is not possible to compare the necessary action of the day with humanitarian concern for the enemy of that day. General hindsight never loses a battle. Hiroshima and Nagasaki are historical facts.

What would have happened in Malaya and Singapore if the British Forces had executed their plans to re-occupy the territories would also have been devastating. The suffering would have been amongst the people we were returning to rescue, and to evict an enemy who had invaded Malaya and Singapore and continued in cruelty of heinous kinds. The attitude to the 'bomb' depends on what side you were on at the time. In spite of what the 'bomb' did, it did not become a deterrent to waging war! On entering for the second time among my many duties was to proceed and ensure that the internees and prisoners of war were not subjected to any harm by the Japanese.

At Sime Road Internment Camp where the men were on one side of a valley and the women on the other side, there were huge cuttings made in the hill-side; two I believe. Perhaps they were potentially mass graves. This was never stated and those cuttings remained open for years, – may still be open.

The family arrival at Singapore on this occasion, January1949, was hectic, had been ever since the order to move from Alor Star had been received over the telephone.

Chapter 7

Normally, when proceeding on transfer or going on home leave and when returning from home leave, accommodation was booked at one of the hotels and a period of three days was authorised at government expense. There would be exceptions but, as I say, normally this was the procedure. However, on this occasion we came off the train at Singapore Railway Station and straight to a Class 2 Government Quarter at 7, Goodwood Hill. To further add to the confusion, the house was occupied by a single man who was about to proceed on leave.

He had one of the bedrooms and was resident for a few days after we arrived. I do not remember ever meeting him or knowing his name.

What I do remember is that we were given a warm welcome by members of the Immigration Department and Pat soon had the situation under control. Amahs were employed and we did get a very good cook. While Pat was busy seeing to the house I was interviewed by the Controller, J.L.J. Haxworth, who put me in the picture with the position at Singapore. It was not a promising situation.

J.L.J. had been my Senior Officer when he was at Penang, following Tony Roach, and in the course of being briefed I was left with the impression that there was another Senior Officer whom Roach did not want at Penang. So be it, I had to report for duty at once and it was with Harry Noble and Tan Kai Cher that I was to spend the next nine months prior to going on home leave.

I wish to say here that J.L.J. was one of the kindest and best superiors you could wish to work with and as for Harry and Kai Cher, they were first class colleagues.

In 1949, for the nine months before going on leave, time spent on duty was intense. I was learning the ropes from the others and there was a recruiting scheme in progress which, as far as I remember, brought in additional Chinese Officers and Eurasians. The constitution of the Immigration Department was amended and new ranks were created to differentiate between the different grades. I was now an Assistant Controller of Immigration, Div. 4. and on the permanent pensionable establishment.

There were further examinations to be taken, especially law, and emphasis was placed on the Criminal Procedure Code, The Penal

Code and The Laws of Evidence. I was most fortunate in finding a splendid tutor, Superintendent Andrew Frew of the Singapore Police. Andrew had been a serving officer in Singapore before the war and was a typical Glaswegian. I had to spend hours with him, always in the evening or at weekends and Pat had to come with me. It is no exaggeration, I was often too tired to drive home.

From 1949 until 1957 proved to be a period that will go down in history as one of the most inportant phases in the life of Singapore. In a way, what Sir Stamford Raffles had foreseen when he took over a forsaken island, with swamps and jungle, mosquito ridden, from the natives at the Johore area of the island Lee Kwan Yew continued and improved with his own charisma and modern technology. Kwan Yew was both a scholar and a practical man and obviously possessed of great courage. It will be written in the course of time how amongst his many feats, he actually enlarged the size of the island and then created tunnels to hold car parks under Raffles Place. But that is a story for those who know what happened. Francis Light had developed the island of Penang in the 18th century with the aid of immigrant Chinese by granting them areas of land on the island. The modern Singapore is also indebted to the Chinese, one of the finest and industrious races of our times. Kwan Yew is now retired and it is reported that his son is following in his father's footsteps.

My time was spent as follows, learning about immigration control in Singapore. Completing my career studies, learning to play polo as a leisure pursuit, appointed as Chairman of the Examining Board of Colloquial Malay in Singapore, twice acting as Deputy Controller of Immigration, Singapore, Passport Officer, Singapore, attending a special course at Liverpool Passport Office and Immigration Control as per U.K. Home Office procedure.

Updating the Malayan Polo Association Handbook on the Laws of the game in English and Malay, Secretary of the Malayan Polo Association and member of the Malayan Amateur Racing Association.

The above will show that there was not a lot of spare time and of course, unknown to any of us, officialdom included, the twilight hours of Colonial Rule in Singapore had arrived. What might have happened to our careers is now hypothetical. Having acted twice in a super-scale appointment was held to point the way ahead.

Indeed, acting once only was deemed to be sufficient but as I look back, I believe my colleague, Tom Mackie, would have become controller, I might have been his deputy. I possessed a volcanic temper and detested negative thinking and procrastination. Decide and do was my own attitude and it rarely failed me. But Tom was a milder man and of an entirely different background to mine.

My 'fuse' is now longer and I am a great believer in the basic grounding of education and secure home life at an early age. Having to concern children with the economic situation at home does not teach them security. Divine providence is manifested time and again during my life and simple Christian faith overcomes all difficulties.

Having mentioned Tom Mackie at this point it is relevant to record how in fact we did come together again in a different country. We both left the Singapore Government under what was called Malayanisation of the Service and received a sum of compensation. Tom did go on to be Controller of Immigration but in Brunei and while he was there the revolution broke out and created certain difficulties for both Brunei and North Borneo.

When the 'dust' had settled, a Plebiscite was held and this was followed by a referendum which I understand, lead to a decision to recall expatriate officers to take over districts in North Borneo (now re-named Sabah).

While Tom was on leave in the U.K. he called at our house in Cornwall to see me but I was up north at the time. Following Tom's visit I acted on the information he had produced and was called to London, Stag Place, for an interview. This resulted in my being accepted and asked to travel by air to Sabah where I was to be appointed as District Officer of Sandakan. The Sandakan Residency had a population of some 80,000 people and in my district there were 32,000 people.

The point of this interlude is I was now District Officer of Sandakan, Tom was on the West Coast, District Officer of Jesselton, the Capital of Sabah. These were the most important Districts in the country, senior appointments, and there was more to come, but I will return to that in sequence.

Assistant Controller of Immigration Singapore

Harry Noble, Tan Kai Cher and Dudley Fox were the Assistant Controllers and had to supervise the main duties of examination in the Port and at the Airport. We were located at the 'depot' on Wharf 44. The Controller, J.L.J. Haxworth was the Executive Authority and responsible for all Immigration decisions, Passport Control, Visa Issues, Certificates of Admission from China, and Temporary Stay Passes. His office was located at Havelock Road and later transferred to Patterson Road. The Deputy Controller, F. Sharp, was responsible for the 'Depot' and all referrals from shipping or aircraft points of entry were dealt with by him. In addition there were a number of 'outdoor' personnel nearly always in what resembled dungarees because of the nature of their duties, i.e searching shipping for illegal immigrants. There were inspectors, also in uniform, white with gold bar stripes on their epaulettes signifying their rank.

The depot was totally responsible for clearing all shipping, from the small craft that had to report at the 44 Jetty having come from the small islands, to the vessels that had to anchor in the Quarantine Anchorage the dangerous Cargo Anchorage and, the Passenger Liners which mainly went alongside at the docks. There was also aircraft to be cleared but in 1949 and for some time after that, there was very little aircraft in and out of Singapore.

Between 1949 and 1957 there was a complete change in The Immigration Laws of Singapore. What we would have called Head Office which was at Havelock Road, this was transferred to Patterson Road. There was a new British Nationality Ordinance brought out in 1949 which was of particular importance to Indians.

It has to be remembered that India had been partitiond in 1947 and the new regions were called India and Pakistan. There was also Bangladesh and of course Afghanistan. There was an interim period during which citizens of those named countries could apply for registration as British subjects. I think that it is no exaggeration to say that practically all 'Indians' living in Singapore and Malaya registered.

Immigration control of entry from India and China was carried out, administratively, at Head Office and Visa Control, British Subjects, (B.S.C. UK. and Colonies) and passport issue was dealt with by the various departments in Head Office. Boarding and clearing of arrivals at Gazetted Points of Entry was the responsibility of the depot. There was also the transferring of ships crews and their repatriation to port of signing on, supervised by the depot.

On the domestic front, Pat was busy with settling in to the ways of Singapore and the constant demands of two infants, Lylie was just over three years of age and Sheila was approaching her first birthday when we arrived at Singapore from Kedah.

1949 was a difficult year as I remember it. In addition to the changes in the Immigration Department procedure, there was the shortage of staff. Men who were on the establishment were given time off to attend advanced education courses at university or college. This resulted in the load falling on the shoulders of the three Assistant Controllers and the junior Inspectors with reference to the outdoor work. The vacancies had to be retained until the 'graduates' returned. While Pat was busy attending to the children and the running of our home, I was spending hours at all times of the day and night, turning out on duty. There was at that time only one aircraft a week arriving at Singapore and it had to land at the R.A.F. station at Tengah before proceeding on to Australia.

There was unfortunately one great drawback. The time of arrival was frequently altered and on many occasions the aeroplane would arrive in the late or early hours and we would be called to clear the passengers. This happened in both directions and then of course there was the shipping. The hours were long and I was out of the house for lengthy periods leaving Pat to manage on her own. As I have said, 1949 was a difficult year both from a departmental and a domestic point of view.

I continued with my career examinations and attended to my share of the duty roster until we were able to proceed on our first 'leave' to the U.K. for a period of six months.

Pat was attending to the domestic needs of the family and at the same time preparing for the journey home in October by the P&O Shipping to Tilbury. We went on leave in October 1949 and during our stay in the U.K. I received a cable message from Harry Noble and Tan Kai Cher congratulating me not only on passing my exams in Financial and General Orders and in Consular Instructions but the first candidate that had ever obtained 100% in Financial Control. There was very little time for leisure pursuits and it must have been due to the fact that Charlie and Mary Renwick arrived in Singapore and took up residence on Mount Pleasant that I found my way to the Singapore Polo Club, as a spectator. Charlie was stabling a horse named 'Singh'.

Arrangements were made for our departure on 'leave'. We still had our K6 (Standard Eight), our first new car bought in 1946. This was traded in against a new Standard Vanguard which we were due to collect in London, Davis Street.

Personal belongings were deposited with the P.W.D. 1st Class passages were booked for all of us and finally, official arrangements were made for me to attend the Immigration Department and then the Liverpool Passport Office at Liverpool. There was also a visit to Southport in connection with Passport Control. (I must have been keen).

After three weeks, we disembarked at Tilbury. We were met by Immigration Officers at Tilbury and received VIP treatment. This had been arranged from Singapore. In those days of rationing we had bought a huge ham on the bone from Singapore cold storage, and brought it home for our own use (it travelled in the ship's refrigerator, immigration perks were quite valuable).

Having collected our luggage and the ham, we were taken ashore and put in a Rolls Royce taxi which conveyed us to the Regent's Palace Hotel, a distance of some 30 miles Fare: £5. (That was 1949, that was). Overnight stop and pick up the Vanguard and on to 50 Caldwell Road, Allerton. We were home.

Mother and Arthur made us welcome and Lylie and Sheila were wrapped in a blanket and sat before the fire. There was one most interesting incident took place almost as soon as the children were sat before the fire. Lylie had spent her baby year in this house and had arrived in Malaya aged fourteen months. On the mantlepiece there were two china ornaments in the shape of a 'King' and 'Queen'.

Lylie spoke and said, "That one shakes its head but the other one does not". She was quite correct, the head on the Queen was loose and rocked while the head on the King was firm. There had been occasions when Lylie was a babe in arms to make the Queen's head rock which had helped the baby to stop crying. And to the amazement of all of us, she had remembered at the age of four years and one month.

October 1949 to March 1950: Visiting Allerton – Newton Village – Allerton – Bridgwater – Falmouth.

Visited Ventnor, Isle of Wight with Harry Butler who had to go there on duty. Crossed from Southampton by Ferry.

Return Singapore. Adelphi Hotel. pending allocation of Government Quarters.

Allocated 13 Malcolm Road (Semi Detached Class IV).

It has to be recorded that much happened at this address. The most memorable event was during the 'Maria Hertog' riots when Pat locked Lylie and Sheila in the bedroom and sat on the verandah with a .303 rifle ready for any of the rioters who were in fact at the bottom of the garden. (It is no idle boast that Pat is a very good shot with a Service Rifle and .22 Competition rifle and possesses 5 in-laid spoons won in competitions at the Singapore Rifle Club to prove it).

Lylie commenced school at 'Deans School', Chancery Lane off Malcolm Road. The uniform was a blue and white gingham dress. We join St. Andrew's Church (the Rev. Robert Greer) I become a member of the Polo Club (non-playing). Pat has adopted a half-bred Alsatian which had been cruelly treated and had arrived at the house where the previous tenant found it cowering at the back of the garage. The lady, wife of a retiring judge, pleaded with Pat to take care of it. She did. More of this later.

I pass my law exams: Laws of Evidence, Penal Code, Criminal Procedure Code (thanks to Andrew Frew). I pass Grade 11 Malay.

Many bribes offered and refused (Pat can tell about one determined character and the 'set of luggage').

'Teddy' no longer with us; the house receives burglars.

Unique method of despatching rats!

Entertain British Troops for Christmas.

Australian Professional Singer as guest for Christmas. Rent Run Run and Run Me Cinema for Christmas Show.

Live Turkey to the Rev. Robert Greer (Perishable Bribe)

1950 to 1952 – Resident at No. 13 until our next leave which was towards the end of 1952.

Pat, Lylie and Sheila, depart for the U.K. by the 'Chusan' while I follow on at a later date. There was an incident at a Gymkhana which affected that journey. After the gymkhana Pat and the girls boarded The Chusan on the Monday and set sail for the U.K.

Pat had received an injection from our own Doctor on the Sunday (Tetanus). Felt stiff and sore during the few days before reaching Bombay. Because Pat felt that if she reported to the Doctor before departing Bombay, she might be taken off the boat, she did not report that her legs were swollen and inflamed. Her main worry was that if she was taken off the boat what was to become of Lylie and Sheila. On top of all this, Pat was running a temperature. The ship duly sailed and Pat reported to the ship's doctor and was told "You should have reported to this surgery at once. You are suffering from a very severe reaction as a result of the Tetanus injection". He gave Pat huge pills (to be taken six in number and then medication to be taken thereafter at three times a day, within a week all was well).

During the journey there was a Fancy Dress party for the children and Pat made costumes from crepe paper for Lylie and Sheila. Lylie received First Prize for her 'Red Riding Hood' costume and received a little sailor doll with 'Chusan' on the cap.

Duly arrived at Tilbury and proceeded by taxi to the Regent's Palace Hotel. Night stop and then home to 50 Caldwell Road.

Two weeks at 50 and then by Train to Cornwall. Pat was under the impression, (which had been conveyed to her in correspondence), that she was moving in to the cottage at Bosavern. Not so.

The hospitality of the 'valley' was such that the Aunts and Uncle Dick were looking forward to Pat and family staying with them at Bosavern. This was much appreciated, but I was soon to join them and it was necessary to have our own place of residence.

Immediately, Pat went to Penzance, bought the local papers and by dint of effort secured a place at St. Hilary by Goldsithney. Pat went to Bill's wedding and Lylie and Sheila stayed with friends. Aunty Mary and Mum returned with Pat from the wedding to St. Hilary.

Thanks to Mum, the canopy over the fireplace (thought to be copper or brass) was restored to its original splendour having been under soot for a long time.

WATER: There was a huge pump in the scullery to produce water in to the sink. There was an even bigger pump in the garden to pump water up to the bathroom – what price pioneers! Lylie started at West Cornwall School as a Day Girl.

In November I arrived in the U.K. and was met by Pat at the Airport. Night stop at the Osterly Park Hotel and proceeded to St. Hilary via Frome.

The children were attending the St. Hilary Methodist Church Sunday School and just before Christmas they had a Carol Service. During the singing of the Carols we noticed Lylie kept glaring at Sheila. We discovered later that Sheila holding the Hymn Book upside down was busy singing "Baa Baa Black Sheep". We spent Christmas Day at the 'Valley' and thoroughly enjoyed the company of Aunty Clara, Aunty Gladys, Uncle Dick. As usual we enjoyed the home produced vegetables and the Cornish Cream. (Uncle Dick had his own cow, 'Bessie', at that time).

In January, we started our journey up north and called in at Liverpool for a few days and them continued towards Edinburgh. At this period in time, Pat and I were faced with a very important decision regarding the girls schooling.

It was the accepted tradition in Malaya that the expatriate children should not be kept in Malaya, on health grounds, beyond the age of eight. It was understood that they should go home to school in the U.K. and come out for holidays only. Our problem was that while Lylie was reaching the 'magical' age of 8, Sheila was only 5. They were therefore both due to be over the age during the next tour of duty in Singapore. What were we to do?

Tommy and Jessie came to our rescue in the following way. We took a house, 'Seton Barns', on a lease and they moved in with their daughter, Janette, and offered to look after Lylie and Sheila until they were of an age to attend boarding school This meant, of course, that the girls attended day school at Cockenzie. While this resolved a major problem for us, it also caused great anxiety and distress at having to leave them behind.

We left Edinburgh for London and then on to embarkation for our return to Singapore by S.S. Glenroy, Captain Evans.

We occupied the state room accommodation on the Port Side and enjoyed the company of some dozen passengers en route. The journey from the time we entered the Mediterranean until we reached Singapore was pleasant and the weather good all the way.

They say that it was very risky to travel on those small cargo/passenger vessels (7000 tons) if there should be a difficult passenger on board. There was a couple on this occasion who upset the Captain by always being late for meals. They were also anti-social in that they did not mix with other passengers. But for the rest of us we enjoyed the voyage.

Passengers and Ships Officers dined together. There was the Captain's table and the Chief Officer's table and the food was excellent. During the voyage, Pat and I held a Cocktail Party for the Bridge Officers on one evening and for the Engine Room Officers on another. This was the 'done' thing on such vessels by the passengers occupying the state room accommodation during the immediate post war days and the cost was not prohibitive, the catering being arranged by the Chief Steward.

Deck tennis and deck quoits provided the exercise and of course walking round the deck when you felt so inclined. Pat thoroughly enjoyed the sports and was good at both games.

It was during this voyage while she was in the ironing room in the company of a lady who was travelling out to visit her nephew, the Resident Commissioner of Johore Bharu, that the possibility of Pat being pregnant was discussed. In the course of time, Pat realised that she was pregnant.

On arrival at Singapore, we booked in to a hotel and shortly afterwards we were allocated a flat in Orange Grove Road, off Orchard Road. Pat reminds me that when the day came to move from the hotel to the flat, I was in Kuala Lumpur playing polo for Singapore in the inter-state tournament. There were repetitions of this type of movement throughout our married life but I insist that they were not managed to happen in this way. They were purely coincidental. The last move into this house, (No.14) took place while I was in hospital for a hip replacement, and that was not arranged.

The previous anxiety mentioned above about Lylie and Sheila was now increased with the knowledge that there was a baby due in the latter part of the year, 1953. There had to be a change of plan and the 8 year age rule would have to be broken.

There was no way that we could keep the girls apart from a new member of our family for up to three years. There was only one thing to do and we took steps to arrange for Lylie and Sheila to rejoin us.

By the time that the necessary arrangements had been made to bring the girls out by air and to find someone in London to meet them from Scotland and put them on the aeroplane, the baby was practically due. It was a race between the girls arriving or the baby coming first. The baby won.

Andrew was born on the 1st of December 1953, in Kandang Kerbau Hospital, Singapore. The girls arrived, having night stopped at Colombo (now Sri Lanka) while mother and baby were still in hospital. Lylie, although only 8 years of age had filled in some of the flight time by assisting the flight hostess to serve the passengers. This raises the question in my mind of how do you occupy children of such a tender age on what was in 1953 a very long voyage? The wife of Squadron Leader Bill Fletcher, Susie, had looked after the girls from arrival at London from Edinburgh until they boarded the aircraft for the journey to Singapore. We were together again as a family and I know that Pat was relieved.

Andrew's arrival had solved a major problem and in retrospect I doubt if we could have put up with the long separation from the girls. The neighbours in the flats were most helpful to us when the girls arrived. There were two families, Young and Hill. It was Margaret Young who took them out to buy suitable dresses for the Singapore climate and at the same time took them to the hairdresser. Then there was schooling. Previously there had been a short spell at Deans School in Chancery Lane. Now I was able to approach the army school which was held at Alexandria because of my connection with the Colloquial Examination Board.

I had been appointed by Government as Chairman of this Board and many army personnel including the G.O.C. Singapore took the test.

The girls were admitted to the army school and travelled by army transport from Orchard Road where they had to meet the lorry at 8 a.m. each school day.

We were subsequently allocated a house at Mount Pleasant during 1954 and we did enjoy that house. The main advantage, in so far as I was concerned, was that we were practically on top of the Polo Ground and At Mo the syce could bring my horse right up to the garden.

In addition to the new baby, we also acquired two Scotch Terriers from people who were about to go on leave, and they gave us a lot of pleasure. On non-playing nights we would go for a walk round the reservoir and the two dogs enjoyed this walk. Dusty and Blackie, as soon as we entered the reservoir grounds, they would run on ahead and disappear out of sight behind the bushes. Shortly afterwards, Blackie would appear under the bushes, looking innocent, and acting as if he had not been in the water.

There was also the zoological gardens, but they were not too popular owing to the monkeys. I believe that they had to be removed all together having become too arrogant and demanding to the point of attacking to obtain the titbits which the people had brought for them. The Tanglin Club was a favourite meeting place for families, especially the swimming pool. This is the same Club that the Japanese had surrendered to me when I had gone looking for Tanglin H.Q.'s on the 5th of September, 1945. My guide had brought me to the wrong Tanglin and I can understand why I had to pay the entry fee of $150 when we came to live in Singapore.

There was the Singapore Swimming Club but we had little or no connection with that Club. We are not a swimming family. On playing nights I was at the Polo Ground and Pat and the children would be there as were the other families of Players and members.

Life followed its normal course until we were once more ready to go on leave to the U.K. in late 1955. I mentioned earlier an incident that happened at a Gymkhana back in 1952. It was in the days when the Polo Club was raising revenue and a new Club House was planned to be built at the side of the Polo Field. The Gymkhana was being held in the evening and there were several events including one where the rider had to have a partner and a wheelbarrow.

A member who shall remain nameless had obtained a steel barrow and in the chaos of lining up on the start line, grabbed Pat to be his partner. The partner was required to sit in the barrow and be wheeled to a start line where the rider let the barrow down and hurriedly mounted his horse to take part in a 'bending' race.

Pat, who was an unwilling partner, might have got away with nothing more than the barrow ride but unfortunately, the rider in his haste had his arm through the reins and as he let the barrow down on the ground, the horse reared.

The reins caught the handle of the barrow and Pat was thrown on to the ground and under the barrow. The horse came down, front feet on to the barrow and then away. Pat was shaken and received attention from the members around her and thereafter reported to our own doctor. What followed on board ship and Pat's anxiety has been explained earlier.

It was always our intention to arrive in the U.K. for our leave during the winter months. The period was usually about six months and so once again we were embarking in October on the 'S.S. Denbyshire' and again we had the State Room.

The voyage home on the Denbyshire was pleasant and comfortable. Andrew had a saying where he referred to his meals as 'num nums' and throughout the journey when the gong sounded for meals not only Andrew but the Ships Officers referred to time for 'num nums'.

It was an uneventful journey until we reached the Bay of Biscay, the part of the journey where rough weather was always anticipated going out and coming home. There were occasions when the Bay was relatively quiet. On this occasion it was rough . . . very rough.

Perhaps because we were nearing the end of the journey the girls had their 'sea legs' and as the ship tossed and heaved they were in the lounge and playing with the cigarette end disposal stands. These were metal stands about 18" high and with a rounded base. Lylie and Sheila had one each and by sitting on the floor at the port or starboard side of the ship, they waited for the ship to rise and as it fell away they would let the stands go and see who 'won' the race. Meanwhile Andrew was in the stateroom and strapped in on the bed. I am almost certain that I would have been in the room and lying on my own bed. There is no fun in being knocked from one side to the other during heavy seas.

Later, in conversation with Captain Simpson, I learned that we had passed very close to a vessel travelling in the opposite direction. As our ship was climbing a huge wave the Captain saw the other ship sliding down and not too far away. Radar was in use but perhaps the weather conditions were having an effect.

As a result of this storm the ship was late in docking at the King George V Dock and we were consequently late in arriving at the Cumberland Hotel where we had made reservations for this particular date. On booking in the receptionist told us that the rooms had been taken because of our "non-arrival". The manager was called for, (it was late in the evening) and the situation was explained to him.

When he heard that we had previously booked two double rooms he was obviously annoyed with the receptionist and we were given accommodation at once. Lylie and Sheila were on a different corridor from us and so to bed.

The late arrival had an ongoing effect until we reached Penzance. The details escape me now but there was a problem with currency exchange and I was short of Sterling. What is clear in my memory is the behaviour of the London taxi driver on arrival at Paddington. He was most helpful, the problem must have been in connection with traveller's cheques. Then the train dining car. The Head Waiter allowed us to take meals and it was agreed that I would meet him on his next tour of duty from London to Penzance and settle the bill. This was done.

The following morning we moved to Harbour Cottage at Mousehole to be greeted by a glorious open fireplace which had been lit by the landlady. Harbour Cottage was a grand place for a holiday and I for one enjoyed sitting in the bay window overlooking the harbour, right on the edge, and throwing crusts of toast to the seagulls as I had my breakfast. I can still imagine the sound of the seagulls when I think of Harbour Cottage. It was a very old cottage and the dining table was a long refectory table made of oak and not one nail in the whole table. Just wooden pegs and morticed joints. There was any amount of room with a small bedroom on the left of the stairs leading to the main bedroom.

There were other rooms and as you entered the cottage there was a stone built in to the wall above and to the right of the entrance showing the date of the Spanish Armada. Uncle Dick and the Aunts from the valley visited us at the cottage and we spent Christmas Day with them.

Lylie and Sheila started school at The West Cornwall School in the January and it could not have been long after that when they had to come home to be nursed because the school matron had been admitted to hospital. The girls had contracted measles. During their fortnight at home, Andrew never knew that they were in the house, but on the day when they were due to be free of infection, Andrew caught the measles.

Pat was next and went down with an unknown virus. Pat is not prone to illness but I do remember Doctor Jock Young meeting me outside the grocer's shop and giving me a fright. He was on his way to see Pat and if he did not find any improvement he was going to have her admitted to hospital. Pat had improved.

The time is easy to remember. It was when the Grand National slipped from the Queen's hand when Devon Loch fell just short of the winning post. Dick Francis was the jockey.

I returned to Singapore in April, the girls had returned to school and on the 30th April, Pat with Andrew moved from Mousehole to Chybran in Penzance.

Major changes were about to take place and although there had been much talk and speculation about Malayanisation of the service, the final decision came as a surprise especially the speed with which it was to be effected. I was 39 years of age and found myself in the top bracket for compensation or what was referred to as a 'golden handshake'.

However, first things first. Roy Bennet had come out to the airport to meet me and as we collected my luggage he informed me that a Polo Match had been arranged between the Royal Artillery and the Singapore Polo Club and that I was down to play. My reply was that it could not be, my horses were out to grass and I doubted my own fitness. "Not so", says Roy, your horses have been in the hands of the 'nagsman', (Sikh horseman) getting fit and look in good form.

I booked in to 'Chequers Hotel' on Thomson Road across from the polo ground and spent the next week, morning and evening, training round the Polo ground and then schooling each horse. We duly played the match and Singapore won by seven goals to five. (I scored three).

Back in the department there was much activity and Tom Mackie and myself were the only expatriates involved in Malayanisation at this point in time. Superscale Officers were on a separate timescale.

I can not remember all that took place, but there was certainly a great deal of administration in connection with pension details and then the 'golden handshake'. There was also the question of where do we go from here. When the details appeared in the local newspapers saying who were among the first to go, I was offered a job by the Sun Life of Canada Insurance Company. Pat and I decided to make a clean break with Singapore and claim our passage home.

At this particular time arrangements had been finalised for Pat and Andrew to return to Singapore and they were due to return in October. It follows therefore that my date of departure had not been decided.

Pat and Andrew arrived at Kallang Airport during October and I met them as they came off the aeroplane. Andrew was carrying his teddy bear and looking very smart in navy blue shorts and open neck shirt.

There had been one incident at Bangkok when Andrew had managed to dodge out of sight and then walked across the tarmac towards the aircraft and right up to the correct machine. Meanwhile Pat having missed him came after him, took him back all the way to the waiting room only to hear that the flight had been called for departure.It was very hot at Bangkok.

We had been allocated No. 18 at Mount Pleasant and moved in. I had kept a surprise for Andrew. The Manager of the Cold Storage Poultry Farm had two Alsatians and I knew that a litter was about due. I asked if I could have the first bitch puppy to be born and this was agreed. Pat and I with Andrew went by boat to collect the pup, 'Jason', and brought it back in a cardboard box. Andrew had named the pup after a dog which he had been friendly with at Paul in Cornwall. Jason came home with us and spent six months in quarantine.

It was during my stay at Kedah in 1948 that I first mentioned polo. I can remember the occasion quite clearly and no doubt this is because the game came to mean so much to me in the years between 1950 and 1957.

It was a typically warm lovely evening and Charlie Renwick was riding a horse which had been a race horse, 'Effingham', but now retired and used as a hack at the Gymkhana Club. Charlie had a polo stick and was quietly knocking a polo ball from place to place. The horse did not seem to mind and I watched what was happening for a few minutes and then asked Charlie about the game. We had a talk about the game and where it was played in Malaya and Singapore. I remember being interested and had at that time become the owner of another retired race horse, 'Tommy'.

Charlie explained that it was necessary to be a competent rider and would take some time to learn the game properly. I was not to know at the time but in the near future I was to be posted to Singapore where there was an active Polo Club. I continued riding 'Tommy' and learning about race riding from Harry Wheeler and Charlie. Practical experience was very limited by the restrictions of the Kedah Club but I had bought the books and paid a lot of attention to what was taught. I had learned how to sit in the saddle and enjoyed what we were able to do. During 1949 I went down to the Polo Club in Singapore, as a spectator, and remember sitting on the edge of the deep drain that ran round the edge of the playing ground. There was no club house and only one wooden seat under a small tree.

Approximately 100 yards from the side of the ground there was a 'lean to' hut for want of better description and one part was used to store the various refreshments, what is now called "juice" and some beer. The other half of the hut was Ali's home. Ali was the one and only employee of the Singapore Club in 1949.

The horses were stabled in the Singapore Police Depot and out at Nee Soon Barracks. One or two were stabled by civilian owners, one of whom was Charlie Renwick and he had a large chesnut horse, 'Singh', behind his house at the top of Mount Pleasant.

Tuesday, Thursday and Saturday were the playing days and Friday, the Muslim 'Sunday', was time off for everyone. As I sat on that grassy bank there was an Indian army officer who advised me that it would take five years to get a polo pony and be fit ones self to take part in a chukka.

I heard what the man said but I was making up my mind what to do when I returned from the U.K. I was not looking five years ahead In 1950 we returned to Singapore and after the usual formalities of moving from the ship to a hotel we were allocated a house at 13 Malcolm Road. This was not too far from the polo ground.

I became a member of the polo club and for a short period I was the Treasurer and assisted by Pat in bringing the books into order. The Club had an overdraft of $7000 with the H.K. & S. Bank and one of the main points of looking after the books was to chase polo players to pay their forage bill in order to stay on the right side of the bank. One unfortunate incident took place and it was obvious that all was not well with the forage account.

The bank manager was a friend of the Club and we invited him to dinner and to go over the accounts in order to trace what was wrong. We found out. We discovered that the two people involved in non-payment, were no longer in Singapore.

It was decided to hold a gymkhana at the polo ground in order to raise funds, but on this occasion Pat decided that it should be 'home catering' and self help rather than employing trades people and reducing the profits. The Club agreed and Pat and Mrs Houghton set about organising the catering which proved to be highly successful. The clearing and washing up was done by the Boy Scouts. The Club had made a profit!

I had started to learn the game and went down to the ground every morning as soon as the first rays of sunlight showed through.

First there was the 'wooden' practise horse inside the practise pit surrounded by wire fencing. It was there that you learned to swing the polo stick and all the strokes on both sides of the pony, The base of the pit was shaped like a soup plate and laid in concrete. This enabled the ball to return to the position at the side of the practise horse. After some time on this practise, it was then necessary to go and mount the pony which the Syce would have brought from the stables.

Schooling. This is a joint venture between horse and rider and I shall deal with a brief introduction for there is so much to observe depending on the experience of the rider and the type of horse being schooled. In the main we were dealing with ex-race horses but later we were able to get some brumbies (wild Australian horses). I was very fortunate to attract the attention of top-class players and I gave strict attention to every thing they said. Schooling brings out what is best and necessary in the rider and patience is the essence.

Communication between rider and horse must be established and every manoeuvre repeated until it becomes second nature and the 'office' to the pony is imperceptible. Control moves from the hands to the legs and the balance of the riders body.

The polo ponies at Singapore in 1950 were a mixed lot and I believe a few of them came in from India when the war ended in the Far East.

There was Ranville, Boater, John, Gray Boy, Singh, Beurie, Jane and Nutmeg. In addition the army used to bring ponies in from Nee Soon Barracks. Many players learned to play on Ranville and Boater including myself. I also had access to Singh which was owned by Charlie Renwick.

In 1992 people talk about the Argentine or Arab ponies being the best for the game. During the '50s those of us who were in Malaya during those years got tremendous pleasure from the game and having learned from our schooling with the original ponies, mentioned above, we were able to train and bring on ex-race horses which also brought pace in to our game.

I remember my first Chukka very clearly. I was scared. There was a good player, Major Chatty, and he kept yelling at me to "Get up . . ." and much else.

He was playing No.4 and I kept trying to do what he wanted. I suppose that I was glad when it was over. Chatty came up to me afterwards and encouraged me to keep at it and to read the books. I kept 'at it'. During 1951 there was to be a change which made a tremendous difference to my game. Two horses, ex-Hong Kong racing, arrived at Singapore, named 'Captain' and 'Pinky'. They had travelled in horse boxes on the deck of a ship and had been subjected to part of the journey through the tail-end of a typhoon. Captain was in reasonable condition but Pinkie was damaged and her hip bone was exposed, requiring veterinary attention. They were un-loaded and taken to the veterinary station for quarantine and treatment. How they came to be ordered from Hong Kong or who brought them I do not remember but they were the first imports during my time.

The army took Captain, but no one wanted Pinkie. In the course of discussion, I believe it was Col. Colin Todd, who suggested to me that if I liked to pay £25 for the shipping of Pinkie, I could have her.

She was a good looking mare and three-quarter bred. Her hip was healing and she had a record of having won a few races at Hong Kong. I paid the £25 and promptly changed her name by translating Pinkie to Merah-Muda and thereafter she was always referred to as Merah.

I spent hours schooling Merah, with advice from another Indian army major who had played in India. Merah was a beauty and had a lovely mouth. She soon took to the game and I was no longer dependant on paying for the use of the army ponies. (although I have never forgotten my debt to Ranville and Boater and partly to Singh). Much happened during the years 1950 to 1954 and I am going to touch on a few of the details.

My game progressed and I was allocated a handicap of 1 to start with. The usual starting handicap is -2. I also obtained two additional ponies, (polo horses are referred to as ponies and at one time there was a restriction to their height, i.e. 14.2 hands). John Willie and a beautiful British thoroughbred, Eriskay. John Willie was an Australian brumbie, wild and unbroken. The manager of the Singapore cold storage had been on a business visit to Australia and had agreed to look for suitable horses for importation to Singapore. Suitable?

John Willie arrived with several other animals and they were all placed in quarantine. Naturally everyone wished to see the new imports and went along to the quarantine station in the evening.

By the time I arrived, most of the horses had been 'claimed'. Colonel Colin Todd was at the station and as I walked up to him he said,"Here you are Dudley, a bargain". I looked in to the stable and saw this horse, not much over 14.2 h., a shaggy long coat, hair over its eyes, quite a sight. I was in no hurry to accept this horse but when we took a closer look at his teeth, we realised that he was still getting rid of his milk teeth which meant that he was very young. "£15 and he's yours" says Colin. I agreed and told Atmo to collect him after the Q period. He eventually arrived at the polo stables and promptly became a pet of the Syces. I had nothing to do with him for almost a year, he spent the time eating and growing and creating quite a fuss if he was not fed first. Eriskay was quite another story. She was nervous and hated the sight of a polo stick. She was out of racing because of her joints. She had to be carefully looked after. I spent hours sitting on her in the school and trying to lift a stick past her face on either side.

In her loose box we had polo sticks suspended from the beams; no matter which way she turned there was a polo stick hanging over her face. In time the problem was resolved. Atmo took great care of her joints, regular hosing with cold water and bandaging and occasionally massaging with liniment. She took to schooling and in time she was playing tournament polo.

As well as having good ponies during this same period, (John Willie yet to be broken) I became Captain of the Club and appointed to office in the MARA, (Malayan Amateur Racing Association) also I became Hon. Secretary of the Malayan Polo Association. The following is a list from 1954. My handicap was also raised to 3 and later to 5.

Malayan Polo Association
Affiliated to the Hurlingham Club Polo
COMMITTEE 1954

STEWARDS PRESIDENT
Col. C.F. Tod, R.A. until 30.6.54.
Maj. F.L. Harding from 30.6.54.

Brigadier H.K. Dimoline – *Selangor Polo Club*
Raja Haji Shahar Shah - *Royal Pahang Polo Club*
D. Gregory, Esq. - *Penang Polo Club*
Lt. Col. C. Spencer - *XII Royal Lancers (Aug. 1954)*
Lt. Col. Wyldebore-Smith - *15/19th The King's Royal Hussars*
Dr. M.A.X. Cocheme – *Ipoh Riding & Polo Club*

Hon. Secretary – G.D.A. Fox, Singapore Polo Club

Representative:
The Hurlingham Polo Club Committee – Major. M. Weipert

MEMBERS

Penang Polo Club,
Ipoh Riding and Polo Club,
XII Royal Lancers (until August, 1954)
15/19th The King's Royal Hussars (from August, 1954).
Selangor Polo Club,
Royal Pahang Polo Club,
Singapore Polo Club.

I remained as Hon. Secretary until my departure from Singapore on the 14th of January, 1957. At Singapore Polo Club on the Sunday prior to departure I was presented with a beautiful Silver Salver by General Festing, Commander-in-Chief Far East. I also became the first life member of the Singapore Polo Club and the inscription on the Salver states why. This Salver, along with five inlaid spoons won by Pat for .22 shooting, sits on our dining room sideboard today. Since leaving Singapore, I have never played polo again and, Pat has never had occasion to hold a rifle again.

Handicap. There were no Hurlingham Handicaps in Malaya during my time there. The reason for making some of us up to 5 was not our skill but the need to make it more even for the majority of players who were of a lower standard.

Finally, I can not leave polo without mentioning John Willie. When Col. Tod said that J.W. was a bargain at £15 he never said a truer thing, but much was to happen before J.W. became a bargain. Our playing evenings usually consisted of two Chukkas in order that everyone got a game. This meant that only one pony was required for club games and I found myself in the potential position of owning three ponies; Merah, Eriskay and J.W. I was made an offer for Merah and the man who wished to buy her was a quiet and enthusiastic beginner. It will be remembered that I had paid £25 to meet the cost of her shipping from Hong Kong. The offer to me was $1,500 (rate of exchange into sterling was 8.5 to the pound). Considering the pleasure Merah had given me and also that she would have an easier time playing slower polo I accepted the offer.

Now J.W. had to be broken and schooled. I spoke to Atmo and said that I was going to start training J.W. One evening, shortly afterwar I arrived at the stables and noticed that there was something diffe I walked round the block and on reaching J.W.'s loose box for empty. Standing nearby there was a fine looking pony, lovely coat, head up. I did not recognise the animal. And the S guessed that I would not, that was why they were waiting reaction. Atmo proudly brought J.W. forward and told r had done. It used to be said that the Boyanese were half animal themselves. Atmo was Boyanese and this term is made as a compliment.

J.W. had been left with his long hair and shaggy looks but when Atmo learned that I was now going to work with him he had arranged with his friends to groom the long hair and smarten J.W. And smart he was. The Syces had got hold of an old car tyre and nailed a part of the tyre to a piece of wood, tread upwards. Then, from the poll to the tail they had 'brushed' the long hair out of the coat. I had never heard of that method but it was most successful. It also revealed that J.W. had a fistulated point on his withers and this was attended to by the vet.

I will now reduce hours of training to a few lines. First I started with a lunging rein and made J.W. walk round me. I used my voice all the time and we progressed from walking to cantering. Then the saddle. There was a spell of anxiety at this point. Not because I was falling off as he jumped around, he showed signs of being a 'rearer'. That is dangerous and the Australians have one way of dealing with the problem which can be fatal and with which I would not take part anyway. As the horse rears high in the air the Australians get behind the horse and pull him right over so that he crashes on to his back. However, I am indebted to a friend for the following advice. Using a strong paper bag containing very warm water, mount quickly while the Syces hold the horse's head and take the paper bag from the syce, As the horse rears, smash the paper bag between his ears. Plop, and the warm water is all over the horse's face. It worked.

From the moment that J.W. accepted me as rider, we never looked back. He was a remarkable horse and learned so quickly, it was incredible. There was a stage at one point where I had to think of a way of making him obey me rather than him anticipating what I was going to do.

I am referring to the 'back hand strokes'. In approaching the ball at speed you have to get there as fast as you can and maintain momentum through the stroke. There is need to make a shift in the positioning of the body and bring the stick up in front of the body preparing to make the stroke. Then there is the 'pull up' or swing away from the 'line' and J.W. had twigged this move and decided to ready for it by slowing down, which was fatal to the shot and a to the other side.

got round that problem eventually by placing a line of polo wn the middle of the ground and then making him approach allop each ball to be played as a back hand stroke. He soon

The next thing that had to be altered was his 'galloping'. J.W. came off the ground with a high 'leaping' move which was a loss of speed and of energy. To counter this it was necessary to teach him to flatten his stride and this is where Merah came to our rescue. A friend of mine helped by taking Merah and we went racing round the polo field with the two horses side by side. I pulled J.W. and as I had supposed he wanted to be up with if not in front of Merah. I kept him back for some time and then let him go. That was quite an eye opener. He took off and we all became aware that he had speed. He did flatten out and soon we were on the field and we both enjoyed the game. He was good.

I have many happy memories of polo and J.W, the small 'brumbie' from Australia shared most of them. He became a great favourite with the public and they delighted in his antics as he left the field after a game, walking behind the Syce without bridle or saddle.

Chapter 8

M y final fling in Malaya was to take part in the polo tournament at Ipoh and played against Pahang in the final. This was my last appearance in competitive polo and I believe we won that tournament. If my memory is correct, it was held at the beginning of December, 1956.

On Sunday, the 13th of January there was a farewell party in the forenoon at the Singapore Polo Ground and I received a great surprise. The Commander-in-Chief Far East, General Festing was there and presented me with a beautiful Silver Salver inscribed as a memento to my 'Service to Polo' and as Club Captain of Singapore Polo Club.

We left Singapore on the 14th January, 1957. It was early in the morning and the sunrise was beautiful.

Salamat Tingal
Repatriation to United Kingdom
14th January 1957

Accompanied by Pat and Andrew we boarded a Constellation aircraft at 0800 hrs on the 14th of January en route to London. Lylie and Sheila were in school at Penzance, The West Cornwall Boarding School. From London, we travelled by train to Penzance and then to Mousehole where we booked in at the Old Coastguard Hotel. A short stay in the hotel where we were very well looked after by the handyman, 'Manny' and then we went in to a house named 'TavisVor' in Mousehole.

We had a thought about buying this house. It sat right on the coastline and the sitting room window faced the English Channel. However, we were not long in discovering that we did not sit looking at the view and within the month we decided that it was not for us.

Meanwhile, the Simpson brothers, who were in business Penzance and with whom we had become friendly over the ye helped us to find a property and we hired a small car until our vehicle was delivered from Sollihull.

Thanks to Duncan Simpson we heard of a house at Gold which had been converted from two cottages and new flooring installed. The owner had intended to move in bu something about insufficient funds. Pat and I went to see the house and decided to buy it. Pat has always maintained that it was the best house we ever had.

We then had to fit the house with furniture and all kitchen gadgets and this was done by a firm in Penzance and a wholesale supplier who was recommended by Duncan. The car, a Rover 60 arrived. We were home.

Throughout 1957 we visited the family and toured around the various shows in Cornwall. Duncan introduced us to the Western Hunt and I became involved with the gymkhanas. There was an attempt to train a musical ride on simple grounds and this went well for a spell. People moved away and that was the end of the team.

I was asked by the Young Farmers if I would school them in polo and this seemed promising because there were polo players at Culdrose Naval Station. I conducted a few evening practises and then the Government called for voluntary retirement from the armed services offering compensation in accordance with years of service. No more mention of polo.

Two men who were stalwarts of show-jumping in Cornwall and connected with the Western Hunt assisted me in buying a horse. I remember also that the younger man had overheard an argument between two brothers in the pub concerning a motor horsebox. One threatened to sell it for £50. My friend promptly offered the £50 and it was accepted. He then asked for time to go home and get the money and came straight to me. I gave him the £50 and we now had a horsebox and a horse. Looking back to 1957 from 1992 I cannot understand how we got what was an excellent vehicle for such a ridiculous price.

'Squire' was young and just 'broken', but completely unaware of motor traffic. He had been bred in the 'black' country on a small farm. He was good and after some time he began to move well. He took to showjumping and won a 'Foxhunter' Novice competition. He also took to hunting and was not afraid of the high Cornish hedges. I had a few good days with him. On the 18th of January 1958 while resting him after the manager had brought him in from a 'Feast' meeting with light galls, I fell off on to some granite stones and broke my right n. I had taken him out, bareback, for exercise. It was a miserable Saturday afternoon and while crossing St. Leven's moors. A Boxer ppeared and frightened the horse. My right arm ended up two horter than the left.

was eventually sold and ended up being exported to Italy to time action as a showjumper. I gave up all interests in nd decided to look for a job.

I approached Holman Brothers, Pneumatic Engineers, manufacturing equipment at three different sites at Camborne and Climax. I remember meeting the Overseas Manager, Williams by name, and offering to be a clerk in the office. After a discussion he said he would be in touch. Three days later I was back at Rosewarne Head Office and met Williams and one of the directors. A further discussion mainly on what I had been doing overseas. Finally an interview with the Board at Rosewarne and I was offered a job as Head of the Pricing Department at Rosewarne. I accepted it.

When I reported for duty I was introduced to Tommy Dunstan and learned that he had been the previous head of department and would be carrying on as my number 2. I did not think this was a very good idea and my first duty after dealing with the preliminaries was to take Tommy out for lunch and find out just what was the position. He soon made it clear that he was relieved to be out of the position as Head of Department. It also became clear that there was a senior woman who had been making his life uncomfortable. Things would have to change.

After a few weeks of being 'carried' I approached the Sales Manager and asked for time off to attend the Training School. This was permitted and I reported to the Training School at No.3 Works. Percy Crocker, a real old timer, was in charge and at the end of the course a trolley, filled with all the parts of the different pneumatic drills, was brought alongside and each of us had to assemble a drill and connect it to the compressed air pipe running round the wall of the workshop. Percy came round and on reaching my position I was asked to 'switch it on'. I did. I was very pleased, it worked. Percy reached over and picked up a spring that had escaped my attention. "And" he asked,"What about this?".

It was the throttle control spring! I suggested that my modification might be accepted? Not long after this course, Tommy was called up stairs by the Chairman and asked to prepare a parts list for a No 30 which he wanted by Monday. Tommy came back and told me what was wanted and added, "Thats my week-end gone". I asked him to bring a No. 3 parts list to my desk and by deleting one part and substituting another, I said, "There you are Tommy, that's your weekend restored." The difference was in the throttle control, a difference of 290 knocks per minute. Tommy replied; "Thirty years I have been in this company and I did not know that". We became good friends.

The senior woman mentioned earlier. I discovered what she was to, mainly creating overtime work for herself. I asked for incinerator supervisor to come down and bring a big bag with

The paperwork which had been causing so much trouble was taken away and disposed of.

We enjoyed living at Goldsithney and Pat loved Carwithen, but as time passed we had come to realise that on behalf of Lylie and Sheila we would have to move to where there was more of a social life for them. We decided to move to Camborne.

I let this be known at the office that we were interested in moving to Camborne and various colleagues said they would keep an eye open for a suitable house. Mr Cottrel came to see me one morning and told me that 25 Pendarves Road was for Sale. Pat and I viewed 25 by appointment and found it suitable. The price was right and we arranged to move in during June/July 1959.

Sheila continued travelling to Penzance by train with a nearby neighbour until she was able to transfer to Camborne and then both girls continued their education at Camborne. Andrew had commenced school at Goldsithney and transferred to the Primary school at Camborne. The move to Camborne certainly changed our ways of life. In 1959 on the 27th of September, Katrina was born in the Redruth Hospital.

The girls did well at school and Sheila gave an excellent performance in 'Quality Street' which was put on by the school for the Public. Lylie completed her schooling and went to college at Plymouth to study Domestic Science. Sheila attended Cornwall Technical College studying art and preparing to enter nursing. Andrew continued his progress towards entering Truro Boys School.

In 1959 I was approached by the Secretary of the Camborne Rugby Club who informed me that the Chairman of the Company, Mr Percy Holman had recommended him to visit me and ask me to consider becoming the Chairman of the Club. The current holder was due to travel to Portugal. The club funds were low and their meeting/changing rooms were in the haylofts above the old stables behind Tyacks Hotel. After a lengthy discussion I accepted the invitation and became Chairman of the Camborne Rugby Club.

At about the same time I was also visited by the General Secretary of the Camborne Show which was a one day show and considered to be one of the biggest in the country at that time.

Holman Brothers had a keen interest in this show and one of the Directors was President of the Show. This time I was being asked to take the duties of General Secretary of the show. From 1959 onwards, after the arrival of Katrina, the whole family were kept busy. The details of my work are far too many to record and looking back they seemed to be confusing and sometimes outwith my remit.

There was one occasion when the Financial Director, a fellow Scot, going to Moscow and it was suggested that I should stand in as his Personal Assistant during his absence. That never happened. Then there was an engineer who came on the scene and his speciality was pumps. Pumping in connection with mining is a very important matter and this man, name forgotten, was keen that I should join his team and, on occasion, I travelled to London and sat in on meetings with him. That came to nothing.

A new department was created at Posewarne by the O & M (Organisation and Methods) specialists to control all details of orders placed and the arrival of raw materials and the authorising of payment of invoices dependant on the original order being fulfilled. I was asked by Murray Allen, Chief Accountant, if I would accept the job as Head of this department. I did. My time, working and leisure, was fully occupied.

O. & M. project: there were a few changes required. These were made. I remember the Chief man's name was Tolman.

There came a period, and at the time I did not notice anything odd, but looking back I realise the 'writing was on the wall'. If I had been ambitious and chasing promotion I might have been aware of what was going on. A senior man was about to retire and his job had been to contact firms who supplied specialist equipment for inclusion in our machinery and see that they met their target dates of delivery.

I heard of his pending departure and my name was mentioned in connection with the job but I treated it as rumour, I had never had anything to do with his department. There was the Buying Department and the No 2 in that department was interested in the job and was probably well qualified to do it. But for me, unbeknown, change was in the offing. Looking back now, I can see more clearly and hindsight is a wonderful thing.

I had gone along to Holmans' looking for a simple job. Since my arrival I had gone from one senior appointment to another, made by the appropriate authority. I had never applied for a senior job. I was also an 'incomer' and local men had been left behind. One afternoon I was asked to go up and see the Administration Director and I received the news, which was shattering at the time, "The Board considered that I was grossly under-employed and qualified for higher responsibility but they had nothing to offer. Therefore I was to take the opportunity to look for new employment and in the meantime I was to continue on full pay".

That was from Mr. John Holman. I was shattered, I can only remember saying one thing to him, "Seems that I have worked myself out of

The Chief Accountant said that he never expected this to h went for a walk and prepared to leave. There may have bee bitterness at the time but I got over it.

There was an appeal by the Air Ministry for a man to take charge of their works development in the S.W. Area and I applied for the job. I was interviewed by a man in Squadron Leader's uniform and after a few questions he wanted to know why I was applying for this type of job.

I replied that I wished to stay in this part of Cornwall. There were several people waiting to be interviewed and he stood up and said,"The jobs yours , we will be in touch" and he walked out. I felt sorry for all the people that were waiting. That evening the General Manager of a Tin Mining Group telephoned and said that he was a cousin of Mr. Percy Holman. He went on to say that he knew I was looking for employment and was I prepared to go to London for an interview. The Company were about to explore the possibility of re-opening tin mining in Cornwall and they were looking for a local person to act as the Local Secretary. I thanked him and I went to London and eventually joined Camborne Tin Ltd. with my new title.

It was a strange feeling to go to an office and have to open it for the first time.There was no one else there to begin with and I attended to such essentials as getting a telephone, a kettle, a teapot and cups, and so on, all the essential equipment of a secretary.

Then appeared Jack Trounson. Jack was a qualified Mining Surveyor and one of the most knowledgeable people in Cornwall concerned with tin mining. I was to work with him for a long time. He produced large tomes from the museums and libraries relating to special tin mines which had been dormant for years.

The purpose was research and I was given direction by him of what to do in connection with 'wheal granville' which was the first to be reviewed. Now my work started and I enjoyed working with and for him.

Next came a General Manager and a South African driller. A lady was employed to work with the G.M. Plant hire contracts were entered into and a company specialising in shaft sinking came on the mine site and started to 'collar' the old shaft. This was all new and interesting. The revolution in Brunei was a long way off and was no concern of mine - or so I thought at the time. Again looking back, it was turning out to be all for the best.

One day Pat saw Tom Mackie coming up the path at 25 Pendarves ad knew there was something important to bring him to Camborne. ranspired that the revolution in Brunei had caused quite an upset. vas away at the time when Tom called but he left sufficient nation to let me know that it was mainly up to me if I wanted to ack into the Colonial Service. I wrote to Stag Place at Victoria ' invited me to come for an interview. That was one of the sant interviews I have ever attended. I was told that I was ed by Senior Expats in Sabah (North Borneo) and we discussed old times in Kedah. I was also shown a map of south east Sabah and the problem of controlling the border was discussed. I answered by pointing out how difficult it is to control an undulating border and how it is necessary to fall back and cover certain 'open' areas. We had coffee and I filled in up to date personal information. After that I returned home secure in the knowledge that I was back in harness. It may seem odd to say secure, but whether I felt that way at the time I do not know. What was obvious, and in retrospect even more so, there was no way forward for me, I was an 'incomer'. This is an expression which is used all over the country and the peculiar thing is, that without 'incomers', the local setting would be hard pushed to find anyone prepared to take on the responsibility of social activities, on a voluntary basis.

I was now about to leave Camborne and I realised that I was leaving the rugby club in much better shape than when I had accepted the office of Chairman. I had personally bought a property with the intention of converting it into a clubhouse with parking space. This was effected by Committee members and players. There were tradesmen of the necessary work required to be done and they did work well. I have to report that Mr P. Holman and the Senior Surgeon of the Truro Hospital, Mr Jimmy Reid, and myself became trustees of the new clubhouse. I was in North Borneo when the clubhouse was opened and the first barrel of beer was donated by me.

In time, the R.F.U. at Twickenham became aware of what had taken place and they took over the responsibility for finance and at a greatly reduced interest rate. It is only recently that Mike Trott contacted me and amended the trustee position. Camborne today (1992) have a modern clubhouse and several playing grounds where we used to hold the Annual Agricultural Show. In the new grandstand I understand that there is a seat with my name on the back of it. The Camborne Agriculture Show was in good health but it has long since ceased to function. It was a good annual event. Happy memories and now I was on my way back to the Far East.

There was so much happening at home in getting ready to depart that as I look back, I realise that I had not grasped the real significance of what I was doing. There certainly was need to move but I w having to leave the family at home, not only because of confrontat but there was no way that the girls could be interrupted at the ti they were at a vital stage in preparing for their future careers also going to be away from Pat for a minimum of two years.

I shall always remember Pat standing on the Camborne S left for London and on to Sabah. Right or wrong, it was r the time, but it hurt.

I attended a service in St. Martins in the field, and then made my way to Heathrow and boarded my flight for Singapore and then by Dakota to Jesselton (Kota Kinabalu). I was met by Tom Mackie and Rosalind and taken to the only reasonable hotel functioning in 1964. I had a sleepless night.

On my arrival, a Sunday I believe, there was a man I mentioned earlier who had been at the Penang residency during the time when we bought all the camera film in 1948.

When Tom introduced me to him, he remembered my name and mentioned how they had been forced to delay the introduction of Identity Cards.

I spent some days at K.K. meeting various Secretariat Officials and being briefed on the political situation which was rather delicate. There were only two parties.

I left K.K. on Board the 'Rajah Brooke' and sailed round the coast via Kudat to Sandakan. We arrived in the early morning and after a brief wait at sea, we progressed into the harbour and alongside the jetty. Gordon Norris was waiting on the jetty to meet me. The new District Officer of Sandakan had arrived and the District Officer of Beluran was there to meet me. We became good friends.

We were both without our families and applied ourselves to a seven day week from the time of our arrival. The government got good value for their money during our stay in office.

We saw the Resident Commissioner during the morning and discovered that we were both invited to the Japanese prawn factory dinner that evening. One of the items on the menu was 'raw fish'. I remember nothing about it and I have never come across the item again. After the Resident I met the man who I was relieving, the Chief Minister's brother, Ben Stevens, a very pleasant man. He had a large family and I was asked to stay at the lodge until the house was ready. I did.

Preliminary senior introductions having been made on the Saturday, the day of arrival; my temporary residence at the Governor's Lodge until Ben had moved with family from the District Officer's bungalow, agreed, I decided to look around on the Sunday morning and get my bearings.

The government buildings lay at the foot of the hill and I walked ᵥn the winding road until I came to a small stone memorial, just de the police station. It was in the usual form of a christian cross e detail inscribed on the pillar referred to previous district They had been killed while on duty. Date and place recorded. s only a small blank place left at the bottom of the stone on ᵥnd corner. I hoped it would still be blank when my time to Sandakan arrived. I saw where my office was, on the ground floor, no doubt for ease of access to the public. The District Office and the Town Board Offices were at the end of the corridor. The toilets were also on this floor. I decided to move upstairs when this might be possible.

Having completed my brief reconnaissance to the edge of the town, I returned to the lodge and discovered that Norris and self were to have breakfast at the Residency. In fact, until we moved to take up our own quarters, we had all meals at the Residency. The Resident, Jim Rutherford and his wife Sheila were most helpful and kind.

On Monday I made further discoveries concerning my office as D.O.; I was automatically President of Sandakan Club, I was Chairman of the Sandakan District Council, Vice-Chairman of Sandakan Town Board, Member of the Sandakan Security Council, Collector of Land Revenue and allocation of Temporary Occupation Leases and Gazetted Magistrate. I decided to edit that lot and got rid of the Presidency and made all else subject to my daily responsibilities as time went by.

During the morning Francis Lingham, my A.D.O., came in and then Bruce Sandilands, Land Surveyor arrived to introduce himself. He was one of the best and most energetic officers that I came to know. Within the week he had arranged for him and myself and some of his field staff to visit an area where the natives were losing crops to the wild pig. We set out on the Saturday morning, exactly one week from my arrival at Sandakan. It is to be remembered that Sabah and Malaya were in confrontation with Indonesia. The 15 natives I met on that Saturday were Indonesian. It was of no consequence to Bruce.

The major scheme that had just began was 'The Sungei Manilla Scheme'. This was an area which was virgin jungle and containing a vast number of commercial value trees. The planning was for the area to be 'logged' by contractors on behalf of the government and, in part payment, the contractors were to make roads, 40 feet wide. The placing of the roads were to be designated by the Survey Department. The total area, when cleared, was to be allocated to native families on a basis of 15 acres per family. The first acre would be cleared and a dwelling supplied. Cash crops would be planted on this acre.

In the first instance it was decided that the 'settler' would clear th remaining 14 acres but I believe this was changed in the light experience. I remember discussing this matter with the Ministe Finance on one of his personal visits to the scheme but it w unofficial conversation. When all the circumstances were cons the change to the 'settlers' way of life and the pioneeri required of people who were mainly fishermen, the t' clearing 14 acres of logged ground must have been a da The ultimate crop was to be oil-palm.

Planning was the order of the day and the 'Red Book' was brought in to being in Sabah during 1964. Each district had its own copy of the Red Book and the main copy was held in Jesselton (Kota Kinabalu). The local planning was reported to the main book office and the residents and the District Officers were responsible for the local planning.

The immediate ground work was straightforward and the needs of long term planning were discussed. One obvious need would be an oil-palm mill and routes of communication to the mill.

The S.M.S. was approached from the 11th mile stone on the partly constructed Telupid Road while a new town was planned for the 30th mile stone on the same road. 30th m.s. was also the turning off point to reach the newly erected landing stage for access to Beluran. The main happenings during my period as D.O. in addition to the Red Book and the S.M.S. were the construction of the landing strip at Kuamut on the kinabatangan south side by the Australian Field Engineers, the rescue of the injured from the logging camp where the vehicle went over a bank on New Year's eve, 1964, the building of a clinic on Tambisan Island in early 1965.

At the time of the logging camp accident the Resident Commissioner was in the Interior Residency where he was taken ill and I found myself acting for him until he returned. The logging company in Sandakan had reported to me by telephone that 22 men had been killed and the person making the report was speaking in Malay. I contacted the Resident at Tawau who was in direct touch with the R.A.F. and asked for the help of a helicopter. The R.A.F. also made emergency preparations at Labuan by removing the seats from a passenger plane with the intention of uplifting the casualties if this should be required. I then contacted Murray Douglas who was located in Sandakan and asked him if he would take me to Kuamat to meet the helicopter. Murray and Gil Singh operated a private charter line from Sandakan.

There was a temporary snag over landing at Kuamut as the strip had not been passed for operative use but the radio telephone communication with Jesselton was so distorted that we had to assume at all was well and due care would have to be exercised when ding. Meanwhile the senior medical officer at the Duchess of Kent tal had arranged a team consisting of a surgeon, nursing sister, urse and an orderly who came out to the Sandakan landing we boarded the Cessna which was piloted by Gil Singh.

nwork was excellent and on arrival at Kuamut, Gil made a during which we saw wild pig wallowing in the S.E. so observed that the grass was very green and he pulled up and round again. This time we were told to brace ourselves and Gil decided to go in diagonally across the strip. With a few bumps we were down and bang on cue the helicopter arrived. The medical team went first owing to the capacity of the helicopter and then came back for me. The situation turned out to be two dead, (one died just as we arrived), four serious head wounds, eight fractures and remainder 'walking wounded'. The dying man had made a request that he should be buried at Sandakan. I believe that this would have been to ensure that a Kathi or equivalent Muslim official would attend to the funeral. After the surgeon had made his appreciation of the situation he returned to the hospital with the first casualties and thanks to the R.A.F., the journey was direct from the logging camp to the hospital grounds. The helicopter carried out a shuttle service and I had arranged that the 'walking wounded' be evacuated by boat.

Finally, I was left with the nursing sister, the male nurse and the orderly and because of failing daylight, the helicopter had to make for Tawau after the last trip to the hospital.

There was a small boat with an outboard engine and we made our way down river towards the landing strip. As we rounded the bend before reaching the strip, we saw Murray leaning against a tree, smoking, and in a strong Australian accent he declared, "Fox comes out of the jungle and what do you know, he has a woman with him".

Murray piloted us back to Sandakan and the press were waiting. The medical team were photographed, (but not the D.O., expats were expected to keep a low profile, out of the public eye) and the press were left to their own method of reporting. I did receive a letter from the Company, which is still with my papers, and a personal visit from the Head of the Company, a Chinese Gentleman of the old school.

The low profile was maintained at official level. I never heard from the Resident nor the Secretariat indeed the incident might never have taken place. I believe and hope that the survivors of the accident eventually made a full recovery and that is what really matters.

Tambisan Island lies in the Suluk Sea and off the east coast of Sabah, south of Sandakan and just where you alter course to follow the coast line to Lahad Datu. I had received information that two young women had been to Singapore on a midwife's course and we about to return to the island having passed the course successf Except for native huts, there was no building or facilities availab them. Survival of the fittest was rampant in Sandakan as els and one man who had been over enthusiastic in his survival required to come to my office. We had a long chat.

He was also a carpenter. He agreed to submit a drawing acceptable to the medical department, and thereafter to timber and erect the clinic on the island. He made a very good job of the building. A lovely thought is that many infants were delivered safely.

Graham Ross, Chief Police Officer, John Anderson, Senior Medical Officer, and myself were the first men to land by seaplane at Tambisan in 1965. On the east coast of what was North Borneo and now called Sabah there is a stretch of coastline between Lahad Datu and Tawau in the Semporna district which in my opinion is one of the loveliest in that part of the world.

While returning from duty, I had occasion to really study and take in the beauty of the area and the corral reef on the eastern side of the sea passage. The ship ran aground! I had been on the bridge with the Captain moments before admiring the beautiful scenery and as we approached the entrance into the sea from the passage. We both left the bridge with one officer at the wheel.

I had collected papers for further action and as I entered the small lounge on the starboard side, I suddenly saw the reef right alongside the ship. We were not travelling at speed, and in a matter of minutes we had ran up onto the reef and stopped with a shudder. There was immediate action by the officers and crew, and the First Officer produced a model craft with what looked like weights and began to prepare a report for the Captain concerning the cargo and its displacement. The Chief Engineer reported to the Captain and the outcome of their discussion was that we would remain where we were until later in the day when they said, the tide would be higher in that area and they hoped to be able to back off using the ships engines.

As the ship lay, partly heeled over to starboard, the view of the water and the myriad coloured fish exceeds description. It is a picture that once seen cannot be forgotten. The fish were swimming in all directions and in and out of the corral. The sun blazed down and for the rest of the day we just lay there on the corral reef. Meantime the Captain had reported to his H.Q. at Singapore and several small ships drew near to see what was happening.

In the evening the tide had risen and a small ship belonging to the ~ame line, "Straits Steamship", had appeared on the scene. A small ~at was lowered and loaded with a rope of large diameter. To this a ~ner rope was attached and they then approached us and ~ually succeeded in getting the tow rope on board. Soon we were ~nd on our way to Sandakan.

~ing and Queen of Malayasia were due to make a visit to ~and this involved every government department in making ~s for their arrival. The Resident was in direct touch with ~t co-ordinating details.

The visit was during 1965 and I was looking forward to the Kings arrival. He was the Rajah of Perlis during my time in Kedah, the only ruler who was not referred to as a sultan. He was also the youngest ruler in post-war Malaya and I remember him sitting beside us when Kedah played Perlis in the knockout tournament for the Malayan Gold Cup. That had been 17 years previously. As I said earlier, Kedah won the Gold Cup having defeated all State Teams in Malaya and Singapore, (the favourites) in the final which was played on the Railway Ground at Kuala Lumpur.

In view of confrontation, security was a first priority and there was a battalion of the Malay Regiment stationed at Sandakan before the Royal Visit was due to take place. They had a very efficient C.O. and one of the Majors was a nephew of the Queen.

The great day arrived and we were all at the Sandakan airport to receive their Majesties. The legislative council and local dignitaries were lined up to be presented by Dato Kew Sek Chew. Next to them was the Resident and his wife and then myself as District Officer with the Regimental Officers on my right. The nephew was next to me. As the King approached where I was standing, he looked at me and smiled and obviously had recognised me at once. He said something about sport and passed along the line.

I have never given it much thought until now, but I wonder what the councillors thought about the low profile of the expat who was the only one the King knew at that meeting? Celebrations went on throughout the day and the royal party paid visits to the large kampongs on either side of Sandakan Town. There was a gathering of representative groups who put on a display in the school hall which was the largest building available to hold so many people. The Filipino dance with the long bamboo poles was a thriller. One mistake and there was bound to be a broken ankle. The visit was most enjoyable and the Royal couple, sitting on the stage seemed to thoroughly enjoy the whole proceedings.

The Residency of Sandakan celebrated the King's birthday on the Padang and there were approximately 2,000 school children formed up on the Padang and making the letters 'Long Live the King'. The District Surveyor had made the outlines for me. I was subsequent 'fined' by the Rotary Fine Master for controlling so many sch children. As the children left the Padang, lorries were lined up each child received a bottle of soft drink and a bag of cakes.

Having arrived at Sandakan early in 1964 and straight in to suppose the tempo must have increased. Being without fam Black Out Bungalow, (Balmoral) to return to in the evening the obvious answer, work seven days a week. We w employed in every department and I remember that commerce and industry were equally busy. There was much that needed to be done, but looking back from 1992 it is now clear that 'ethnic cleansing' was a must in the political calendar. Expatriates had to be removed from executive posts.

The Resident Commissioner of Sandakan in my period of duty there, was the last expatriate to hold the post. My successor, Andrew Brooks, was the last expatriate to be District Officer of Sandakan. This 'cleansing' continued in all departments and expatriates were posted to advisory positions.

The Resident Commissioner of Sandakan, Jim Rutherford, was a dedicated officer and a christian gentleman. Quiet and thorough in his approach to his duties and good at his leisure pursuits, golf and bridge. He was ably assisted by Sheila, his wife.

At another time and in another day there could have been a very healthy atmosphere had HMOCS been responsible for the government of North Borneo, but prior to the war the colonial office had no jurisdiction for the territory.

Previously North Borneo had been administered by a chartered company and it was about 1951 that the change began to take place and by the early 60s development was the order of the day. I hope the people continue to benefit from the original planning.

During one of the rare absences of the Resident Commissioner, I was acting for him for about a week I think. I remember on one occasion when I had to change out of my bush shirt and put on a suit and collar and tie and travel out to the airport in a large car flying the Union Jack.

Protocol must have been involved, but I have no memory of any particular occasion. At that period also, a Royal Navy vessel, a survey ship, called in at Sandakan and I met the Captain when he came to the office. I was invited to dine with the officers and when I arrived at the ship in the evening I was piped aboard in recognition of the office I was representing and entertained to a fine meal followed by a cinema show which was located on an upper deck. Looking back, it was along way from the pit and the coal face. I owe much to my instructors and e training over the years.

here was one other incident during 1965; remember my ioning the small christian cross with the remaining small blank the right hand corner which I hoped to leave blank when my luty as D.O. ended? It was early in the morning and I had just t the office, which was now upstairs, when the Head of nch appeared, Ted Pearce, a most efficient officer who had service at Cyprus during the Eoka period.

Ted sat at the other side of my desk and then quietly asked me if I would like to see my replacement in office. He went on to tell me that this replacement was in the local gaol with several other men who had been arrested during an early morning raid. Ted revealed that they had been under supervision for some time. He then produced a document and handed it over to me. "That", he said, "is a list of the people who were to be assassinated". The list contained the names of all the executive expatriates and my name was second from the top. The Resident Commissioner was first and then on to police and government departments.

I did not visit the gaol. I did give much thought to what had taken place and was particularly reminded that we were in a state of confrontation with a Communist backed Indonesia. It had a remarkable affect on my christian thinking. If they had been able to carry out their intention of assassination, they would have bound us hand and foot and placed a blind-fold over our eyes. We would have been helpless. But, while they did all of this they could not alter what was in the mind, and if death was certain, we could say, "O Lord, my God, how great Thou art". Nothing can separate us from the love of God. But, again, would I have had sufficient courage and nerve to stand still and defy them? I shall never know. But, they made me think.

The Resident Commissioner was posted to an advisory post at the secretariat and was in the process of preparing to hand over to his successor, when news reached me that my stepfather had died suddenly. I requested permission to return to Scotland to attend to the funeral arrangements, etc. and this was granted.

I had to move quickly and transport was a problem. There was only shipping, out of the question, and the Dakota service which arrived morning, lunctime, evening. It was necessary for me to get to Jesselton and board the midday Comet for Singapore and then on to the U.K. Murray Douglas came to my aid. I took a small grip and went out to the airport only to learn that the charter plane was somewhere between Sandakan and Jesselton. The pilot knew that I had arrived and called in. "Tell Dudley not to worry, I shall be right back". I was taken immediately to Jesselton and managed to board the Comet and away to Singapore.

It was to prove to be a hectic journey. Comet to Singapore and th another Comet to Heathrow and a Britannia to Edinburgh. An missed the funeral. I had been assisted all the way from Sandak Edinburgh and it was unfortunate that I missed the funeral, but give me the opportunity to attend to necessary details a inevitable documentation following death. Having hired a c able to complete the necessary registrar and insurance business, and then made my way to Camborne to spend a few days with Pat and the family before returning to Sandakan. Once again air travel from Edinburgh to London with the intention of being in Camborne by dinner time. Not so. There was delay at Heathrow and the small transport 'plane which was supposed to take the passengers to Plymouth, did not take off until dusk. Looking back that was a peculiar arrangement. There was only eight seats available and although there was the usual left and right hand seats for the pilots, there was only one pilot on board and he was wearing an ordinary top coat.

We duly arrived at Exeter and discovered that there was no luggage on board; the 'plane was not going to Plymouth and we were being taken on the rest of the journey from Exeter to Plymouth by taxi. Seems unbelievable, but that is what happened in 1965. I had contacted Pat by telephone and eventually arrived at the hotel in Plymouth very late. I was on such a limited time at home that I never thought to check up on that peculiar flight and my luggage was delivered by a carrier I had booked through a travel agent.

It was a fleeting visit to 'Shawthorne' and while I found Pat and the family in good health, it was an upsetting visit after being away since early 1964. Pat had been forced to move house, 25 having become too large to manage, and 'Shawthorne' was a neat and easily-run house. The knowledge that I was only there for a few days seemed very odd and I was soon on my way back to Sandakan. Not a happy memory.

The journey back was uneventful and in Sandakan there was much activity with 'Red Book' Planning and meetings with those concerned. One of my last proposals for the new township at 30th mile was to mark of a site for a christian church and a Moslem Surau. At the time it was pointed out to me that there had been no provision for a cemetery. The main requirements of health, education, religion, provisions, transport, water had been noted and it seems appropriate that in the end there would have to be a cemetery.

Much of the preliminary work in preparing for development and re-settlement of families and the opening of estates to grow oil palm will have been implemented, the oil mill will have been built, the infrastructure created and amended and expatriates relegated to istory. The moving finger writes . . .

It was a Saturday afternoon and there was to be a concert at the dakan Club. The performers and musicians were no doubt off one e passing ships and this was a rare occurrence. I decided to go and as I was entering the Club one of the expatriate women er to me and said that in future they would have to 'crave an '. I asked her what she meant.

It appears that 'leaked government documents' is no new practise and there is always someone who wants to be first with the news. Apparently I was to be appointed the new Assistant Secretary of Finance and posted to Jesselton (as it was at the time) during the coming week.

Chapter 9

I had no idea about this posting and the subject had never been mentioned in my presence. Furthermore, I would never have applied for such a job and at that moment I found it difficult to believe what I was being told.

All through my working life, ever since I had joined the army or at some time during my service life, I had found myself doing minor duties connected with money. During my immigration service I had come in contact with revenue collection in a small way and there was my time with Holmans at Camborne and then Camborne Tin Mining. At no time had I ever applied for a Job connected with accounting or finance.

On arrival at Sandakan to take over as D.O., there was one interesting moment when my predecessor produced a ledger which he referred to as the 'flood relief fund' He explained what it was and how it came to be in existence and when I asked how many signatures were required or how the money was dispersed he replied, 'Just the D.O.s'. There was thousands of dollars on balance. As I said earlier I had passed my government exams while in the immigration department and knew just what had to be done. On Monday morning I appeared at the Chartered Bank and opened an account which could only be operated by the Chairman of the Sandakan Town Board and myself. At no time was this account to be the sole responsibility of one person. Being keen to get rid of sole responsibility, I overlooked the need to inform the Ministry of Finance! On Monday, I was told that I had been appointed to the Ministry of Finance as A.S. (F.).

Andrew Brooks, D.O. at Tawau, was posted to Sandakan to take over and I duly left for Jesselton. Andrew was the last expatriate to be D.O. at Sandakan. I never met him again but he was studying law at the time of his posting with the view of becoming a lawyer.

I reported to the Permanent Secretary of the Ministry of Finance at the Secretariat and received an introduction to the directives outlining my duties and a brief discussion of what was happening at the time. I went along and met the man I was to relieve.

Handing over, taking over procedure was completed and I was on my own.

The office was right out of a travel brochure. At the top of the Secretariat Building and glass to the front and along the side of the building. The top of the glass was tinted and as one looked from the office the view was an inlet from the China Sea with small islands dotted irregularly and leading shorewards. Between the Secretariat and the sea, the main road ran from the airport into the town with one junction leading inland.

The next move was to make contact with the people working in my part of the Ministry and with the Accountant General and the Director of Audit. This was a pleasant exercise and I found them all to be helpful. In the course of time I realised that my best contact was the Director and Deputy Director of Audit. I also met the Attorney General, a large bluff Welshman with lots of ideas about development.

Administration: There were open files, confidential files and in my office there was a contingency file always up to date and permitting expenditure up to $1,000,000. Beside this file on the same table were the annual estimates for every department in the government.

Budget and financial control was operated from this office. There was the 'flimsy' file which held the copies of inter-ministry letters and kept the Secretariat in touch with what was happening in all departments.

I had a personal staff of Personal Assistant and a lady secretary and they were efficient. In addition to being A.S.(F) I had other 'hats' to wear from time to time, e.g. Chairman of the Tender's Board up to $1,5 million and Secretary to the Tender's Board above this figure. The Chairman was the Permanent Secretary.

The State Tender's Board procedure was thorough and strictly disciplined. My P.A. was well versed in dealing with tenders. On the day and at the time when tenders had been called, the Tender's Board would meet in my office before the tenders were collected.

Skinner, the P.A. and myself would then go to the special steel cage at the front of the building, unlock the padlock with the key which was in my possession and remove the locked container of tenders. Returning to the office, the container would be unlocked and opened before all members and the contents spilled on to the floor. Skinner would then call out the details and I would personally prepare the schedule.

At this point, the technicians and specialists concerned with the tender would hear the offers made and then decide which to accept. Low tenders would be carefully studied and the quantity surveyor would report whether the tenderer was equipped to meet the special demands of the tender. A final decision would be made by the Board. Financial or material disputes were referred to the higher board, chaired by the Permanent Secretary. The secretary was a Chinese lady, and we soon had a working system in operation. I made no attempt to keep to my predecessors methods and from my own experience of dealing with known efficient staff, trusting them to do the normal routine creates its own atmosphere. The decisions and responsibility are mine. Among my other 'hats', there was the duty of appointing Boards of Survey. These fell in to different categories. All government stores and equipment held on inventory had to be accounted for and when it had to be disposed off, it was necessary to follow a procedure of 'write off'.

The other type of Board was a Surprise Board which really appointed itself. I simply kept a rota and then named the officials who were to attend and carry out the Surprise Inspection of the various banks in the area.

Boards of Survey are usually routine and a method of balancing the books. There is only one Board appointed during my time which had an amusing conclusion with regard to material. The Agricultural Department wanted to dispose of a quantity of barbed wire which had been used for protection of crops from wild pig and they had applied for a Board of Survey to be appointed.

The Board was appointed in the normal way, calling on officers employed in that area and appointing a senior officer as Chairman of the Board. In this case the decision was to load the barbed wire on to a flat craft and dump the wire at sea. I agreed.

During the intervening time of getting a suitable craft to dump the wire, a Chinese contractor approached the Agricultural Department and offered to purchase the wire from them. The Chairman of the B.S. accepted the offer and reported to me saying that he did not know how to account for the money received.

I replied and told him to credit the full payment to general revenue and congratulated him on his initiative. The wire had been disposed off at the buyer's expense, government had been saved the cost of floating the wire out to sea, and general revenue had benefited.

The amusing conclusion; I was walking along George Street in Edinburgh some time afterwards and suddenly heard my name being called. It was a tall, red-haired, bearded Scot who had been the Chairman of the Board.

It transpired that when he agreed to sell the wire after receiving instructions to dump it, the Senior Clerk had told him he would be in serious trouble with the Ministry of Finance. The letter of congratulation from my desk was framed and hung on the wall of the office. I was entertained to a very good lunch, just off George Street.

The P.A.C. – Public Accounts Committee. This Committee is without question the most powerful committee in any government. The composition of the committee consists of Government Ministers, Permanent Secretaries, Nominated Heads of Government departments, Legislative and Executive elected Members. On one occasion the under secretary and myself attended on behalf of the Ministry. At the end of a long and tiring day and when several officials had been 'spoken to' about irregularities, we were sitting with the Director of Audit among others and just as we were getting ready to leave, the D. of A. said; "There is one item that keeps coming up of a large sum of money on deposit in the Chartered Bank at Sandakan but not under a specified Revenue Heading".

I had learned quite a bit since arriving at Sandakan to become District Officer and as I heard what was being said, I wanted to disappear. Instead of being a junior member on the Board I should have been in front of the Board.

I admitted that I knew what the deposit was. I also admitted that I had wanted nothing to do with it and had got rid of it as soon as I arrived having found that it was being operated over one signature, the District Officer's. Of course I knew now that I should have reported the action taken to the A.S.(F). The silence was deafening, but I survived.

Of the many matters that came my way for decision there were two with the Medical Department, one with the Social Welfare Department, and two with the Road Traffic Department that are worthy of mention.

Just after my arrival at the Ministry the Doctor for Medical Health in Sabah came in one afternoon and said there was a serious situation developing in the Beaufort area from a contagious disease. His problem was that he had a limited supply of serum available, certainly not enough for the population of North Borneo (Sabah) which was estimated in 1964 to be approximately 500,000.

He went on to say that he could get what he required in Singapore, but it was necessary to arrange special expenditure to meet the cost. That the purchase would have to be made quickly and confidentially. The amount required was stated and within the hour, the Director of Medical Services and the Permanent Secretary having been consulted, the Medical Officer for Health was on his way to obtain the serum.

The second Medical Department requirement was common sense. The doctor concerned came in and said that there was a suitable electric generator standing idle and had never been used since its arrival. He had made enquiries and was told that it could be used as an emergency generator in he case of normal supply failure. He was asking for authority to transport it to the hospital. It was done. Until I left I never heard of it being used, but I had a ready reply for anyone who might object to the expenditure. Social Welfare – Government Estimates fall in to three categories: Above the Line; Below the Line; Special Development. In certain cases Virement (adjustment) is permitted above the line and the mechanics of this procedure means that the grand total is never exceeded. But all adjustments must be completed by the 30th of September. The new estimates for the following year must be made and submitted for approval after that date.

The Deputy Director of Social Welfare had come along to discuss and present the estimates for his department. When dealing with the Old Peoples Home, he referred to the diets for the year and then said to me that he was surprised to find that the old people had not received an egg during the past year. The question of eggs was settled and added to the diet forthwith.

The Road Transport Department. It had been decided to build a bridge in the south of the country and do away with the ferry which was unsuitable and unable to meet the demands of the increased population.

As the day for the opening of the bridge drew near the contractor realised that it was not going to be ready. He was worried about what would happen in the area where the people had been promised free access over the bridge instead of having to pay the ferry fare.

A final date was agreed for the opening of the bridge and as a concession to the public, the ferry would be free for the brief interval until the bridge was open.

The second issue with the Road Transport Department had undertones of lack of co-operation leading to stalemate. It concerned an important Revenue Collection, i.e. road tax. There was an extant method, but it was proving to be uncertain in effect and very difficult for the public to reach the office in view of the location which shall remain nameless.

I called on the Road Transport Officer and listened to his problems. It was obvious that he was being intentionally awkward and while there were regulations to deal with him, the matter would be further delayed. The whole matter boiled down to his alleged inability to have the documentation ready in time and there was no available site to build an office in the proposed area. I removed the task of typing from his office and went on a tour of the new area. There was no site as he had claimed. There was however, a small Government Building built on stilts. By enclosing the open space between the four corners, allowing for doors and windows, the P.W.D. could submit drawings and create the new office. It was done. The office opened on time. In addition to Budget Control and Finance there were many duties to be attended to on a daily basis and as I said at an earlier stage Development in every direction was the order of the day.

This involved capital plant and a significant problem had arisen. Machines costing hundreds of thousands of dollars (Malayan) were seen lying around the countryside, broken down. I was asked to look in to this problem and started by contacting the P.W.D. Department. On my first visit to the central workshops, I saw a large engine belonging to an earth moving machine lying on the floor. The foreman informed me that it only required a small part and they were waiting for it to arrive.

On further investigation, the few skilled engineers explained that the native engineers were not conversant with the modern machines and the smallest fault could result in the whole machine being put out of operation. There was reference to what was called a 'German system' of constructing engines in sub-assemblies and recognised by using a colour scheme. Thus if a small assembly contained the faulty part, this would be removed and a total assembly slipped in to its place.

In consultation with engineers and the importers of heavy equipment, the position of residual values and replacement at a given working life of the machine, (based on working hours) was considered. It was decided that visits should be made to Sarawak, Kuala Lumpur and a report submitted on how they dealt with this type of problem. Consequently, the Accountant General and myself left for Kuching one Sunday afternoon and commenced our visit on the Monday morning.

Kuching had no similar problem at that time and we carried on to Kuala Lumpur. We had two meetings there. The first meeting was totally lacking in interest by the majority of officials present. As the meeting broke up we got into conversation with a small group and they showed a different attitude to the problem. Ian and I went off to lunch at the hotel and during lunch we received a telephone call from the Secretariat asking us to call back in the afternoon. We did.

As a result of the afternoon meeting we contacted a Secretarial Agency and hired a secretary to compile a report from our notes and dictation. I was about to proceed on leave to the U.K. and was glad that I had made some progress. I did not return to that office and do not know how the matter was finally resolved.

There was a bonus from this visit to Kuala Lumpur. An old polo playing friend of mine suggested that I should visit the polo ptables in the evening. I did and met John Willie. It was unbelievable. 1957 when

I left Singapore and now, here in 1966 he was still going, but not playing Polo. He was owned by a bank manager's daughter and was held in high esteem for his gymkhana skills.

I had entered the Ministry of Finance with a great deal of trepidation but I need not have worried. I was leaving to go on holidays with my family in the U.K. a much wiser man than when I had taken up the post and on reflection it was simply a case of relying on past training and common sense.

I had been given an extended contract for a further two years and permission to return by sea accompanied by Pat and Katrina. The family situation had been partly resolved; Lylie and Sheila were established in their careers and Andrew was in Truro School for Boys. Andrew was able to come out to Sabah twice a year at government expense.

My final investigation on behalf of the Ministry of Finance was to seek for information regarding the high cost of imported goods to Sabah.

The goods mainly food-stuff, came from Malaya where they had been imported from Australia and the U.K. and some other countries. The handling charges were obviously a factor and I called for a meeting of representatives from the major importing companies. The result of this enquiry was interesting. We had taken a tin of milk powder as an example imported from the Port of Swettenham on the West Coast of Malaya.

From Swettenham to Kota Kinabalu we considered the shipping, C.I.F., port charges at Kota Kinabalu and in to the shops, the distance, approximately one mile from the docks. According to the report made by the agents representatives there was an increase of 114% .

I left in June of 1966 and went straight to Camborne. We were due to return to Sabah in October and 'Shawthorne' was to be sold and the furniture put in store at Redruth. Arrangements were made for passages by P. & O. and the uplifting of heavy baggage and then we went visiting, a must, when home from overseas. With one exception, it was a pleasant holiday at home. The main reason for returning to the Far East had been accomplished and there was no longer an overdraft to worry about. Pat had kept her car in excellent condition. The tyres after two years had hardly any wear on the treads. We made an arrangement with Taylors', our regular Garage in Penzance, to trade the car in against a new car when I finally came home from employment in Sabah. Meanwhile we were given the use of a 3 litre Rover for the remainder of our holiday and we proceeded north to see the various relatives.

We had a lovely time at Inverness and Frank joined us, staying at a separate B. & B. He and Lylie obtained bicycles and toured around Inverness. They were both keen to see the 'monster'.

Loch Maree was the highlight of that visit and as we sat beside the Loch, with the birds landing on our outstretched feet, you could hear the silence. Peaceful.

Eventually we arrived back at Camborne and made final arrangements for our departure. The day of departure arrived. Lylie was in London, Sheila was at the Royal Masonic Hospital where she was commencing her training and Andrew was at Truro School. Pat, Katrina and myself had booked in to one of the hotels in Camborne.

It was fortunate that we had not moved away to a hotel nearer our port of embarkation. We had asked Mr Jimmy Reid, a senior surgeon at the Truro Hospital, to look after Andrew, health wise, and given our consent in the event of accidents for him to act as he saw fit.

We had just finished lunch when there was a telephone call to say that Andrew had been admitted to Truro Hospital with acute appendicitis. That was the exception I referred to earlier. It came as a blow and just as we were about to leave the country. We went to the hospital and saw Andrew. As I remember the visit, he put up a good show, he was only thirteen and knew that his parents were on their way to the Far East. It was not an easy farewell for any of us.

On arrival at Southampton we were informed that the ship would be delayed for a few days and we were to be accommodated on the Chusan until the departure date. We spent the time walking round the town and I had my application for an Irish Sweepstake ticket returned asking me where the money should go. I replied "To hospital charities". We left Southampton and had a splendid journey to Singapore, where we booked into a hotel on Orchard Road, quite near to where we were living when Andrew was born. I called in at the Sabah Government Agent's office to make arrangements for the onward journey to Jesselton and was informed that we would be in Singapore for a few days. I was also told that I could have expenses for myself, Pat and Katrina. I refused to accept expenses for Katrina, who was only seven years of age, and was quite adamant about that when I signed the voucher for Pat and myself. This simple act was to have far reaching results.

We boarded a Straits steamship vessel and continued our journey to Jesselton. It was not a bad crossing, but Katrina was conscious of the difference between the P. & O. and the smaller vessel and I do not think she enjoyed this part at all.

We booked in to the Borneo Hotel on arrival and in a short spell we were allotted a large flat close to the shore. We were to stay there until the end of the tour. I reported back to the Ministry of Finance, and found myself dealing with specialist tasks and the most unlikely title of Financial Advisor to Lands and Survey. Previously my duties ha been in connection with the State of Sabah and the development within Sabah, but now I was to be involved in a much wider field. Sabah was politically in two parts, Federal and State. Financially, it is very important to note and remember the significance. At the moment, 1992, in this country there is mention of federal from time to time in connection with the E.C. and I wonder if the people are aware of the need to avoid what federal would mean to this country.

As I acquainted myself with the new situation, I discovered that an American advisor had been brought in to advise the Permanent Secretary on economics. He called in to tell me how fortunate we were to have him and that he was always available to assist. I never saw him again.

During this tour, there were three things that occupied my time. The establishing of Secondary Industries in Sabah, advisory role to the Director of Lands and Survey and, a four wheeled drive up-country when the boys were out on holiday from school.

Secondary Industries: This incurred Federal Involvement and having to travel to Kuala Lumpur to attend conferences and special meetings, and then back to what was now Kota Kinabalu commonly referred to as K.K.

There was a lot of suggestion and planning, but I never saw any factory or industry in or near K.K. However, in Federal H.Q., I have no doubt there would be plans pinned on the walls. There was one major industry under discussion, copper mining, and the Japanese were said to be interested in this project. I was never involved in this, but I heard the buzz within the Secretariat and that tests were being carried out. Then the 'file' was 'called in'. Federal interest would be keen and the subject disappeared from even the State Buzz.

Lands and Survey: I do not know if the Director asked that I should be seconded to his department, but I was glad to be involved with him and we became good friends. The situation in Lands and Survey was a complex one created by the difficulty of access to most of the country which had been developed piecemeal, and applications had been made to the District Officers who had the authority and rightly had issued Temporary Occupation Leases to the applicants. While scores of such documents had been issued to the applicants, mainly natives, who had trekked in for miles by jungle paths to obtain them, the D.O.s did not have the staff to follow up the processing of the leases and consequently the full leases were lying, awaiting collection in the D.O.'s office.

It is almost certain that the holder of the T.O.L. was under the mpression that he had sufficient claim to the holding and he had no rther need to approach the office where the D.O. (also the ACLR),

Assistant Commissioner Land Revenue was waiting to levy the Fees for the Land.

In fact, the T.O.L. was just that, temporary, and expired six months after issue. I set out to try and redress this situation, using 'bush radio', but left before it got of the ground. There must have been heavy losses of revenue. The legal documentation referring to land was in a mess.

Throughout the country there were small holders occupying land on what was called a T.O.L. (Temporary Occupation Lease) and these were severely restricted to six months. They could be and should be extended to full lease conditions, but this had not taken place in spite of the Lands and Survey efforts to achieve completion of the title and of course to obtain the resulting revenue.

The answer from all the Districts was that they did not have the staff to send out to deal with the settlers who were mainly in difficult parts of the country, accessible only by foot. My own experience of Sandakan as D.O. was now going to be of value to me and to Government. When I arrived at Sandakan I had been shown a cupboard and when they opened the door, paper showered out on to the floor. The paper was T.O.L.'s and other land documents which 'could not be processed because of staff shortages and far distances from Sandakan". Sandakan had one Process Server.

The Chief Clerk at Sandakan had proved to be efficient and there was another young Chinese cadet who had been sent to Sandakan to gain experience.

The Process Server was a wizened man, short in stature and could probably walk all day. The cadet was gaining experience by leaning on the counter. It was decided to make a change and all were agreed that the land papers must be attended to at once. One Process Server but four points to the compass. By equipping him with necessary supplies to be away from the station for some time, in order to serve notice on the small holders who were no doubt sitting on 'their' cultivated land, he was able to go to the furthest point and the news would be out that if the revenue was not paid the lease would be cancelled.

Where T.O.L.'s had not been exchanged for title, the land was available for re-allocation. The Cadet worked in with the Chief Clerk and the Process Server and progress, slowly, was made.

While I was in the Ministry of Finance, I heard that the Chief Clerk had become an Assistant District Officer and the Cadet was about to become an Assistant District Officer. With that past experience, we started the same procedure in all the Districts, 22 I believe, and we go results. They were not all amicable and some with strange results.

Politicians families suddenly appeared on the scene and complained to the Director about the issue of the titles or of reasons why they should have extensions of time. The Director showed sympathy, but pointed out what the law required. The Registrar became busy, titles were prepared, T.O.L.'s were surrendered and modern equipment was introduced to the office. Xerox was on hire and there were several occasions when the paper in the copying machine sent out smoke but never actually caught fire. Then there was the first contact with computers and numerous 'teething' problems.

In 1966 there was a problem of removing a mistake from the memory of the computer and on one of my visits to Singapore I saw, what on 20-20 hindsight is obvious, a very complicated method of correcting the fault.

Today corrections are a simple matter. You only get out what you put in. It was agreed that I should go on a countrywide tour of Land Offices.

It was getting near the end of my contract period and I had already made enquiries about returning to the University at Edinburgh to study for entry into the Church of Scotland. The schoolmaster of the secondary school in K.K. was Cannon Rusted, (Rusty) and he was also a member of the K.K. Cathedral. I shall return to Rusty but first let me complete my tour of Land Offices.

With the exclusion of the interior and Beluran and the south District of Sandakan on the Kinabatangan river, the remainder were reasonably easy to approach. If you think of the coastline of Sabah being formed in the shape of an equilateral triangle with the left hand angle at Beaufort (facing the China Sea) and the right hand angle at Tawau (facing the Suluk Sea) with Kudat at the apex pointing due east, China Sea to the north and the Suluk Sea to the south, this will give an idea of the layout of the country which, away from the coast, is mainly dense jungle and sloping up to steep hills and of course Mount Kinabalu.

The Land Offices at Beaufort and Keningau were reached by rail car, (memories of Bukit Ketri in Perlis), and they had their different problems but not quite so complex as on the east coast.

Beaufort was more open and had a large settled population. Having visited the south west I returned to K.K. and booked my passage on the Straits Steamship, which proceeded from K.K. and sailed up the west coast calling in at Kudat and then on down the Suluk Sea to Sandakan, Lahad Datu, Semporna and Tawau. Norris, the D.O. from Beluran, and Thomas, from the Kinabatangan District, would have me to Sandakan to discuss the problem and as far as I can remember, they had the situation well in hand.

I was accompanied by a Chinese Officer on this tour and he saw what was required. However, whether he was appointed to this duty I do not know because I prepared to leave Sabah shortly afterwards.

Cannon Rusted: I must have come to know Rusty through my attendance at the Cathedral, where I had become a sides-man and took my turn at reading the lessons on the Sunday Evening. I first went to see him during 1967 and discussed my interest in becoming a minister. His advice was for me to write to Edinburgh and ask for details about 'mature' entry and theological colleges. He also loaned a book which he suggested I should study, a simple act and one that was to change my whole attitude to the basic understanding of the Christian Faith.

I sent off what really amounted to a curriculum vitae to the Secretary for Education of the Ministry at 121 George Street, Edinburgh and received a prompt reply. Most of what was required of me could be attended to when I returned to the U.K. The first step being that I would be required to attend a selection school.

I was encouraged to do selected study pending my return to the U.K. I shall always remember the meeting I had with Rusty when I returned the book to him. I said that the most interesting thing about the book was that it had made it quite clear God was not only transcendent but also imminent. Rusty looked at me for a few seconds and then replied, "You have learned that from reading only one book, when the day comes for you to be ordained, I want to know and I shall attend the Ordination".

I believe that I now understand more clearly why Rusty was so impressed at the time. That was in 1967. I was Ordained at Ballantrae in Ayrshire on the 21st of September 1972. Rusty was there. Rusty had returned to Croydon where he was Cannon Emeritus and in the Diocese of the Archbishop of Canterbury, Archbishop Ramsay.

When Rusty asked for leave to attend my Ordination. He had to explain to the Archbishop the background for his request. On hearing what Rusty had to say the Archbishop approved the request and added, "and give that young man my blessing also".

I suppose that makes me one of the few ministers to be Ordained with the blessing of The Church of England and The Church of Scotland.

Before leaving Sabah I want to mention how Pat and Katrina coped with Sabah and of Andrew's visits to Sabah from school in Cornwall. I have always been well supported by Pat in whatever I attempted to do, but I have only become fully aware just what that meant since writing this autobiography. Having reached this point of life in Sab

I realise now how much Pat disliked the restricted way of life, but she did not surrender to the restrictions. On the contrary she took a keen interest in what Katrina was doing both at school and in the 'Brownies'. At school there were only six or so expatriate children and this showed in various ways. The Brownies consisted of mainly native children and the 'Brown Owl' was a Chinese woman.

This also revealed some amusing moments. e.g. The chorus, "This is Tommy, this is Tommy . . . very well, I thank you". Katrina came home on one occasion having learned this chorus at the Brownie meeting and repeated it to us, but it was interpreted, "Velly well I tank you, Velly well I tank you . . ." and it was some time before Pat was able to persuade Katrina to accept the occidental interpretation.

Katrina also had dancing lessons and French outwith the school curriculum and Pat took her to the different locations in the area of the town to attend the lessons. Pat was also involved in voluntary work with the Health Department at the Family Planning Clinic and periodically took her turn at cleaning the brass in the Cathedral.

During 1967 we had the happy, yet disappointing event, of Lylie's wedding to Frank which had been postponed from 1966. Disappointing because we were not able to be present.

Bobby Norris came to live in Jesselton (K.K.) and proved to be a very good friend of Pat. Neither were interested in being 'Club types' and spent most of their time with the children. The highlight of Pat's sojourn in Sabah was the arrival of Andrew from school in Cornwall when he came out on holiday. I'm not sure how Andrew felt on arrival at K.K. We used to go straight to the barber from the airport and the improvement was worth the effort.

Prior to Andrew's arrival for Christmas in 1966, Pat, Katrina, and myself went for a short holiday trip by sea from K.K. to Sandakan on a Straits steamship vessel and returned by air from Sandakan aboard a Fokker Friendship, the aircraft which had replaced the DC3 (Dakota).

While Andrew was with us, Pat saw to his measurements for a kilt and outfit to attend Lylie's wedding in the coming March. During the holidays there was the usual activities at the Jesselton Sport's Club and it was on this occasion I believe that Andrew surprised Dudley Smith and Ian Melville when he was invited by Dudley Smith to try a shot from the third tee. We stood back and watched. The shot was good and went about as far as the rest of us. I believe that was Andrew's advent to golf and he and Dudley Smith played together at various courses during the following years, not continuously, but at home or when on holiday to Sabah. There was one occasion when Frank joined them for a round at Gullane. Andrew takes kindly to sport but cannot be accused of dedication to any particular form. I should like to have his swing at golf but that was not for me.

During Andrew's visit, we went on a few short journeys out and about K.K. and he pottered about in his mother's mini on the beach which was right alongside our block of flats. He acquired quite a useful experience of driving which stood him in good stead in later years. The end of the holiday and Andrew was back to Truro School. We returned to normal and my duties were as I have described.

The major event in 1967 was the wedding of Frank and Lylie in March, with Pat and Lylie in regular correspondence. Lylie was in fact organising her own wedding reception, making her wedding dress and the wedding cake. We managed to send a box of orchids via Robinsons from Singapore. Andrew arrives for the summer holidays and this time I have a visit planned for a 4-wheel drive to Kudat. We also invite the sons of the bank manager to join us.

I had been told that there was no 'road' as such between K.K. and Kudat, only a track, but with a four wheel drive vehicle it should be possible. John Fryer had an Austen Gypsy 4-wheel drive and agreed to let me have it for the trip. John was the Head of Department of Lands and Survey with whom I was working at that time.

We loaded the vehicle and set off for Kudat. As it turned out the journey was uneventful and my memory of the track, that while it was uneven and broken in parts, it was quite easy to navigate. (much simpler than the track from Ban Sadau across to Padang Besar in Malaya). What was really surprising was the areas of open space. From the sea on one side and then jungle, no trees or foilage between the sea and the edge of the jungle at all. We did not see many people on the journey and eventually arrived at Kudat where we were booked into the rest house.

The boys enjoyed the visit and there was the knowledge that not many teenagers (expatriate) had arrived at Kudat in a 4-wheeled vehicle from K.K. On the return journey there was one incident which gave cause for concern. There was a fire raging on both sides of the track and seemed to extend for quite some way on both sides.

The track was open and I decided to drive on, but the question of the petrol tank which was at the side of the vehicle and full of fuel might present a problem. I asked the boys to hold on and went through as fast as I could depending on the surface. I was hoping that I would not have to stop for any reason and as it turned out, there was no need for concern.

We got back to K.K. and from there until the end of the holiday the clubs held different events involving families and sporting competitions. Golf, swimming, table tennis, cinema shows and parties. On Andrew's third visit we decided to visit the interior which we were able to do by rail jeep. We went from K.K. to Beaufort and walked round the market place.

It was here that Andrew bought a huge brimmed hat and I believe he has that hat to this day. There was a rubber planter at Beaufort with a young family and Andrew disappeared with the boy to be shown around the shops, etc. When we left Beaufort, Andrew was given a present from the boy. It was a piece of wood shaped in the form of a machine gun. That 'gun' was in Andrew's possession for quite a long time and I think it actually came back to this country when we returned.

The passage up to the interior will always be remembered. The rail track ascended up a very steep slope with several bends and then on into Keningau. While there we visited the missionary. David Smith, who was the only son of friends of my parents. On the return run I was sitting at the rear of the rail jeep and Pat with Katrina and Andrew were near the front.We hurtled down that track. Hugh Teo, Director of Public Works was sitting beside me and I wonder what he made of that journey. As I write tonight it is Christmas Eve, 1992. On Christmas Eve 1965, 27 years ago, I was Father Christmas and arrived at the Jesselton Sports Club riding on a Kerbau, not an easy thing to do and the keeper of the buffalo must have been there to lead it for those animals do not like Europeans, including Father Christmas. The choice was obviously influenced because I was without my family and the younger children would have no idea who I was.

The sons of the late Dr Cecil James, Deputy Director of Medical Services were among the children and I shall always remember that it was the elder son who came across the verandah to ask if I would like something to eat or drink. It was a happy occasion for the children, but my thoughts were far away.

47 years ago I had been faced with two riots in the afternoon and evening of Christmas Eve. They were summarily dealt with and subsequently there was no further trouble. The National news has just informed us in 1992 that a number of prisoners in an English gaol have decided to go on a hunger strike from Christmas Eve. I hope they are not disturbed. During 1968, we were busy making arrangements to depart for the U.K. and there was much to be done with packing for sea transport. There was also passages by air for Pat, Katrina and myself and financial arrangements to settle final payment to the Inland Revenue before our departure. We left K.K. on a Comet flight and it must have been by coincidence that Bobby Norris was on the same flight with her sons. We arrived at Singapore in the afternoon and departed by B.O.A.C. VC10 in the evening for London Heathrow. Bobby would have gone on to New Zealand.

The flight was uneventful and comfortable. But the end of the journey was to give us something to remember for all time. It was in the month of November and there was severe frost and fog. As we approached Heathrow and came lower and lower, I became aware that the orange lights were getting brighter but we were still flying fairly fast. Suddenly, the nose tilted upwards and the Captain's voice came over the broadcast system, apologising for the sudden change and explaining that he could not see the ground and was aborting the landing at Heathrow. He was going on to see what it was like at Manchester. Shortly afterwards he announced again that Manchester was no better and we were on our way to Prestwick. As we approached the sun was shining and we could look out to sea, we were going in to land. I had suggested that perhaps Customs and Immigration could clear us and let us disembark instead of flying back to London. A number of the passengers in addition to ourselves were bound for Scottish destinations. Permission was given by the authorities.

We were served with coffee in the arrivals lounge and the Captain of our flight came and spoke to us. He explained about being talked down and how at a certain point it was up to him if he could see the landing strip and if not, he abandoned the landing and went to a different airport. We were all very glad to be safely down. I went to one of the hire car services to get a vehicle and was told by the young lady that she had been unable to start the only car available at the time. I had a surplus of sterling in my wallet from the changing of Malayan Dollars and offered to pay the cost and suggested that she should show me the car. She settled the paper work and then took me to the car. There was no problem, the engine fired and we loaded the back of what was an estate car and so we arrived at my mother's home one very cold winter's morning. We had arranged a short lease on a furnished house at Crowhurst in Sussex, and after a brief visit, we departed for Crowhurst by train handing the car back in Edinburgh.

Pat, Katrina and me, we arrived at Crowhurst in the evening and the place seemed to be deserted. The house was not too far from the station and I seem to remember that we walked to it and returning for some of our baggage thus completing our journey. Having attended to the initial details of settling in, our next move was to travel to Truro to attend Andrew's School Carol Service and to collect a Rover 2000 from Taylor's Garage. The car was delivered to the hotel where we were staying.

Unfortunately, that journey by train was not a success. Pat and Katrina were taken ill as a result of the meal served on the train. It had been Silverside beef and both were attended by a doctor in the hotel bedroom. We met Andrew and managed to attend the Carol Concert.

Prior to going to Truro, I had telephoned the Church of Scotland at Edinburgh and they expressed delight that I had telephoned and that the selection school was meeting that week. Would I make every effort to get to Glasgow to take part in the selection process. There would not be another school until later in the year. I promised to make every effort. But what an experience.

Poor Pat was still not fully recovered and she had to travel with Katrina by train from Truro. I had to take the car to Crowhurst and then get on the train to Glasgow.

Pat has told me that the return to Crowhurst was a nightmare and on reflection I wish it had never happened. We seemed to be rushing all over the place at the end of 1968 and there was Christmas looming up and Frank, Lylle, Sheila, all coming to Crowhurst. We survived and I was successful in being selected to train for the ministry. But that news came later.

We were home. Just in time for Andrew's Carol Service. We had collected our Rover 2000, and I had attended the selection school at Glasgow and returned to Crowhurst. The house was comfortable and we were quite near large shopping areas, which we visited in preparation for Christmas. Andrew arrived home from school and the others arrived to complete the family group. Christmas, then New Year and we were in to 1969.

The holiday period would have been a rest for all of us but the hustle and bustle for Pat, Katrina and myself was far from over and it is a good thing that we never know completely what lies ahead.

The letter arrived informing me that I was accepted for training for the Church of Scotland ministry and laying down conditions to be followed. Returning to Scotland and taking up residence in Scotland, I was also to join a Church which in turn would be responsible for me to the Presbytery. There was more about finding a college and details for preparation to enter the college in October 1969.

We immediately took steps to finalise our short lease on the Crowhurst House and made our way to Scotland, visiting on the way. Pat and Katrina travelled by train and I went by car, fully loaded. There was a Poinsettia plant which had been given to Pat and it travelled remarkably well considering the snow and frost.

Late in the evening I experienced a tyre blowout on the nearside rear tyre. This lead to difficulties because the ground was unable to support the jack and there was no planks of wood or anything else to assist me in getting the wheel changed. In the course of time, the A.A.

sent a garage vehicle out to me and with his special under body jack. The wheel was soon changed. I remember being pleased with the behaviour of the car when the tyre blew out. She answered to the controls and enabled me to pull up straight and on the side of the road. Unfortunately the ground proved to be too soft.

I discovered from the mechanic that I was only a few miles from a motel and made my way there where I booked in, garaged the car under lock and key and the receptionist managed to supply filled sandwiches. In the morning, I made a good breakfast and proceeded to Darlington where I replaced the tyre and then on to Scotland. I was able to get to the Waverley Station before Pat and Katrina arrived and then home to my mothers at Newton Village. Still in January 1969.

New college at Edinburgh University was my choice and while I was in the office I made enquiries about housing for the family. It transpired that there was a plan to assist people attending university to find housing, newly built, at Barnton.

Pat and I went out and met the caretaker at the houses and then went round with him deciding on which type we wanted. Looking back it seems so easy but we actually found what we wanted and set about the paperwork to enable us to move into 101 Craigmount Avenue, North (nr. Barnton). Pat has reminded me that there was a co-ownership arrangement between the university and the builders of the houses. They were modern and central heated from a main source which was oil fired. The heating was conveyed by a pipe system and metered at each house.

Our old friend, Douglas Cochrane of Alston, Nairn & Hogg, Solicitors in Edinburgh attended to the legal formalities and as I remember the situation, there was a deposit and thereafter a monthly payment by standing order.

Meantime I was busy preparing a route map for the carriers to transport our furniture and crated effects from the depository at Redruth in Cornwall to 101 Craigmount Avenue. When we were in Cornwall to attend Andrew's Carol Concert, I had gone to the depository and collected a fleece lined suede coat and other outer winter garments for Pat. While at the depository, I observed that there was a cylindrical power type paraffin heater being used inside the depository. It was also noticeable that the separation between the different stocks of furniture consisted of flimsy sack type curtains, trailing from the roof to the floor.

I believe that I mentioned something about the heater, but I was not too sure when thinking about it at a later date. I posted the route map from Redruth to Edinburgh about the end of January, 1969.

Mail: Because of our movements from Sabah and temporary residence in England we were using the head office of the Bank of Scotland as our c/o address until we were settled. At the beginning of February, '69, Pat and I called at the bank to collect our mail and there was one from Redruth.

As we stood within the entrance to the bank, talking with Mr Gow, manager at the time, I opened the Redruth letter, read it, and stood quite still to allow the contents to settle in my mind.

We were informed that on the 31st of January, 1969, the Depository had been destroyed by fire and was declared a total loss. Explanations and regret. I had cause to immediately remember that paraffin heater but it was strongly denied by the owners. Correspondence between the lawyers followed. The insurance company baulked at paying full settlement, arguing that we were under insured. They had collected the premium from the bank every year for years, and when we left for Sabah in 1966, we commenced paying rent to the depository. Never a word about the need to increase the premium and, I have to confess, it never crossed my mind to increase the annual payment.

Before leaving the bank, I was interviewed by Mr Murray of the Personnel Department and obtained temporary employment while waiting to enter new college which was not until October '69.

The position now was that Andrew would continue at Truro School until it was possible for him to transfer without upsetting his final preparations for the higher levels. Katrina would once more enter a primary school at the age of nine. If change of schooling created a handicap then Katrina was certainly put to the test.

1969 was a very difficult year what with moving Katrina to a new school, forward planning for Andrew to move when we knew where we would be settled, and my own arrangements for entry to New College. The main problem was money and as for preparation to enter New College, my whole time was taken up with work and on occasion, overtime.

Pat was fully occupied with obtaining new furniture and setting up home from scratch. Besides Edinburgh, we were introduced to a firm at Musselburgh and they were most helpful.

My mother was living at Newton Village, about eight miles from our house and of course we visited her from time to time. From February until October 1969 I worked in the Head Office of the Bank of Scotland and assisted Alan Jessiman who was engaged in the introduction of computers to the Accounting Department primarily at the Head Office. The hours were from 8am until 5pm and there was overtime on many occasions. My method of travelling from Barnton to the office was by bus in the first place, but then I became friendly with the manager of the Inland Revenue Branch of the Bank, Jim Lithgow, who lived close by and I travelled with him into George Street and then walked up to the Head Office.

It seems that we had just returned to this country in time to attend to my mother's future because of her health. In addition to all the other matters which seemed to be crowding us in 1969, I received a call from my mother's minister, the Rev. Bob Logan, saying that in his opinion, mother should no longer live by herself. Mother was then 81 years of age and according to Bob she was failing and required care and attention. He went on to add that she was a woman with an excellent and strong spirit and he hoped that it would not be broken.

I went out to see him and discussed the position with mother. It was recommended that she should apply for admission to Wedderburn House at Musselburgh and with her agreement procedure was set in motion. Tommy agreed and mother would be living quite near to him. It was in the latter part of the year that mother moved to Wedderburn.

Before going on to deal with my commencement at New College, I will relate what happened at Wedderburn. Mother had only been there for a matter of weeks when I received a message from a fellow student that there was a telephone call to say that mother had collapsed and was admitted to Bruntsfield Hospital in Edinburgh. She did not recover the ability to be able to speak and died ten days after her collapse.

Chapter 10

Her funeral took place at Seafield Crematorium on the 30th Jan 1970. Tommy was ill and unable to attend the funeral. Helen came up from Cornwall and was able to visit the hospital before mother died. Jim Sharp, our stepbrother, attended the funeral at Seafield Crematorium.

It was some considerable time after the funeral that Tommy and myself took the casket of ashes to Dingwall and, in accordance with our mother's wishes, scattered them on the waters of the Cromarty Firth. Before going down to the Firth I had asked the Minister of Castle Street Church, Rev. Buchannan, if we could hold a brief service in the church and this he had agreed to do. We had taken the road which passes on the left of the railway station and travelled down past the hospital to the edge of the water. We walked forward to a suitable point, opened the casket, said the Lord's Prayer and scattered the ashes on the water. When we looked up there were seven swans formed in a semi-circle in front of us and we had not heard them arriving.

Entry: New College, Edinburgh 7th Oct, 1969
Even now, as I look back, I can remember the awful uncertain feeling that I might not be able to qualify as a minister. There had been many people who said that it was asking too much to allow mature students to return to university in their 50's and meet the demands of the curriculum. (Failure was implied). I have met with failure as I have met with fear. They are both to be defeated.

I parked the car somewhere near Abercromby Place and as I walked along the street I caught up with Douglas Cochrane and his son. The son is an architect and Douglas was not only the solicitor that had proved to be of immense assistance to my family, he was also a friend. It must have been a good omen.

I arrived at New College on the Mound and reported in to the office which used to be just inside the entrance on the right. I was directed to the hall where the new students were assembling and there we listened to a member of staff, Dr Gray. We were given the name of our personal Director of Studies and a great deal of information. The usual "any questions" and then further matriculate procedure which was being carried out for the whole university in Adams Building, Chambers Street. Grant-aid cheques were cashed. I was in.

I had continued to work right up to the time of admission and I was assured that the job would be there between terms and between years. This was to prove to be a big mistake, (addendum explaining initial 'steps' to the call at back of Biography).

The day came when we were to attend lectures and it may have been the same day that we met the various student groups and were encouraged to consider joining one or more of them. We met in the Common Room and it was there that I first met Eddie Simpson. Eddie was the Vice-President of the New College Students Union and Ron Ferguson was the President. I am using the word 'Union' and hope this is correct. During my time in New College we only met the people from 121, on one occasion, a General Assembly Committee, in connection with the Theological Colleges maintaining a contact with 121. Eddie collected the New Students to show us the way around the different lecture rooms and where the facilities were to be found. New College in 1969 was quite different from what it is today. I suppose that it depended on your personal outlook but to me it was a cold and foreboding building of grey stone. On the right hand side of the steps leading up to the assembly rooms there was a turret type of structure with a doorway leading to a winding stairway and this seemed to be the main entry for students proceeding to the Common Room and the cloakrooms.

On the opposite side of the assembly steps, immediately past the John Knox monument, there was an entrance to the library and a corridor leading off to a small chapel where morning prayers were held at 8.30 each morning. In the corridor there were stone busts of one time prominent people scattered around and obviously in the way. This, to me, was evidence of the neglect apparent in the lower parts of the building. Upstairs there was warmth in the Common Room, an open fireplace, and the dining room was approached by a few steps just past the Common Room. There was also lecture rooms and the staff room on this level. But the overall first impression created many questions. Once the term started we were too busy either hurrying from one lecture to another or making our way to the library which was a lovely spaciously laid out part of the building. I have never forgotten my first impression.

There was a paradox. The building and many of its parts were hostile, but this was completely nullified by the staff, professors and lecturers, senior students, lady supervisors in the dining room and rooms of residence, in all these places and from the staff there was kindness. And Eddie was the first of the line. There was something else that we could not have known at the time. The 'year' in front of us had several students who were destined to be 'giants' in the life of the Church of Scotland. There were a number who went on to Phd. and many hold prominent positions in the academic world of the church. Let those who wish criticise our academics, but I for one give thanks for our scholars. It is a great talent.

I also believe that we were able to learn much from association with fellow students, at all levels. During the first year, 1969 - 1970, all students appeared for the lectures at O.T., N.T., doctrine and dogmatics and history. There may have been a few who were not regular, but we soon settled down and I found myself in the company of three other 'mature students'. There was a Senior Inspector of Schools, a man with an awesome appetite for work and an inspiration to many. There was the retired chief engineer from the Ugandan Railways, a son of the manse and one of the most genuine people you could wish to meet. There was the proprietor of a small Road Haulage Transport Company, keen and knowledgeable but who, it transpired, did not enjoy good health. I made the fourth member of what came to be known as "Dad's Army." We enjoyed sitting near the front of the lecture room and, thanks to the wife of one of our group, we also shared each others company from time to time when invited to supper.

There were three children, one at primary school and two not yet at school. Today one is a doctor of medicine, one a civil engineer, and the third approaching his finals in psychiatric medicine. A grand result from the sacrifices their parents made.

Dad used to cycle to New College and parked his bicycle beside the Stone Busts where it was reasonably safe. The Inspector of Schools went on to obtain his PhD., our transport colleague died when his health broke down completely, my railway colleague and self went on to hold two charges each. He is still active in the Church and I have joined the ranks of the retired clergy.

From the moment I entered New College until I was licensed to preach at St. Giles in accordance with the Church of Scotland procedure, it proved to be one of the most demanding periods in my life. The hours were long and in addition to lectures and note preparation and long periods in the library, there was the student attachment to a designated church, which meant that you had duties assigned by the minister of the church. These were mainly pastoral and taking one or two services during the term.

My first sermon was preached in Murrayfield Church and among the congregation, there was Mr and Mrs Scott, my schoolteachers, who had played an important part in my life. As I write I can say that the text had nothing to do with their being present, the passage was about the Good Samaritan and I remember how I thought that it is a parable about how the Church failed and our master came to our rescue. Perhaps this parable should be preached once every year, say at Easter.

At the end of the first year, having struggled with term exams and the demands of the college, I went home on the Friday and reported for duty at the bank on the Monday. The first academic year had ended in April 1970, and as I look back there was two very happy events. Lylie was expecting her first baby and Sheila and Jeremy were to be married at Craigsbank Church on the 18th of July. Keith was born on the 1st of November.

The year had started with the death of my mother, I was trying to cope with New College and there was the schooling of Katrina and Andrew. Andrew did not present a problem as he was in to the final stretch of his formal schooling and being transferred to the Royal Academy at Inverness ,he was able to proceed with his highers and indeed, did very well.

But if ever a child was submitted to a changing primary education, Katrina must have had some bitter experiences. In 1969, Katrina had entered Clermiston Primary School when we resided at Craigsbank Avenue. Approximately eighteen months later she was admitted to Lochardil Primary School where she remained until 1972. Preparations were began for the wedding and Pat was kept very busy, in touch with Sheila and Jeremy, finding a suitable hotel for the reception, attending to invitations and finding accommodation for the friends who were coming up from England. Jeremy's father and mother came up and I remember they were very happy and cheerful. Jeremy also had a minister friend who came up and shared the ceremony with the Parish Minister, Rev. James B. Donald. The venue for the reception was the Barnton Hotel and eventually all the guests arrived. They were a very happy crowd.

It had been decided that there was to be communion immediately after the marriage and this proved to be of interest. Taking communion is not a normal practise at weddings in Scotland. As the ceremony commenced, many of the local population entered the church and took their seats in the back rows. The guests and ourselves were at the front of the church. When the marriage was completed and the ministers prepared the Communion Elements, the family and the invited guests moved forward to take Communion and to our surprise, and delight, many of the people who had come into the church and witnessed the marriage, came forward and joined with us in the Communion. I never saw that happen again.

A very happy time was spent at the hotel and in the normal way of things, the happy couple left on their honeymoon which, we subsequently learned, was spent at Spein Bridge. Perhaps I should add that this is north of Fort William. We decided to take a holiday and exchanged our Rover car with our neighbours who loaned us their VW Caravanette. It was our intention to go to Skye, but bad weather forced us to make a change and we went north, ending up at Rosemarkie, next to Fortrose.

While visiting Inverness, we noticed in the local paper that there was a new bungalow for sale at Lochardil and decided to go and have a look at it. It was ideal and the price was right. We telephoned the solicitor in Edinburgh and agreed to raise the money and purchase No. 5 Garth Road. The month was August and we had to move fast, I was due back at New College in October.

Andrew moved from Truro School to enter The Inverness Royal Academy and to enable him to do this he had to stay with Aunty Ara until we could arrive. We settled up with 101 Craigmount Avenue and Pat and Katrina with 'Tammy' travelled by train to Inverness, I went in the car.

It must have been a hectic move, but we got there and settled in time for me to go back to New College. I had arranged to move in to Salvesan Hall which was a University Residence adjacent to New College. The 1970–71 year began, and this time I was attached to Junction Road Church, (Dr. Rudolph Ehrlich). This proved to be a good attachment and I was given a prepared schedule for visitation and preaching. I was given a great deal of advice which was to come in really useful in view of what lay ahead and best of all, I was given a present of books, Calvins Institutes, Vol. 1 and Vol. 2. It was from these that I learned about the dual nature of our Lord Jesus. For me, this information opened a lot of doors and helped me to understand much that had never previously been explained in such a way.

It was another full year and during the year I was interviewed and the Director of Studies, learning that I was now resident at Inverness, commenced procedure for me to be attached for my Probationary Year to the Ness Bank Church. On the 31st of May, 1971 I reported to the Rev. George Elliot, Ness Bank Church, Inverness. New College had been quite an experience and there were many who had cast doubts that at my age I would be able to stand the pace.

There had been periods of long hours lasting in to the early morning and I had come away with some memories of students, quite young, who had fallen by the wayside. They were from the U.S.A. and from Europe as well as the U.K. The Christian faith is not an easy faith and when the fundamentals are subjected to exegesis, there can be devastating results as we saw during the time at New College.

However, I had passed. I was given my exeat certificate and I departed from the building which I had found cold and depressing. But my memories of the professors and lecturers are pleasant and I learned much from them, although my ability to prove this fact on paper was limited.

There were many individual acts of kindness and on occasion, encouragement when problems arose whether at college or within the family as I discovered at the time of my mother's death.

There was one statement made by Dr. Gibson at the opening of one of his lectures. Dr. Gibson commenced every lecture with prayer and on this particular morning he started by saying, in broad Scots, "You are not entitled to the simplicity of the Old Buddy who sits by her fire reading her bible". I have not forgotten that statement and it may have been at the time, or shortly afterwards, when I came to the conclusion, 'Perhaps, but we are all eligible'. Above I said that the Christian faith is not an easy faith, but from my point of view, approached in simplicity, in the words of Jesus, "Follow Me" is sufficient. The proof is easy to find.

At Christmas, 1970, I received Calvin's Institutes, Vols. 1 & 2 from Dr. Ehrlic and on the 16th of June, 1971 I was presented with a complete large edition of the New English Bible when I was licensed to preach the gospel in St. Giles Cathedral, Edinburgh. Now I could wear the clerical collar.

As an assistant to the Rev. George Elliott, my Ministry began with a shock. I had reported to George on the 31st of May and on the 6th of June George was in the Royal Infirmary, Edinburgh, under intensive care following heart surgery. When I had reported to him he handed to me a prepared schedule of pulpit supply which he had made out before he knew that he was to have a probationer attached to him. It so happened however, that the Sunday in June when I had to step in, was also the Sunday when five infants were to be baptised.

I remember writing their names on a postcard and placing the card on the Communion Table. That was 22 years ago. George made a good recovery and to my knowledge never looked back.

I stayed with him until September 1972 and greatly benefited from the attachment. The probation period had been for one year but the board agreed to pay my probation stipend until I received a call to my first charge. And when that call came the congregation of Ness Bank presented my wife and myself with a most generous cheque. Pastoral care was well organised and during the winter of 1971 there were problems with the coal delivery. George organised how we should visit the members by him taking one side of the river and myself the other. The object was to discover if any member was in difficulty over fuel and if so, we were going to arrange for a delivery of logs to be made. I do not remember having to make one delivery.

Hospital visiting was another well organised activity and each of the three hospitals had different coloured cards which the Hospital Chaplain's Secretary posted to the patient's minister. The benefit of such a system is obvious. Funerals had, on occasion, to be arranged for people living in remote parts of the Highlands and who wished to bring the deceased to Inverness for burial. There was also one occasion when I had to travel to Callander to conduct the funeral of one of the oldest members of the congregation. I had heard of traditional procedure in some parts of the Highlands when carrying the coffin from the house to the cemetery. There would be a number of bearers who would take it in turn to carry the coffin. Each time the bearers changed, it was said, "The whisky bottle" would be produced and the carriers would take a dram. The coffin would be lifted and carried for the next stage and so on until they arrived at the cemetery. I do not know who organised the 'stages'.

On one occasion I was required to conduct a funeral at Tomnahurich Cemetery on behalf of a family who lived north of Helmsdale. The hearse duly arrived followed by private cars and six very tall men carried the coffin from the hearse and laid it beside the open grave. As I walked between them, three on either side, the reek of whisky revealed that they must have had to carry the coffin some way to reach the hearse. They stood steady and straight and with a minimum of conversation.

There are funerals that leave an indelible mark on a minister's memory. A baby accidentally killed by its mother and the little white coffin carried to the grave where the parents and grandparents are standing on either side. The cremation of the husband and only two people at the funeral, the widow and the daughter. Finally, a well-loved member of the town is followed to his grave by the population. The extremes.

Pat and Andrew were involved in the activities of the church, particularly the Sunday School. I had a brief contact with the Boys Brigade when their Captain was taken ill. We enjoyed Inverness. There was one particular event which took place that I wish to recall. While a minister is on his probationary year, he is not available to make nor to accept a call from a church which has a vacancy. In my time the regulations stated that no application could be made before the 1st of January following the probationary period. This of course could lead to long delays and a period of unemployment after the year was completed. An advertisement appeared in the newspaper calling for a secretary for the A.A. Anticipating that I may be some time before I received a call I applied for the post, and got it.

When I told George what I had done he promptly convened a joint meeting of session and managers (UP constitution) and the outcome was that I continued as assistant until I received a call. They also agreed to pay my stipend. No A.A. and I was grateful.

Today is the 20th of January 1993. This date will be remembered for different reasons by many people, but in Kelso it will be specifically remembered as the date on which representatives of the Nations Fire Service gathered in the Old Parish Church to pay tribute to the late Ian Bruce who was killed on the 14th of January when the fire tender crashed over the Kelso Bridge into the River Tweed while proceeding to answer a call for help.

The pews on the ground floor of the Old Parish were fully occupied and the pews upstairs, on both sides, were occupied. It is questionable whether any member of the present congregation has ever seen such a turnout. The community of Kelso had turned out to express their sympathy to the widow and members of the family. To my mind this was a sincere tribute and demonstration of sympathy to be paid in the presence of Almighty God. Kelso had turned to the place of original worship, the Parish Church.

Throughout the world much is said and written about religion, faith, whether there is or is not a God. But when tragedy and disaster strike there is only one word - Prayer.

To Whom - Why?

Clergy, Doctors, Ambulance Services, Police, Fire Services, the young, the old, the halt and the weary, they were all there and paying homage to Almighty God and reverential respect to a brave man. (the young may die and the old must die, the wisest knoweth not how soon). Time giveth way to Eternity. Thanks be to God.

I left off at the point where the combined Board of Managers and Kirk Session of Ness Bank Church had decided on my future pending the Call to a Charge of my own.

I had been apprehensive, possessed with a feeling of insecurity but as it turned out I did receive an invitation to preach for a vacancy from a well-known church and duly attended on the appointed Sunday. It turned out to be an interesting experience.

Pat was with me and after the service we were entertained to lunch and met committees and sub-committees of the various organisations. I remember that 'raffles' and gambling was a burning question. There was doubt about gambling and lottery. It was a very pleasant lunch. We then went to see the manse which was under structural alteration. Pat was asked if she preferred gas to electric cooking? Questions about the kitchen. I was asked if I was happy with the location of the new garage. Pat and I could be forgiven for thinking that they had made up their mind about the new minister. I was told that the vacancy committee were meeting on the Monday and they would be in touch. I learned later that "Edinburgh had appointed a minister". I was to learn that this was not an unusual practise. A few weeks later while out on pastoral visiting, I was asked to visit a patient who was in Raigmore Hospital. This was to prove to be an incredible coincidence. The patient was the brother of the man who had introduced me to polo in 1948. David was making a steady recovery from his operation and while I was with him, the ward sister approached me and said that there was a patient due for an operation on the following day and would like to speak to me. I went over to him and we had a conversation. I explained that I was the assistant minister at Ness Bank Church and in the course of time I hoped to have my own church.

It transpired that as a result of that conversation I received an invitation to preach for the church at Ballantrae in Ayrshire. I accepted the invitation and Pat and I went to 'Maidens' for B. & B. on the Saturday and then on to St. Andrew's Church in Girvan to conduct the service on the Sunday. After the service ,Pat and I met the vacancy committee, answered their questions, (the main one being, "If you called at a house and were offered a drink would you take it?". Answer: "If I was on pastoral duty, no. But if you had invited me to dinner and I was your guest, I would behave as a guest".) Pat and I had lunch in The King's Hotel, Girvan and returned to Inverness on the Monday.

A period of time passed and then I received a letter from the Session Clerk saying that I had been accepted as the sole nominee. I confirmed my acceptance and in due course proceeded to Ballantrae, where I went through the procedure of preaching as sole nominee and then being 'removed' from the church while the congregation voted. I was waiting in the Royal Bank House opposite the church, the home of the Treasurer of the Church when I was then 'recalled' to the church to be told that the result was 'unanimous' yes. The procedure leading up to receiving a call is quite lengthy and when the appointment of being sole nominee is communicated, the period can be tense. For me the result was a tremendous relief, I know that I had confused thoughts and a realisation of the responsibility which now lay ahead of me. Lunch had been arranged at Corseclays, the home of Mr and Mrs Robbie Stevenson, Robbie being the Session Clerk and, as a farmer colleague of his described him, "One of the most embarrassing, generous men you could ever meet". It was a very happy luncheon party. From Corseclays we were taken to Auchairne, the home of Lord and Lady Ballantrae where we had tea and reminiscences of the war and the Black Watch. Once more we returned to Inverness.

The date for my Ordination and Induction was the 21st. of September 1972. Pat and I sat down to work out the move from Inverness to Ballantrae and there was need for precision in choosing certain dates, once again there was the transfer of Katrina from Lochardil Primary School to Girvan. But this time Katrina and ourselves were very pleased with this proposed move. The school at Girvan was to be Katrina's first and only secondary school and she would be starting on level terms with the other children, no more changing systems and having to catch up! The opening date for the school was earlier than our due date of arrival at Ballantrae, but that was easily dealt with. We had been introduced to Mr and Mrs Billy Britain who kept a Bed and Breakfast home at 'Davaar'. They also had two daughters, Jean and Katrina Britain, who were attending Girvan School. Our first priority was to arrange for Katrina to be in Ballantrae in time to start school and she went to 'Davaar' as a guest to await our arrival. I took her down and returned to Inverness to assist Pat with the further details of our move.

We had to say farewell to the Ness Bank Church congregation and they were most generous, presenting us with a cheque and wishing us well at a farewell social.

We had an Alsatian at the time and she presented a problem, she loathed travelling in the car. The vet however came to our rescue and 'Tammy' made the journey under a general anaesthetic given to her just as we were leaving Inverness.

I have to add here that she had company in the form of a West Highland Terrier which I had rescued on the day before our departure. The owner's of 'Glen' were emigrating to South Africa and rather than risk Glen going to a bad home they had decided to 'put him down'.

I had gone to collect a small chest of drawers which they had advertised for sale and as I was about to come down stairs, this little white head appeared at the foot of the stairs. A conversation followed from which I learned what was to be his fate. I succeeded in assuring the lady that I could give Glen a good home and he came home with me. I wish I could remember what Pat said when I arrived home with a new dog and us on the point of moving. Today Glen and his son are both at rest after long and happy lives and West Highland Terriers are Pat's favourite dogs.

Transport for the removal had been agreed with a firm in Inverness and proved to be more economical than anything from the South.

What with loading and then the journey it meant that the men would be away from home overnight. On arrival at Ballantrae they were given dinner at 'Davaar'.

After breakfast on the following day, Pat and I walked round to the manse and witnessed a grand form of welcome. Mrs Peggy Kirk and Mrs Margaret Neil had just placed a box of groceries on the front doorstep. Meanwhile there was Andrew and in his case events had turned out well. Andrew had applied to enter the Customs Department and was called to Edinburgh to sit the Civil Service Entrance Examination.

The place of examination was somewhere in the vicinity of the Haymarket Edinburgh and I had taken him there by car. I remember that when he rejoined me he said that they had given him 50 questions and a time limit. He had completed the paper in record time and we left for home. A letter arrived to inform Andrew that he had passed the entrance and that he was to report to an address in London. He was now a Cadet Executive Officer in H.M. Customs.

We settled in as quickly as possible and let our close friends know the date of Ordination. I heard from the Presbytery of Wigtown and Stranraer and received instructions in connection with the Ceremony of Ordination and Induction.

It will be remembered that my first contact with anyone about becoming a minister was with Canon Rusted in Jesselton (K.K.) Sabah. He had said that no matter where he was at the time of my Ordination he would make every effort to be present. 'Rusty' had returned to the U.K. and in 1972 he was Canon Emritus in Croydon. He had to apply to his Bishop for permission to come to the Ceremony the Bishop, being no less a person than the Archbishop of Canterbury, Ramsay. When he learned from Rusty about our long standing arrangement he replied; 'Go and take my Blessing to the Young man'. I suppose that this makes me one of the few men who were Ordained and Blessed by both denominations? Pat who had and has always supported me in my career efforts since the war, accompanied by Andrew and Katrina were present and representing the rest of the family.

The important guests at my Ordination were my schoolmaster, Mr William Scott and Mrs Scott. They had both known and tried to educate me as a schoolboy just out of primary school at Newbattle. There was also Dudley Smith, one time controller of Inland Revenue, Sabah. On the 21st of September, in the evening, I became the Rev. G. D. A . Fox, Minister with charge of Ballantrae Parish Church. The last five years had been long and difficult.

Six days later Anne was born, 27.9.72, and Pat went down to look after Keith until Lylie and the baby came home. Anne was the second grandchild and in November Jeremy and Sheila were blessed with their first child and our third grandchild, Philippa, born on the 27th November 1972.

The final quarter of 1972 was a busy period getting to know the parish and attending to the paperwork making necessary returns for 121 George Street. The parish of Ballantrae was an ideal parish for pastoral visiting and in so far as the village was concerned members were able to reach the manse easily when they required to contact the Minister. However, there were a few out-lying parts of the parish and to reach them you had to travel a long way round to reach the people. On one hand it was necessary to go via Colmonell and Barrhill, past the Barrhill Railway Station and out across the moors to reach an isolated holding. In the other direction, it was necessary to go south of Cairnryan towards Stranraer and turn of left and again, cross the moors until reaching a small grouping of cottages. I kept in touch with the people but the only time any of them were seen at church was on the main seasons such as Christmas or Easter or if they had a special need. It was easy to understand their position and while it was necessary for me to pass through two neighbouring parishes to reach them, geographically they were in Ballantrae Parish.

During 1973 I completed visiting every district accompanied by the Elder for the district and this was a rewarding duty. To meet people in their own homes and hold an ordinary conversation with them helped to bring us together and to obtain their confidence and remove any 'stiffness' when dealing with personal difficulties. There were occasions when prayer would be asked for, when parts of the Bible would raise questions, when sometimes I would be asked about some part of the sermon. If I reached the end of a visit I would suggest that we part in prayer, and there would be times when it was obvious that prayer would not be appropriate. I made it a rule that prayer was never forced on people.

Each Minister will have his own way but for me I felt that the christian faith should be part and parcel of the ordinary way of life, that there should be no embarrassment when the Minister arrived, and I am glad to remember that there were very few occasions when prayer was absent from a visit.

There were two major happenings in 1973. We were called upon to register for petrol coupons and complete forms indicating our needs. The coupons were issued but never used. Today, in 1993, I still have my issue of coupons.

The second major happening was the appointment of the Senior Elder of Ballantrae Kirk Session as High Commissioner to the General Assembly of the Church of Scotland.

Lord Ballantrae was the Senior Elder and I remember that on the night when it was made known to the kirk session, Lord Ballantrae walked the short distance to the manse gate with me and asked if I would mind if he invited his brother to be his Chaplain during the General Assembly.

His Lordship's brother was the parish Minister at Barr Parish, the Reverend Simon Fergusson. It is the High Commissioner's privilege to appoint his Chaplain and it was kind of the Brigadier to ask for my agreement. It will not happen very often for a High Commissioner to the Church of Scotland General Assembly to have his brother in a position to be his Chaplain. I was happy to agree. It was also a great honour for Pat and myself to be invited to Lunch at Holyrood Palace on the day of the Garden Party and for Pat to be seated to the right of his Lordship, myself to the right of Lady Ballantrae. Lord Ballantrae was constantly referred to as 'The Brigadier' even when his former title had been Sir Bernard Fergusson, the Ballantrae folk referred to him as the Bigadier. He was a war time hero and Colonel of the Regiment. The Royal Highlanders (Black Watch). He was also the War Time Commander of 'B' Column of the Chindits who had operated behind the Japanese lines in Burma.

From the moment it became known that Lord Ballantrae was to be the High Commissioner to the General Assembly, arrangements were made, in accordance with His Lordship's wishes, to invite the whole of the village to the General Assembly Garden Party at Holyrood Palace. Pat and myself were invited to lunch with Lord and Lady Ballantrae on the Saturday of the Garden Party in Holyrood Palace. To be part of this historic occasion in this beautiful historical palace is a memory treasured by both of us.

After lunch the High Commissioner and his guests proceeded from the palace and joined with the Garden Party waiting in the grounds of the Palace. It was a beautiful sunny day and our own folk from Ballantrae were thoroughly enjoying themselves. The journey from Ballantrae had been in a luxury coach and every thing was going to plan. I am sure that no one who was there that day will ever forget the experience. The General Assembly closed on the following Friday and we all returned to duty in our respective Parishes.

My diary informs me that there was quite a lot happening in all walks of life. The every day requirements of the Church, the night I had to interrupt a Session Meeting to detail Elders to attend to a domestic disturbance caused by 'Scottish Wine', the need to increase the size of the session by Ordaining new Elders. It is a matter of fact that when I look back much was brought or referred to the Minister, which should rightly have been dealt with by the police. I was very much involved with family disputes, and with vandalism, with much that was not really within my remit, but Ballantrae was/is a close nit community of fishermen and farmers and looking back, I am glad they came to the church when they needed help. At the foot of Bennane as you begin the approach to Ballantrae on the level road there is a cave which may still be there and on the opposite side of the road there is a 'cairn' with an inscription on a metal plate inserted in to the cairn. The cave was the home of 'snib Scott' known as the local tramp. His real name was Henry Torbet (may have been Tarbert) and he was popular with the people in Ballantrae. He was quiet and known to be scrupulously honest.

One outstanding occasion was when a tourist had stopped off to look at the cave and the surrounding area. When she went away she left her handbag on top of the dyke. Snib found it and took it in to the Post Office at Ballantrae. There was discovered to be £40 in the handbag.

I went to visit Snib and as I reached the entrance to his cave, I called and asked if there was any one at home. There was a shout and I replied, "It's the Minister".

"Oh, it's you, come in". I made my way round a pool of rainwater at the entrance and walked up a slight incline towards a fire which was a large piece of driftwood which he would have found on the shore. His worldly possessions were piled in a heap on the left side as you approached the fire and there was a mattress, folded on top of the pile. We did not hold a conversation about anything in particular but I was satisfied that contact had taken place.

I called again on a few occasions and saw some of the things he was doing, but the purpose was beyond me. I also knew from information given to me by the village folk that he had been friendly with a man who was now in hospital as the result of an operation that had proved to be unsuccessful. It may have been a coincidence but Snib was said to have been employed in a bank in his earlier days and the man, who was a permanent patient in hospital, had also been employed in a bank prior to the unfortunate operation. It was decided on the 70th birthday of the patient to take a special birthday cake and a card to the hospital. A few close friends set off from Ballantrae and we stopped at the cave while I went in and asked Snib if he would sign his name on the card.

He did and I have to report, it was a firm and legible signature. On the way back I called in again and handed Snib a huge piece of the cake and greetings from his friend.

Prior to my arrival at Ballantrae, Snib had been involved in an accident and broke his leg. I understand that there were problems at the hospital concerning clothing and bathing and these were duly settled. I was asked what would happen to Snib if he had an accident that could prove fatal or, what was to be done when he died. I let it be known that he would have a christian funeral and I was to be informed when he died.

Snib died in his cave and was found by the policeman. Snib had been missed from his usual walk in to the village. I was notified and informed that the Ballantrae folk had decided to open a fund to meet necessary expenses.

Snib was given a christian funeral and the cairn was erected to his memory by the people of Ballantrae. My family contributed to the fund for the cairn.

Snib never begged. He was quietly cared for and looked after by the community and especially at Christmas and the New Year by the manse and the nearby farmers.

I was taken to hospital in 1980 with a suspected heart attack. When I came back to the manse, Snib used to walk up and down passing the manse. I was standing at the window one day, he walked past, looked over the wall and I waved to him. He was satisfied, he did not come again.

Ballantrae School. Mr Martin was the Headteacher when I arrived in 1972 and he made me welcome. It was not generally known at the time but if the headteacher of the school did not want the Minister to enter for the purpose of religious instruction, the Minister was not allowed entry.

I arranged to be available every Tuesday during term time and Mr Martin decided that I should take Form 6 and 7 together at 9.a.m. Not only was the Minister made welcome, but I discovered that at the end of each academic year it was the custom to hold a Bible reading competition which was judged by two Elders and the Minister. The winners of P6 and P7 would then read the lesson on the following Sunday in church at the Morning Service. The custom had not lapsed during the vacancy and I hope that it is continuing. I remember being told that when the Gaelic speaking Highlanders were being taught to speak English, the first book used was the Bible. I enjoyed the morning session every Tuesday and there were interesting occasions, too numerous to relate here, but one I will mention.

A boy appeared one day and was placed in P7. He had just come to this country having previously resided in a Kibbutz in Israel. He promptly distinguished himself by standing up and stating that he would not say The Lord's Prayer.

What might have happened with any of my colleagues I do not know, but I remember being quiet for a short spell and then agreeing that he did not have to say the Prayer if he did not want to. (his father was a Jew and his mother was a Scot). The headteacher thought that perhaps it would be better to give the boy other work during the R.I. period, but in the end the boy was allowed to stay. About two weeks later another boy, the son of a policeman, spoke up and said that the new boy should say the Prayer with the class. What might have become a devisive subject was settled when the new boy came in one Tuesday morning and joined in with the class in Prayer.

At the end of the year our new boy took part in the Bible reading competition, P7, and came top. Now I was faced with a problem, how was he going to read the lesson, in a Christian church? I visited his parents and explained the position. They were a charming couple and saw no objection to their son reading the lesson. He did and did it very well.

I wonder what became of him, he will be in his twenties now. And the question remains, what if force had been used? We should all remember that reconciliation is offered free by God. There is one other necessity about R.I. Co-operation. Football. To speak to anyone about Religion particularly a captive audience aged from 10 to 12 years of age can prove to be a boring and absolute waste of time. The subject that can generate a heated discussion is football. If you really wish to employ football as a 'starter' for a religious lesson, get the score between Rangers and Celtic the wrong way round and then sit back for a few minutes.

I used this method over and over again, acted and deliberately appeared foolish. I would remark about the game played on the previous Saturday and what a splendid game Celtic had played and deservedly won the match. The class, comprising boys and girls and all of whom had listlessly trudged in to the classroom at 9 a.m., suddenly came alive. I was promptly, and scathingly, corrected. The merits of their heroes were pointed out and the correction came from the girls as well as the boys.

I made my apologies and asked them to open their Bibles at the chosen part and then proceeded to get them to deal with the lesson in the same way as for the football match. There was an easy approach in discussion, not a stilted or mumbling answer to suit the Minister. And they were learning all about the love of God for them through Jesus Christ. I know that I made many friends at Ballantrae School.

Life in Ballantrae was very full and busy and on occasion there would be unusual incidents where the Minister would be involved whether he wished it so or not. I had become used to a pattern of living in Ballantrae and when there was any real difficulty, the Minister was consulted. As my time during the 70's was drawing to a close and my mind was becoming engaged with the question of retirement, there happened three events which I will recall, each having left an indelible mark in the history of my Ministry at Ballantrae.

VANDALISM: One evening at dusk, a woman came to the Manse and asked to speak to me. She came in and soon I was listening to a report that three boys had set fire to a wooden building on the outskirts of the village. I stopped her and explained that it was not me but the police to whom she must report. Her reply was one that I had heard all too often; "I will only speak to the Minister". She went on to say that there had been a witness and she thought it was a man who I happened to know very well.

When she had gone I called on the witness and he confirmed what the woman had told me and identified the three boys by name. They were in fact teenaged youths and well known to both of us. When I asked the witness why he had not tried to stop them I received the reply that was to become all too common through the 80's and continuing. "I did not want to become involved and besides there were three of them and we know what they are capable of". I contacted the parents of the three and invited them to call at the Manse on the following evening. They came.

The meeting with the parents had its amusing side as well as the seriousness of why I had to call them.

The owner of the wooden building that had been destroyed had contacted me earlier in the day by telephone and must have guessed what I had in mind. He stressed that he did not want the building to be replaced.

When I had explained to the parents what had happened, I was met with the usual denials that it could not have been their sons. In one case, the parents were adamant that their sons had been in the house all evening. The other denial was based on the statement; "It's aye my son when anything goes wrong". The third parent, the mother spoke up quietly. "What the Minister has told us is correct. Both my sons were there, but the oldest one came home and refused to take part in burning the hut. He told me that his brother was one of the group responsible," and turning to the parents who were certain that their sons had been in all evening she said, "and your boys were there with my son". There was silence and then the reaction; the father of one said " It's aye my son", and was going to go home and he would, " B . .. well kill him".

The adamant parents were stunned and had honestly believed that their sons were at home. They did live in a large house with more than one entry. The mother was not one of my congregation. I told the father that he would not "kill his erring son" but I hoped that he would treat the matter seriously.

There was not much that I could do in view of the owner's request and so I instructed the parents that their sons were to appear in church for a number of Sundays, sit in the front pew and think on what they had done. I do not remember how often they appeared, they did come, but it was in the gallery front pew, where they sat and placed a copper penny on the plate as their offering.

It is with deep regret that I remember two of these youths ended up in prison for serious offences. One of them had the makings of a good man and when I visited him in prison he told me, speaking quietly, "You know, Mr. Fox, it's my own fault that I am in here".

Coal Strike: The main factors of that particular period were three in number. The miners were in dispute and Mick Mcgahey was negotiating on their behalf. The coal yard at Girvan was empty. There was a very bad storm and on the morning following the storm thirteen houses were damaged, all by rain water, the roofs had been opened by the force of the gales.

The houses were the homes of elderly widows and all depended on coal fires. Accompanied by Brian McIlwraith, I went in to Girvan and discovered that the coal yard was empty. On further enquiry I learned that there were three waggons of coal lying in a railway siding between Girvan and Ayr. Of the thirteen houses damaged, one person had the presence of mind to use a screwdriver and punch a series of holes in the ceiling thus releasing the water and saving the ceiling from collapsing.

The immediate problem was to get the three waggons from the siding down to the Girvan coal yard. I made contact with Jim Sillars, MP (at that time he was a member of the Labour Party) and an approach was made to Mick McGahey re the moving of the coal waggons. There was also contact with an official of the Coal Merchants Association and it all proved to be agreeable and the waggons were moved.

While the man in charge of the coal yard was not exactly hostile, neither was he helpful and I remember being sceptical when he asked me to leave the delivery from the waggon for the people at Ballantrae, to him. I did not agree. We, Brian and I, were only concerned with one waggon and when, to add to our difficulties, the unloading 'grab' machinery broke down, (I suppose that it did breakdown?) it meant that the waggon had to be unloaded by shovel.

Brian and I managed to get a shovel and with the Yard Foreman looking on, we unloaded the coal into coal sacks. The coalman who did the normal delivery in Ballantrae assisted and supplied the transport. We then made the delivery to the anxious widows and set in motion the need for emergency repairs.

There was a follow up to this shortage of coal at the Girvan Coal Yard and the strike still to be settled. I telephoned to a friend of mine, a solicitor in Edinburgh whom I had known since the war, and explained to him that the village was in need of coal. Was there any source that I could approach to collect a load? Just one telephone call and the next thing I knew there was a vehicle coming to Ballantrae with 45 tons of open-cast coal.

Arrangements were communicated to the open-cast office re route to follow and a meeting place with a request for approximately time of arrival.

There was a large shed at the end of the foreland which had been in use by the local fishermen and Brian was able to obtain permission for us to store the coal inside the shed. The vehicle duly arrived and the driver was most co-operative. He manoeuvred into the shed and tipped the whole load with difficulty but progressively until it was all on the floor of the shed. Brian locked the shed. My diary shows that there were two men in Glasgow who had co-operated with my solicitor friend in arranging this immediate delivery. There was not one penny charged by them. I wish to record our thanks and pay tribute to them by name.

Solicitor: Mr Douglas Cochrane
Associates: Mr Bill Dodds and Mr Jim Deakin

Today, 20th February 1993, I found the telephone number recorded in my diary and telephoned to Glasgow to enquire if the man who had helped us out was still in business. It turned out that the name I had recorded was the name of the Company . The individual names are now recorded above and we, Bill Dodds and myself, had a very pleasant conversation. I was unable to contact Jim Deakin.

I now draw near to the close of my ministry at Ballantrae and there is so much more that could be written about the daily life of the village and the people in it but it is suffice to say that my wife, family and myself were very happy during our time from September 1972 until we left. However, before I leave off writing about Ballantrae, I must mention how we left the church building and the Manse.

Before I arrived at Ballantrae, the office bearers and the congregation had re-decorated the inside of the church and attended to the pews by removing the dark brown varnish, so common in all churches throughout Scotland, and re-varnishing the woodwork in clear varnish. Carpeting had been renewed, red making the inside attractive and comfortable.

During my time the session decided to recover all pew cushions and suitable cloth was purchased from a firm in Girvan. There was a lady who worked at the firm and was also an office bearer of the North Parish Church in Girvan, who attended to the negotiations for the cloth. We were next assisted by a team of members, lead by the Session Clerk of the North Parish, in making the new cushion covers and fitting them on to the cushions. John McIlwraith, Session Clerk, Robby McNally, Elder and myself were instructed in the task of covering the Cushion Buttons and then threading them in to position with a special type of tool for the job. The Lady who had negotiated the cloth also measured the Pews and made the covers. The Minister of the North Parish Church at Girvan was my old friend Eddy Simpson of New College days.

The work was carried out during the Winter months and the Girvan people had to journey 13 miles to reach Ballantrae. This was truly a magnificent example of co-operation between the two Communities and perhaps happens elsewhere. I like to think it does.

The external walls were usually Snow Cemmed by way of decoration. When the walls were examined it was noticed that at various parts there was a hollow sound similar to what was referred to as being 'Boss' in mining language. It was decided that Snow Cemming was uneconomical and of a limited period before it had to be done again. Meetings were held and advice sought from different Builders. It was decided to strip the walls and replaster with cement coating. Tenders were called for and a Firm in the Stranraer area was given the contract.

When the original wall was revealed it was found that the wall was built of stones not unlike the stones found on the beach at the foreland. This also accounted for the 'Hollow' sound because of the rounded surface of the stone and the uneven size of the different stones.

The whole of the Building was stripped to the original stone and then three coats of cement facing, coat after coat and a drying out period between each coat, was applied until there was a flat even finish. The final coat was of a special mixture requiring a Pinkish Colour sand to mix with the cement. The end result was referred to as 'Canterbury Pink'.

The Manse eventually received the same attention and in the finished stage was completed in 'Esna ? White Chip'. The Manse had also been rewired and when I think how the cost of such work has increased over the years, we were fortunate to have embarked on the work at that time. The whole venture from renewal of Pew Covers, refacing the external walls of Church and Manse, is a memorial to the members, ladies and gentlemen and Manse family, of their pride and care for their place of worship, and greatly appreciated the ready help and assistance given by the friends from Girvan North.

The 17th of December 1979 will be remembered as a Black Day in the lives of the People of Ballantrae.

Gales are not unknown to Ballantrae. The Wind howled and tore at the buildings, the Waves were towering in height, Shipping had come in close for shelter, trees were being uprooted and snapped off close to the Main Road or along the country lanes leading to the farms and private properties, the elements that day were fierce. And about one hour after 12 Noon, Lady Laura Ballantrae was killed by a fallen tree. The silence which greeted the news of this tragic accident was louder than the Gales.

The lane leading to the house was blocked but I knew of a seldom used farm track and hoping that it might be open set off to see Lord Ballantrae. He was by himself, sitting at a desk and when I went in there was only a few words, the best I could offer was company and silent prayer.

The Ballantraes were held in the very highest regard by Ballantrae and Lady Ballantrae was loved by all. One of her last acts of Charity was to sit all night by the bedside of an old lady who was dying in a cottage in the village.

Chapter 11

The tragedy and the effect upon the Ballantrae community caused by the accident which removed Lady Ballantrae from their midst, was shared worldwide and spread as the ripples on a large pond when a small stone has been dropped at its centre. At this time of writing I am in possession of the facts relating to the Auchairne Branch of the Fergusson Family, (Lord Ballantrae of Auchairne and the Bay of Islands, Lady Laura Ballantrae and the Honorable George Fergusson), I refer to the untimely death of Lady Ballantrae and what was to happen before another year had passed.

The funeral of Lady Ballantrae took place at the Ballantrae Parish Church and the service was conducted by the Moderator of the General Assembly, the Right Reverend Robin Barbour. The Interment was conducted by the Rev. Simon Fergusson at the Kilkerran family burial ground and this was private.

The Church was at 'overflow' and people from all over had travelled to Ballantrae to attend the funeral. The Duke of Buccleuch was brought to the front of the Church in his invalid push chair.

Arrangements were then put in hand for a Memorial Service to be held at London. This Memorial Service took place on the 10th of January 1980 in the Royal Hospital Chapel of Chelsea Barracks and was conducted by the Rt. Rev. Bishop Victor Pike, former Chaplain General to the Forces and Bishop of Cherbourne, assisted by the Rev. Walter Evans.

There were representatives of many nations and the Royal Family, Queen Elizabeth the Queen Mother was represented by Lieutenant Colonel Sir Martin Gilliat and Princess Alexandra the Hon. Mrs Angus Ogilvy by Miss Mona Mitchell. The New Zealand High Commissioner and the Colonel of the Regiment, (The Black Watch) Brigadier Monteith, also Sir Michael Herries representing the Scottish Trust for the Physically Disabled of which Lady Ballantrae was a Founder Member. "Representing the Community of Ballantrae which Lord and Lady Ballantrae made their own was the Minister, the Rev. G.D.A. Fox" (extract from the Carrick Gazette and Girvan News). The Hon. George Fergusson read the Lesson, Romans 8 v.31 to the end, and Miss Kiri te Kanawa sang; " I know that my Redeemer Liveth " from Handel's Messiah. In New Zealand there was an Ecumenical Service in memory of Laura Fergusson, Lady Ballantrae, held in

Wellington Cathedral on Friday, 21st December 1979 at 12.30 p.m. Lady Ballantrae was a member of the Episcopalian church in Scotland and attended the periodic services which were held in the Ballantrae Parish Church as well as regular Sunday worship with the community.

The Ecumenical Service in New Zealand closed with the singing of the following hymn;

> I vow to Thee, my country, all earthly things above
> Entire and Whole and perfect, the service of my love:
> The Love that asks no question, The Love that stands the test
> That lays upon the Altar the dearest and the best;
> The Love that never falters, The Love that pays the price,
> The Love that makes undaunted the final sacrifice,
>
> And there's another country, I've heard of long ago,
> Most dear to them that love her, most great to them that know;
> We may not count her armies, we may not see her King;
> Her fortress is a faithful heart, her pride is suffering;
> And Soul by Soul and silently her shining bounds increase,
> And her ways are ways of gentleness and all her paths are Peace.

The family connections with the Royal Hospital is strong. Lady Ballantrae's grandfather, General Sir Neville Lyttleton, was for 20 years Governor of the Hospital and Lady Ballantrae herself was baptised in the Chapel in 1920 in the presence of her grandparents. Laura Margaret, Lady Ballantrae, was the youngest daughter of Lt. Col. Arthur Grenfell of Deale Kent. During the Second World War she was secretary to Lady Reading, co-ordinator of the Women's Vouluntary Service.

After the war she edited The New Elizabethans, a publication for young people. She and the then Brigadier Bernard Fergusson were married in 1950 and moved to Auchairne. As well as her work for the disabled, Lady Ballantrae was well known in Scotland for her activities in the guiding movement and also as President of the Girl Guide association of New Zealand. (Tribute from N.Z. - " The fire that warmed us has gone out. Our Guiding Lights will glow bright with her memory. May we warm others as she warmed us.") I returned from London on the 11th of January and having just completed the form for the 'adoption' by the Ballantrae Sunday School of a girl in the Middle East, I collapsed and was taken by ambulance to Heathfield Hospital. It was thought at the time that I had suffered a heart attack.

I was out of the pulpit for months and several people rallied round to attend to the business of the Church. I was encouraged by the M of

M at 121 to take a holiday at Crieff Hydro and this we did. The remainder of 1980 progressed in the normal way until about the last quarter. We were negotiating for a building to house the Youth Group when we received news that Lord Ballantrae was ill. The people of Ballantrae had observed and commented upon the appearance of Lord Ballantrae since the loss of his partner, for that is exactly what Lady Ballantrae had been, his partner as well as wife. He had lost weight and his jovial nature had changed. Word had reached the village that Geordie had become engaged and it was hoped that this would give his father a 'lift'. It may have done, we shall never know.

Lord Ballantrae of Auchairne and the Bay of Islands died on the 28th of November, 1980. At the time of his death, Lord Ballantrae was recovering from the effects of a stroke at his flat in Chelsea. In July, he had written to me explaining that he was going to visit Jerusalem to take part in the 50th anniversary celebrations of St. Andrew's Memorial Church. He was expecting to depart from London on the 28th of November. This was normal procedure for Lord Ballantrae to inform me when he was not going to be present in Church at Ballantrae.

Geordie came home to Auchairne and brought his father's ashes for interment in the family burial ground at Kilkerran after the service which was held in Ballantrae Parish Church.

Once more, in less than one year, the community of Ballantrae were shocked, to have lost Lady Ballantrae under such horrendous circumstances had caused great grief, and now The Brigadier had passed from time to eternity. His mourning had been deep and the cruel twist of fate that had taken his Laura from him had persisted and crushed the will to live without his partner. That first verse of Ecclesiastes Chap. 12 comes to mind; "Remember now thy creator in the days of thy youth, while the evil days come not, nor the years draw nigh, when thou shalt say, I have no pleasure in them".

The Church was filled to capacity for the service and I conducted the service. Later the private family interment was conducted by the Rev. Simon Fergusson of Alton Albany, Barr.

Simon was not well at this time but insisted on conducting the interment of his favourite brother's ashes in the top right hand corner of the grave of Lady Ballantrae. It was right that he should and I stood just behind Simon during the ceremony which was performed with quiet dignity. A sudden ending to the lives of a splendid couple who had meant so much to so many people right across the world. As Brigadier Sir Bernard Fergusson, Lord Ballantrae maintained a family link with New Zealand by serving as Governor General there from 1962–67. He was the fourth member of his family to become the

Governor General. His grandfather Sir James Fergusson, the sixth Baronet of Kilkerran, held the post from 1873–75.

Lord Ballantrae's maternal grandfather, the seventh Earl of Glasgow, was Governor General from 1892–97. And Lord Ballantrae's father, the late General Sir Charles Fergusson, was Governor General for six years until 1930. Lord Ballantrae has served as Lord High Commissioner to the General Assembly of the Church of Scotland. He served in the Middle East and India during the second World War and then joined the Wingate expeditions in to Burma with the Chindits. He retired from the army in 1958. Lord Ballantrae was known for his keen sense of fun and I have one example sent to me when he was Lord High Commissioner and in residence at Holyrood Palace. He had left his dress shoes at Auchairne.

MA SHOON

"O what can ail thee, Knight at Arms,
Alone and palely loitering?
Art thou perturbed at dread alarms,
Or some sic thing?

Doth some sepulchral ghaist pursue
Thee through some weird ancestral hall?
Perchance the Inland Revenue
Hath thee in thrall?

Then up and spake that hapless Knight,
Sat at the Queen's right knee:
– A really bloody awful plight
Perplexes me."

With drear, doom laden voice he speaks,
"I hae my hat aboon;
I hae my jaicket, sark and breeks,
But whaur's ma shoon?

It's no a beldam sans merci
Has me in thrall, or on me sits.
It's waur nor that, for- mercy me! -
I hae nae buits

A gallant Knight I may hae been;
A gallant Knight 'maist a'thing tholes;
But O! I dannae face my Queen
In stocking soles."

The word gaed forth across the land
(For this auld Knight was no that blate);
There's a close link, ye'll unnerstan,
Twixt Kirk and State

Word sped across the barren rocks
Twixt Enbro toun and Ballantrae.
Gleg to respond were Dudley Fox
and Hamilton (Hay).

So thanks to Dudley's wark, and Hay's,
The Monarch didnae have to gaze
Forfochit and in dire amaze
Like Cortez in those earlier days
Upon those un-clad hammer-taes
(Prehensile) which are Ballantrae's.
Shoon move in mysterious ways.

.... THE ANSWER

Just a word of thanks to you,
Brigadier, for your poem which we received today,
and though some words were mighty queer,
I think we know what you meant to say.

You seem to have been in quite a state
with no shoes or boots or slippers,
but when you tend to stay up late,
What better for a K night than slippers?

And when a Queen would ask you out
to lunch or even suppies,
with all the corgies there, there is no doubt
she'd not look twice at Hush Puppies.

I hope you don't mind receiving this verse.
And if you do I beg your pardon,
but my afternoon could be a lot worse
being stuck in the Manse back garden.
Hay-Hamilton.

Perhaps the last thing Lord Ballantrae ever wrote appeared in the November issue of the Church's Life and Work Magazine.

I referred to it in my eulogy at the Ballantrae Funeral Service.

"I hold in deep strength the belief that the Scots Kirk and presence in Jerusalem may have more to contribute in the future than it has in the past. It stands between the past and the future. It bears the scars of past fighting it takes no sides in disputes. It enshrines the memories and recalls the presence within its walls of devoted men and women. It radiates sanity as well as sanctity". There is one last tribute to pay to Lord and Lady Ballantrae and this took place on Remembrance Sunday in 1983. My health had been erratic throughout 1980 and 1981 and I was thinking about retirement at age 65. But it was not to be. There was still work that had to be done. I am recording the final tribute here for the sake of sequence.

MEMORIAL ADDRESS
DEDICATION OF MEMORIAL PLAQUE
TO
LORD AND LADY BALLANTRAE
13/11/1983

On the 2nd of December 1980 in this Church I said, "It is impossible on this occasion to pay tribute to the memory of Brigadier Lord Ballantrae in the full sense of recognising his services to God, to Queen and Country. In the fulness of time this will be done and services of thanksgiving for the life of Lord Ballantrae will be held in the near future."

Today, Remembrance Sunday 1983, we are taking part in the 3rd of important services which have been held at home and abroad. Just about a year ago a plaque was placed in the Church of the 1st Battalion The Black Watch, at Werl, West Germany. That plaque was commissioned by the Regimental Kirk Session, recording Lord Ballantrae's service as Lord High Commissioner to the General Assembly, Colonel of the Regiment and Elder in its Kirk Session. In St. Andrew's Church in Jerusalem, the framed portrait of Lord Ballantrae has been hung on the wall beside that of Lord Allenby.

And now, we are gathered to dedicate a Memorial Plaque, in the Church of Lord Ballantrae's chosen home. And in the month of November.

In November 1980, the Scots presence in Jerusalem was to be celebrated by St. Andrew's Church, their jubilee, on St. Andrew's day, the 30th of November. Lord Ballantrae wrote in his apology for absence from Ballantrae; "On the 28th November I fly out to Jerusalem with the Moderator, to represent the Church of Scotland at the 50th Anniversary of the Scots Kirk there on St. Andrew's Day. I will enjoy this the more as it is 43 years since I first worshipped in that Church. I was an Elder there and also stand-by Organist in 1946–47 ".

In the November copy of Life and Work 1980, there is a full article written by Lord Ballantrae. It was to be his last contribution to the Church of Scotland's Magazine. It is a moving and prophetic writing, and on the 28th of November, Lord Ballantrae departed not for Jerusalem, but to join his beloved wife, Laura in the presence of our Heavenly Father. It is impossible for anyone who knew Lady Laura Ballantrae and especially for those of us who lived with her here at Ballantrae, to think of her as other than a happy Woman. Lord and Lady Ballantrae were a great team. Lady Ballantrae was really loved by the people of Ballantrae. She took part in everything that went on in the village, she had great compassion and visited the sick It will be particularly remembered that when the last of the Hucknell sisters was dying at home, Lady Ballantrae took part in sitting up through the night with Miss Hucknell in her cottage on the Foreland.

As we look back at the concerts, the night Joyce Grenfell gave her solo concert, the Guilds, the Red Cross, the Guides, wherever she appeared the atmosphere was brightened.

On that Monday, the 17th of December 1979, entered in my diary as 'Black Monday', there was a storm that the older people claimed was the worst they had ever known. The sky was darkened from early morning, the gale was fierce, damage was extensive and approximately in the middle of the day, Lady Ballantrae was killed by a fallen tree. The tragic news sped across the world and deep mourning was felt wherever Lady Ballantrae had been known. One elderly local lady claimed; "God was short of Angels that day . . ."

Tragic was her death, but she can only be remembered as a happy person giving happiness wherever she went. The Laura Fergusson Trust Home in N.Z. where a crippled man was resident, summed the situation up with true feeling. He, through a retired but unknown taxi driver, wrote to Lord Ballantrae and said,"What a Lady".

Lord Ballantrae's favourite prayer
"We seem to give them back to Thee, O God, who gavest them to us. Yet as Thou didst not lose them in giving . . . "

At the beginning of my ministry at Ballantrae I discovered that my predecessor had been a pipe smoker and came to the Session Meetings with 'loaded' pipes of tobacco. There were a few heavy smokers on the session and when I pointed out that there should not be smoking during a Session Meeting, they appealed to Lord Ballantrae as Senior Elder to 'have a word' with the Minister. He did and he supported the Minister.

He had many favourites in hymns and psalms and I have letters from him making constructive suggestions in the choice of tune. Recovering from illness on one occasion he asked me to put Ps. 103 on the Praise List. I did.

There are two Plaques which have been placed in two churches; A Plaque in memory of the late Lord Ballantrae was placed in the Church of the 1st Battalion, The Black Watch, at WERL, West Germany. The inscription on the Plaque records Lord Ballantrae's service as Lord High Commissioner to the General Assembly; Colonel of the Regiment, and Elder in its Kirk Session. The Plaque was commissioned by the Regimental Kirk Session.

The other plaque is in the vestibule of Ballantrae Church. The inscription reads:

IN HONOURED MEMORY OF
BERNARD FERGUSSON
BRIGADIER THE LORD BALLANTRAE K.T.
1911–1980,
GOVERNOR GENERAL OF NEW ZEALAND 1962–1967,
LORD HIGH COMMISSIONER TO THE GENERAL ASSEMBLY
OF THE CHURCH OF SCOTLAND 1973–1974,
AND
AN ELDER OF THIS CONGREGATION,
ALSO
OF HIS DEVOTED WIFE,
LAURA MARGARET GRENFELL
1920–1979.

The Plaque was commissioned by the Ballantrae Community and paid for by public subscription.

Truth stranger than fiction. The young Subaltern from Sandhurst and the run away teenager arrived at the Perth Depot of the Black Watch in the early thirties.

This is the biography of that teenager.

We came together at Ballantrae, servants of Christ – Minister and Elder.

1981 was to prove a very active year and in the beginning there was nothing to indicate that a major change was about to take place. As I have said I was thinking about retiring at age 65 and communication was made with several housing associations in connection with renting a property. Also, with the church and other authorities who had special plans for purchasing property on behalf of pensioners, and charging interest (fixed) on the capital.

However, having attended to the external condition of the manse the question of central heating was raised and this lead to several meetings, but the internal architecture was such that alteration to suit central heating would have placed a major expenditure upon the congregation.

There was also the need for a hall and this gave rise to the possibility of building a new manse and a hall. Again, expenditure although this time there would be various sources of grant aid if a suitable scheme should be approved. The young people of the village were asking for a place to meet as a 'Youth Group' and this was receiving consideration.

It has to be borne in mind that the village hall at Ballantrae was in constant use throughout the week and there was the age old attitude of the adult population that the 'young people" would damage the hall. The greatest opposition was against indoor football. In spite of the rules governing this type of sport, accidental damage could easily take place and lead to costly repairs.

Dances and concerts were held to raise funds for the church fabric fund and a flower festival was held during the summer based on the theme 'Life'. The Annual Fete took place in July when there were open-air events on the foreland on the Friday evening and the sale stalls in the hall on the Saturday afternoon which was the Saturday ending the first week of the Glasgow Fare.

In addition to the youth clammering for a hall of their own, I received an undertaking from the young 'marrieds' that they were prepared to be involved with the village youth. It was just after the annual event that we received news that Pat's eldest brother had died.

During October I received an invitation to attend a Ministers In Service course at Carberry Tower from 10th to the 17th November and this I accepted. At the same time it was brought to my attention that there had been difficulty at Kelso where the Union & Re-adjustment Committee had attempted to close the Old Parish Church. I was reminded of how I objected to closing Old Parish Churches.

On the 30th October 1981 I made telephone enquiries in connection with the vacancy of the Old Parish Church at Kelso and learned that the church had been vacant since 1979. After further enquiry I decided to go to Kelso and hope to have a look inside the church so on Monday, 2nd of November, Pat, Katrina and Andrew accompanied me and we set off from Ballantrae and decided to make it a day out.

We arrived in the early evening and found the church next to the car park. There were two ladies standing at the front gate and when I asked one of them to direct me to the manse she replied that there was no one there, but the session clerk was in his shop in Bridge Street and she would show me where that was. That was a chance meeting with Lucy Scott, who was in fact the wife of the Elder, Convenor of the Fabric Committee and a man who was to prove to be a key man in the restoration of the church.

I then met with Ian Wright, Session Clerk, and explained my interest in wishing to see inside the church. Ian had received my written enquiry and laughed as he handed over his answer which he had been about to post. He promptly closed his shop and we went round to the church, where Pat, Katrina and Andrew were waiting. Ian gave me an outline of the problem facing them and as he opened the Church door on the south side we went in and I shall never forget that occasion.

There was an odour of dampness and inside the blackout blinds were still on the windows, some hanging askew. There was a hole in the ceiling near the centre and as we walked round it was noticeable that the plaster of the walls was peeling off and large flakes were lying on the floor. The atmosphere was one of neglect, no doubt attributable to the struggle that was going on between the congregation and the parties concerned with U & R.

The external walls were showing wear and the stone work was 'shrinking' in places at ground level. It was not encouraging but it was the ongoing church from the Kelso Abbey which had been built in 1128 and this particular building had been built in 1770.

Ian had given me a very fair account of what was happening and as we stood at the east side of the pulpit, he was looking at me, probably waiting for my reaction. I walked forward to the Communion Table, knelt on the step and prayed; "Father if You want me, send me".

We had the dogs with us and we made a good and happy journey home to Ballantrae via the service station where we all enjoyed an excellent meal. It rained all the way from the M8 and Pat did the driving, (it was her turn). The company of A & K and the nonsense with the dogs provided a lot of laughs. On the 10th of November the Minister's In Service Course assembled at Carberry Tower and this proved to be most helpful for in addition to what turned out to be an excellent course, I was able to meet two of the principal people from Edinburgh dealing with the Kelso Old Church. I remember that they were not too keen on my interest in the vacancy and said much to dissuade me from going ahead with my application.

But there was one Minister there from the same Presbytery and who knew the Kelso Old Church. His attitude was in favour and on the outcome of our conversation I decide to press on. I understood that there had been other applications for what had been approved as a 'Terminable Appointment' over three years. I was aware that the session and the congregation intended to keep their church going and in presenting my C.V. to them I had made it quite clear that if I was 'called' it would be my intention to have the church restored to full status.

I received an invitation to come and preach for the church on the 22nd of November and the Interim Moderator informed me that he had arranged for the service to be held in St. George's Church, Hawick at 6 p.m. The Kelso Old Session Clerk, Ian Wright, wrote advising me of the procedure at Hawick.

On the 22nd of November I conducted the morning service at Ballantrae and after a light lunch, Pat and I set off for Hawick, a distance of 139 miles.

We arrived in good time and as previously arranged we went to the manse of the Interim Moderator, the Rev. David Wright, and Mrs Wright provided an excellent meal. David was the minister who had borne the brunt of the prolonged vacancy and he gave me quite a lot of information during dinner. A hostile confrontation during a vacancy is something to be avoided and Christian charity difficult to recognise on both sides.

After the service, Pat and I met with the vacancy committee from Kelso and the meeting continued until 8 p.m. We set off for Ballantrae and arrived, very late and very tired.

The 22nd had been dull and overcast and the 23rd dawned wild and with lashing gales. This continued through the 24th and resulted in flooding the surrounding area. Transport was stranded in the village and help was required in the village.

Once again, fuel was short and a supply of logs was brought in to the village. The youth came to the assistance of the elderly and logs were delivered on the 13th of December. On the 14th of December I received the news that I had been accepted as the sole nominee for Kelso Old Parish Church.

In accordance with the un-written procedure of the Church of Scotland it was now necessary to inform the Kirk Session of my intention to be translated from Ballantrae and that I had been accepted as the sole nominee for the Kelso Old Parish Church. A Kirk Session meeting was called for on the 20th and I reported to the session that I would be preaching for the vacancy at Kelso.

There was surprise and discussion and I believe that it had been more or less taken for granted that I would continue as Minister at Ballantrae until my retirement. The usual procedure was then followed where session informed Presbytery of my intention.

There is an amusing part of the proceedings at this stage in accordance with Church Law arising from an incident which took place in the distant past. When a Minister decided to move from his charge or to retire, the Presbytery appointed two fellow Ministers to 'wait' upon him and to ensure that all was well with him. In other words to ensure that he was of sound mind before Presbytery took any action in connection with translation or retirement. The 'wait' meeting ended with tea and cake and my fellows were satisfied that I was of sound mind.

The remainder of December was busy with trying to tie up the loose ends and reach conclusions on outstanding matters, the youth application for a hall, the retention of the supplementary roll, being the most important. Meantime, Kelso were busy arranging a date in January for the sole nominee to be heard by the Congregation in the Kelso Old Parish Church and this was duly set for the 10th of January, 1982.

The first week in January was giving concern because of severe bad weather. On the 4th the radio broadcast that Kelso was flooded and cut off by snow. Pulpit supply for Ballantrae had been arranged and we decide to leave for Kelso on the 8th in order to allow for the weather and be at Kelso for the 10th. Our route was via Carlisle and then by A7 to Hawick and on to Kelso.

It was a difficult journey and as we approached Moss Paul, a dreadful area in winter, we saw the wind forming drifts of fine snow across the corners of the road. We arrived at Kelso in the evening and were made welcome by Naomi and Ian Wright, (Session Clerk) where we were guests over the weekend.

There was apprehension that the people would not be able to turn out on the Sunday morning, the roads were covered in deep snow and there was no sign of pavements at all, the conditions under foot could not have been worse.

On Sunday we set off for the church and I must have felt terrible. The weather was atrocious and yet, there was a full turnout of over 200 people to support the church and I was elected unanimously.

Oh the relief from tension. Looking back I remember thinking would they want a minister of 65 years of age. There can not be many ministers who were elected to a charge at that age. By way of explanation the point about "un-written procedure" refers to when any minister contemplates a move he is forced to keep it strictly confidential for the sake of his congregation. The reason being that if he was to give prior notice of his intention and subsequently failed to be accepted,the relationship between minister and congregation would be disturbed in the future. Once he is accepted as sole nominee he is then in the positive position of being able to tell all concerned. Rarely does the sole nominee fail to be accepted.

It is a necessary act of Presbyterianism that the members of the congregation shall confirm the vacancy committee's choice of minister, the committee having listened to a number of Ministers preaching in their own Churches. After the 10th of January 1982 it was all systems go to move to Kelso and take up residence in the Old Parish Manse. There was the necessary administration between the two Presbyteries, Ayr and Jedburgh. I have explained that the Presbytery of Ayr had 'waited' upon me and were satisfied that I could be translated to Kelso. In addition to the normal form of translation there was the requirement for me to resign my charge at Ballantrae and thereafter I would be 'introduced'to Kelso Old as Minister without Charge.

The reason for this procedure was because Kelso Old had been placed on a terminable appointment of three years. Once this has been done by the appropriate authority it is said that terminable means what it says and the minister who is 'introduced' would either revert to the Presbytery from whence he had come, or to the Presbytery where he had been Ordained at the end of the terminable period. I was aware of this possibility.

However, at the end of a very long vacancy, the Kelso Old Kirk Session and the members of the congregation were in no mood to see their church closed and it was my intention to join with them and accept the challenge to defeat this act of Terminable Appointment.

It is said that Christianity flourishes under persecution and there is historical facts to support this claim. It can be said that the people of Kelso Old saw the action of the Union and Readjustment as persecution. Having repealed the power of Ad Vitam Aut Culpam in 1973 there was no way that a minister entering a Terminable Appointment could be inducted to that charge; having resigned he was now without charge. I have felt for some time that a great deal of what takes place in Church Administration is questionable. Today, the practise of Terminable Appointment has been reviewed and I believe that I am probably one of the last persons to have been subjected to the risks incurred by taking on such an appointment. The task facing us at Kelso Old Parish was formidable. The objective was clear but the priorities had to be placed in order and much required to be done. The family were now in Kelso, let work begin.

The first meeting was a joint meeting of Kirk Session and Congregational Board and the necessary extracts of minutes were made and forwarded to Presbytery.

The next and most important step was to brief me on what had been happening during the extended vacancy. It must have been difficult to decide where to start but after reference to the minutes and observations from certain members we were able to agree what the first move of the minister should be.

Among the many decisions to be made two were important and involved several factors. They both came under the Congregational Board and it was agreed that the Secretary of the Board should accompany me and examine what the situation was. Both were potentially Revenue Earning and this was to be our main consideration for the next few years.

The Secretary, Mrs. Jean Cormack, met with me and we carried out a reconnaissance of the Glebe field (4.9 acres) and a lane which was referred to as 'Poo Alley' because of the dog fouling which took place. The Glebe fencing was not stock proof and the stone wall had a breach of 18 yards caused by frost where the wall had collapsed. It has to be stressed that the period of vacancy caused a situation of limbo and while the Session Clerk and church officials were aware of what required to be done, under the threat of closure they could not even act on a care and maintenance basis.

There had been negotiations to purchase land from the church to make a road running the length of 'Poo Alley' but these had been suspended. A major obstacle to the road project was the demolition of the extant 8 ft. wall which divided the lane from the Manse Garden. It had been muted that if the wall was taken down it would be necessary for the Council to erect a similar wall at the edge of the new road bordering the remaining part of the Manse Garden.

An estimate had been received for the repair of the Glebe wall only. I decided to recommend to the Board that a new estimate be called for to stock proof the entire circumference of the 4.9 acre area, that the fractured wall be demolished and the rubble removed. The Board approved and a five wire tensile fence was erected with barbed wire top strand on top. The cost of the estimate was similar to the proposed repair of the breached wall, some £850 approximately. The situation with the road problem was not practicable and I recommended to the Board that they accept the offer of financial compensation for the land from the Council. To demand the erection of a similar wall was not advantageous and a fence with Beech Hedging in support would suffice and the new road would be an asset to the general public.

The recommendations were accepted and the information passed to all concerned. I have to confess of one blunder in that it did not occur to me to sell the top soil. Thousands of tons had to be removed to form a base for the road.

At this point I have to mention one elder who played a leading part in these initial proceedings and in fact continued to be prominent in the total restoration of our church, I refer to Mr Sandy Scott whom, I regret to report, has just died.

Having got something going from the first meeting my next important action was to get to know the Office Bearers and to let them know what I intended to do. It was imperative that we acted as a united team. The following requirement was to meet the members of the Congregation in their homes. 1982 was a very busy year.

The acknowledged ideal size of an Elder's District is one of 12 households. What I discovered was that the Districts were too large and the obvious way to deal with that problem was to increase the size of the Kirk Session. This necessity was placed before the Session and the usual procedure followed which does take time from nomination to the final Edict which is read out to the congregation prior to Ordination to the Eldership.

In due course the Session was nearly doubled and the ideal of 12 households or near to that figure, achieved. Meanwhile, a district visitation programme was drawn up and I was able to visit every household of the Congregation in the Company of the Elder. The men and women of the Kirk Session were splendid and willingly gave of their time and made arrangements to enable me to meet each member.

In my opinion this was absolutely essential in view of what had been happening since 1979 and it was to prove fruitful. The next move was to keep every member informed of what was happening in our church affairs and a monthly letter was issued by me and taken by the elders to their members. This also kept elders in touch with their members each month.

The interior of the church building was next. It was dreich, dowdy and totally without appeal. It was in a way evidence that in the minds of some people the building was finished, even the black-out blinds were still hanging, at varying angles, above the windows. Each Sunday morning the Church Officer, Mr Tom Cairns, would go round with a bucket and hand shovel clearing the flakes of wall debris before the Congregation arrived.

It was nearing the end of 1982 when another man appeared on the scene, not a member of Kelso Old Parish. He was an architect, Mr Duncan Cameron from Galashiels. I met Duncan, accidentally, as he walked towards the church from the Butts car park. Divine providence? We got in to conversation and having introduced myself, explained what it was we hoped to do to get the Old Parish restored to full status.

It transpired that Duncan had been a member of the Church of Scotland Advisory Board on Artistic Matters, the Committee who advised on the decoration of church buildings. Duncan looked round the church and offered to help with the internal decoration. I explained our state of funds and that I would report to the Session. He was asked to proceed and in time he produced plans and colour schemes. These were discussed by the Session and the Board and when they had agreed on the colour, Duncan was asked to proceed with the decoration after approach to the Artistic Committee.

When I knew that the work was about to begin, I obtained permission from the Abbey Row Centre Officials to hold morning services in the ARC and this was readily given. We held our morning services for the following six weeks in the ARC and according to members of the congregation it was much appreciated, cosy and bright. Having removed the congregation from the church building, I looked in while the work was in hand and received a shock. The scaffolding was throughout the building from floor to ceiling and hardly any space to walk except round steel supports. I did not go back until the decoration was completed.

During this period I was also concerned for the Sunday School which met one hour before the morning service in the church and consequently were interrupted by the arrival of the members for the service. The facilities for the children to sit or use writing/drawing materials were nil. Heating left much to be desired. There was also the absence of secondary schoolage children and I decided to try and hold a Young People's Church to attract the older children and avoid the word 'school'. With this in mind, I approached the Abbey Row Centre Authority again and was pleased to receive their encouragement to go ahead.

Thanks to the help of one of the young elders and a few senior teenagers, our son Andrew and daughter Katrina, a Young People's Church took shape and played an important part in the life of the church until the natural wastage, which affects all young organisations, caused by further education and leaving to take up employment took its toll.

Prior to returning to the church the Young Mother's group, the Woman's Guild, Members of the Board and Session aided by equipment from Messrs. Neves, entered the Church and cleaned the whole of the interior and polished the wood block floor. Everything was bright and welcoming. The black-out blinds had gone, a symbol of the past.

It was about this time that we received an invitation to an Elder's Conference at Carberry Tower. 50% of that course were from Kelso Old Parish. Every church official was involved in what was happening to the Old Parish Church, and members who were not in any of the organisations of the church, were always keen to help in the ongoing activities. The church building is a Listed Building and this presents difficulties when attempting to improve or modernise such a building. There was a need for an indoor toilet and washbasin. I was going to say 'urgent' except that would sound foolish considering what had been the situation since the building of the church.

What was behind the thinking of the officials of yesteryear I can not imagine, but there was no provision for women or children. On the south east corner of the building there was an ornate extension jutting out from the side of the church. There was no roof but there was a lead lined trough leading to a soak away drain. That was it.

Leading from the Session Room there was a large opening which had been in use when there was a pipe organ in the church. It was now vacant since there was no longer a pipe organ. By reducing the interior of the Session room and utilising this space we could have our toilet facilities without disturbing the fabric of the Listed Building. It was agreed.

The Session room had become too small and today we have what can be referred to as a rest room in emergency and hot and cold water with hot air drying for hand use.

In passing, when I first proposed that this inside toilet should be installed it was said that it was not possible because it would be necessary to "dig down 13 feet and go under the wall right across the Butts road". It was agreed that the situation should be examined and we are indebted to Mr Ballantyne for his expertise. He carried out tests with a 'die' and found that there was drainage within a few feet of the old external latrine. Today there is drainage right round the church with down pipes from the roof guttering.

The speaker for the "13 feet" defended his statement with the old, "It has aye been said in the past . . ." The toilet conversion took place in April 1983 and it was now time to think of increasing revenue. There is provision in church procedure to purchase increased endowments. But it can only be done with 'new money'. Donations had suddenly appeared, large and anonymous. I will not go in to detail suffice to say that the outcome is capital remains intact and the interest is credited annually to the church. Capital is not refundable. There is the incentive that the new money being used to purchase the 'increased endowments' is accepted at two for one and it is on the gross figure that the interest is calculated. The benefit of this is shared by the whole congregation.

Our secretary of the Congregational Board, Mrs Jean Cormack, agreed to visit Edinburgh and establish contact with the Historic Buildings Grant Aid people and similar organisations concerned with aiding Listed Ancient Buildings. There was also the General Trustees of the Church of Scotland. Jean has been indefatigable in her efforts on behalf of the Kelso Old Parish and when, at this stage, she visited Edinburgh, it really was on a fact finding mission. But it turned out that we were making the right moves. While we were on a terminable appointment I doubt if there would ever have been any grant made to the Old Parish. But we were met with the utmost courtesy, and we were on record.

That is important because there is likely to be a long waiting list of applicants seeking aid. On one occasion when I was in an office the woman looking through the index mentioned that there was no trace of any other application from Kelso.

I had been given to understand differently but it was none of my business, Kelso Old was my only interest. We had decided to hold a series of Manse lunches after the morning service and these were held at the Abbey Row Centre and in the Tait Hall.

A stated annual meeting which is on a compulsory dated period can be a very boring and routine matter and it was necessary to maintain interest in what was going on in the church and what was needed for the church. Consequently the Stated Annual Meeting was advanced to being a social evening in the second half. We had a good turn out.

On the 6th of March 1983 after the decoration and works had taken place, a re-dedication service was held and the Interim Moderator of the Long Vacancy, the Reverend David Wright, was invited to preach the sermon. Throughout 1983 planning was taking shape and revenue was coming in. Donations were being received, still anonymously, and Duncan Cameron had produced a detailed estimate and plans for the restoration of the external walls of the building. The sum estimated was £158,000. There was 'oohs' and 'ahs' and you will never get that amount of money Mr Fox.

There was more than one '13' footer on the touchline but they would be hard to find now. Duncan Cameron had made the estimate and carried out all the work to date without receiving one penny or asking for payment.

Messrs. Sandy Scott, John Wilson, Bill Ford, Bobby Hossack, Jim Thomson, all of these Elders voluntarily attended to the Manse Garden. I believe that they also had kept it in order during the three years of vacancy.

Mr Ian Wright, Session Clerk; Mrs Jean Cormack, Clerk to the Board; Mr Tom Gray/Mrs Peggy Ford, Treasurers were constant in their attention to their official duties and a tremendous help to me.

The Elm Tree which had been in the centre of the Glebe Field for years was destroyed by the Elm Disease. When Her Grace, The Duchess of Roxburghe, heard about this she asked the Head Forester for a replacement tree and on the 7th of April 1983, planted a Red

Lime in the field. During the planting members of my family were present and we were all caught in a flash hailstone shower. We had a pleasant tea party to follow in the Manse. As 1983 drew to a close everything that was possible to be done or put in hand during that year was attended to. I had been the Chaplain to the Kelso Boys Brigade, (later I became Battalion Chaplain from Selkirk to Langholm) re-joined Rotary having been a Vice-President in Sandakan. We had made enquiries about cleaning the Regimental Colours of the Blues and Royals which had been on the walls of the church since 1927. They were placed there by the Duke of Roxburghe's brother, Lord Alistair, Commanding Officer of the Regiment, by command of H.M. King George the V.

To arrange for the cleaning was no easy matter and the guards sources in London and at Windsor were unable to be of much assistance. Fortunately, Ian Wright had information about an expert cleaner, a Mrs Susan Rodgers of Aberdeen.

We were able to contact Mrs Rodgers and thanks to our Provost of the day, Mr Sandy Blair, the Colours were taken by car to Aberdeen and some time later they were returned to Kelso by Securicor in early 1984. Again, when Her Grace heard of this action re the cleaning of the Colours, she settled the invoice.

The family enjoyed their holidays at Crieff. 1982 and 1983 had covered the period of arriving at Kelso and once introduced to the charge and proceeding with the matters in hand and planning for the future the time had gone by quickly.

On looking through my diary I am truly astonished at what happened in 1984. The Terminable Appointment was due to expire in March 1985 and I had felt the pressure of that limited time factor ever since my arrival. But it is now that I realise just how much had been achieved in what I now see as the preparatory years to achieve the full restoration of the church.

The following is the progress, date by date:

Firstly, there was severe weather conditions and travel on occasion had to be postponed. The Young People's Church Conference at Carberry had to be cancelled and the Deposit Transferred to a later date.

On the 11th January the Young People's Church produced a concert for church funds. Mrs Elizabeth Findlay commenced taping the morning service for distribution to the Housebound members.

March 15th: Presbytery quinquennial visitation. Rev. Lindsay Thomson, Rev. Jim Strachan, Elders: Mr. McQueen, Mr. Irvine.

March 18th: 'Kelso Volunteers' History Picture.

March 29th: Mrs. Isobel Reid & Band for Church Funds @ S.A.M.

April 29th: 13 miles sponsored walk.

May 2nd: Presbytery recommend release from suppression!

May 12th: New garage doors fitted by Sandy Scott and Bill Ford.

May 16th: Auction Sale - Church Funds.

May 20th: H.G. Duke of Roxburghe and Lord Robin replace Colours in Church.

June 10th: Manse Garden Fete - Young Peoples Church Young Women's Group donate £100.

June Initiate plans for New Manse. (discussion stage only).

July 10th: Rev. G. Watson, Presbytery Clerk. Rev. L. Thomson, Member. Presbytery Representatives to meet with Session and Board in Church 'To report to General Assembly M. of M. Committee in October recommending that Kelso Old Parish be restored to Full Status".

There was a full turn out of Elders and Board members and the Presbytery Representatives expressed their appreciation of a very happy meeting.

July 14th: Flower Festival in Church.

Aug 14th: Jean, Ian, Bill McKechnie with Inspector to view possible new manse site.

Aug 22nd: "Hallidon" Tea Party Church Funds

Aug 27th: Official meeting with Duncan Cameron at 2.30 p.m. in the Church Subject "Grants for historic Buildings" Decision "A letter from the Church signed by the Session Clerk stating intention to restore external walls of the Church and instructing Duncan Cameron to set the project in motion, also to send the full cost of conversion of the Session Room."

Aug 29th: Boys Brigade to arrange for the Ministers of the North Parish and the Old Parish to supply the Chaplain on alternate years.

Sept 3rd: Glebe Field – Mr J. Elliot accepts to farm the Glebe for five (5) years.

Oct 26th: Extract minute from General. Assembly – M. of M. Committee that the Suppression of K.O.P. Church had been lifted. Presbytery ask me to appoint a date for my induction to the Kelso Old Parish Church.

This book is dedicated to my wife, Pat, I asked for her birthday, the 16th December, 1984.

On the 23rd of December the first Service was a family service.

The objective of the whole exercise had been achieved, the Kelso Old Parish was once again a charge with its own minister, but there was now much more to be done by way of consolidating the position in finding a site and building a new manse. Tentative steps had been taken and reconnaissance with the proper authorities gave us a very clear idea that this question was not going to be easy to deal with.

Now that the term 'terminable appointment' had been removed, the Kirk Session and the Congregational Board were now in the position of making a positive approach to the authorities concerned with disposing of the old manse and further financing the church restoration and building of the new manse.

It was decided to form a 'think tank' to attend to the necessary details and we were in the favourable position of having professional people in our midst.

Architects, lawyers, bankers, doctors, chartered accountants, industrialists and from their number a working 'think tank' was selected by the joint Kirk Session/Congregational Board. This arrangement was successful and the 'TT' reported to the statutory meeting of the combined Session/Board either, what progress was made or for further direction. The Minister, The Session Clerk, The Clerk to the Board, The Fabric Convenor were ex-officio members of the 'TT'.

An application to build a manse on church ground, (referred to as 'Manse Garden') was, to our surprise, refused by Regional Planning Authority. An appeal was lodged and that too was refused.

A second appeal was lodged and this resulted in a public enquiry which was heard in the Town Hall, Kelso. The architects, with the church consent, had approached Town Planning Consultants to attend the public enquiry on our behalf. However, when the fees were made known to the church, this presented a problem and it looked as if we could not proceed. We owned the ground and we had submitted all the relevant points, there were no new factors and we were therefore not in a position to risk large financial loss. After further discussion the Town Planning Consultants decided to proceed and waive their fees on 'professional grounds'. The public enquiry ruled against the church and we had to think again.

In February 1985, Duncan Cameron produced elevations for the restoration work. These elevations plans were accompanied by a further estimate of £169,955. It was also at about this time that Duncan introduced us to one of his colleagues, a young architect by name Simon Longlands. Simon applied himself with enthusiasm and professional interest in ancient buildings. We soon realised that we were in 'good hands'.

We were equally fortunate in co-opting Mr George Young, a chartered accountant to take over the balance of the fabric account and open the Kelso Old Parish Church Heritage Fund. Her Grace, The

Duchess of Roxburghe became our Patron.

Mr Muir Sturrock, a legal consultant agreed to act for us if and when required. Now we were ready to proceed from a different angle and this time I requested that we make no claim to 'our ground'. Let us approach the authority and having presented our problem, ask how we should go about obtaining permission? Times had changed. Staff at planning had changed. An appointment was arranged to see an official of the Planning Department and our Board Secretary accompanied by a member of the 'TT' attended the meeting. The result was favourable and today the new manse stands on a part of what was called 'Manse Garden'.

Meanwhile the parish work was continuing and in addition to local revenue earning, by members and their friends in the community, negotiations were in hand for grant aid by 'The Historic Buildings and Monuments Fund of the Scottish Development Department', 'The Scottish Churches Architectural Trust', local authorities and special trusts interested in Listed Church Buildings. It was not just a case of making an application. The above fund and trust organisations have special rules and the applicants must comply. Perhaps the greatest consideration is given to those who make every effort to help themselves.

Garden fetes and coffee mornings had been held throughout the year. The fetes were in 'Halidon' Garden the home of Drs. Mr and Mrs Trainer and, at the manse by the members of the Young People's Church.

There was also concerts and visiting choirs and exhibitions in the church. An auction sale of items that were no longer required by their owners, there was every kind of activity by all of our members.

The final cost of the restoration of Kelso Old Parish Church was £344,353.18.

During 1986 I was nominated and elected Moderator of the Presbytery and requested at the end of the first year to continue for a second term. I was then elected as Moderator of the Synod thus completing a period of interesting and sad duty. It is ironic that having taken so much trouble to keep an ancient church open, I became Moderator of a Presbytery that was ordered by the General Assembly of the Church of Scotland to reduce the number of Churches in Hawick.

Hawick Old Parish foundations were discovered to be unsafe and in the end the church was reduced to rubble. While I was Battalion Chaplain of the Borders Boys Brigade, the Annual Oversea's meeting was held in the Kelso Old Parish Church on the 14th November ' when all the Units in Scotland attended and handed over their cheque for £41,000 to the Moderator of the General Assembly The Right Reverend Archie Craig.

As Chaplain to Lyle & Scott at Kelso I attended the Industrial Mission at Carronvale, Larbert during 1986.

Epilogue

When I began to write this Biography nearly three years ago I decided on a period covering 1921 to 1988. It was on the 31st of December 1988 that I became officially retired after the extensions, which had been granted to me at my request, to enable me to see the church fully restored and the new manse built.

Planning permission, after refusal, appeal, public enquiry, refusal, was eventually granted to build the manse and after that it was all downhill. The activities of all Agencies of the Church continued through 1987 and 1988.

The Rev. Haisley Moore was appointed as Interim Moderator and preached the Church Vacant in January 1989. I continued as locum giving pulpit supply and pastoral assistance when requested, until the minister was inducted on the 25th of August 1989. I wish to pay my personal tribute to all concerned with the successful return of the Kelso Parish Church to its rightful position as a Full Charge.

To those families of the Kelso Old who read this epilogue I want you to visualise a circle round the church with you at the centre. Whether as a child, or as an adult, employed or a pensioner, whatever your status and means, each looking from the centre will find all parts of the circle equidistant. It was a grand effort from Sunday School to the oldest member and assisted by many who were not on the roll of the Parish Church.

Dear Lord, Thy Will be done. Not mine.

Addendum

Called to the Church
Detailing "Steps" to the Call

When I arrived at Sandakan it was on a Saturday morning and there was the usual business of disembarking and collecting the luggage. I was met by the District Officer of Baluran who had come to meet me and take me to the Resident's lodge where we were both to stay prior to being briefed by the Resident. Gordon Norris, District Officer Beluran, was also without his family and we became good friends during the following months as we tackled our various duties.

On the Sunday morning I walked down to the Government Office and as I acquainted myself with the various buildings I noticed a small monument in the shape of a christian cross situated in front of the police station. The inscription on the monument referred to the Districts Officers who had been killed while on duty. The Japanese had not disturbed this monument and there was a small space left at the foot of the cross. I hoped to leave that space when my tour of duty was completed.

It was about a year later in 1965 that the memory of the monument was dramatically brought to mind. It was early in the morning and the head of the Special Branch came to see me. Ted Pearce was a most efficient officer and had seen similar service in Cyprus during the Eoka political uprising. He sat at the other side of my desk and in a quiet voice asked, "Would I like to see the person who was to replace me as District Officer?" Continuing, he informed me that the replacement was in gaol with several other men who had been arrested during an early morning raid. He handed a document to me and said that the people in gaol had been under supervision for some time. Pointing to the document he said, "That is a list of the people who were to be assassinated". The list contained the names of all the executive expatriates and my name was second from the top. the Resident Commissioner was first and then followed the police and heads of government departments.

I did not visit the gaol. Perhaps the political situation had reached a point of being taken for granted but if so, we were forcibly reminded on this occasion that we were in confrontation with Communist Indonesia.

What would I have done as a Christian. If the communist terrorists has been successful in carrying our their intention of assassination they would have bound us hand and foot and placed a blind-fold over our eyes. We would have been helpless.

I do not remember exactly when it came to mind but the question of Faith did arise and I remember the thought that came to me, whatever they might have done, they could not reach the mind, and if death was certain, the last words could be, "O Lord my God, how great Thou art". Nothing can separate us from the Love of God. But, again, would I have had sufficient courage and nerve to stand still and defy them! I shall never know, but they made me think. The small space on the monument-cross remained empty.

There is another cross which is empty because the Saviour of mankind defeated death and dwells among us having said, "I am the Way, the Truth and the Life". Faith will not be denied. Not for the first time my thoughts turned to asking that I might be allowed to enter the Ministry of the Church of Scotland. Ever since childhood my family had a close connection with the Church and in my personal case, until I left home for the Army, I had grown up within the Church and taught in the Sunday School.

There is even an amusing family story that I preached my first sermon when I was a five-year-old at Bran Castle.

But now the simmering has reached the boiling point.

It was necessary for me to go on a visit with a number of my Land Survey people and we had travelled some way in to the jungle and walking alongside a river when we had stopped for a rest. Our conversation was conducted mainly in Malay and I remember leaving them chattering as I moved along the river bank and stood looking up at the high hill in front of us. The river was the usual dark brown water flowing quite fast, and the hill stood high and daunting. My thought turned to the Highlands of Scotland; the beautiful clear running water, the magnificent mountains, the silence around Loch Maree. And then I thought of the Power of Almighty God, as we look at the towering waves of the stormy sea and the Majesty of God shown in the height of the highest mountain.

I knew then that I was going to approach the appropriate Church Authorities, the Call was becoming louder.

Here I was in N. Borneo (Sabah) district Officer of a vast area and responsible for the well-being of some 32,000 people. If the Church will let me enter the Ministry I can surely bring this experience to the benefit of my Native Land. As the decision took a firm hold I found myself looking back and realising that my life had been saved on many occasions. Yes, I am a firm believer in Divine Providence. The were minor incidents such as brakes failures and crashing in to a wall but when I went to work in the coal mines, there were serious incidents.

Being dragged by the collar of my jacket from under a steel hutch. A roof fall where the slabs of rock crashed down right up to the coal face blocking the entrance and sealing a miner and myself behind the fall. During the War there were the normal hazards but the nearest one to death must have been the time while travelling in to Burma seated in the mid gunners seat of a Halifax Bomber, suddenly there was a mountain in front of us. The pilot turned the aircraft on its wing tip out of the direction of the mountain. We were saved.

I obtained the address of the Rev. Mr. Fleming in Singapore where he was working with the Rev. Robert Greer who had been our minister when we resided in Singapore. I received advice from Mr. Fleming and prepared an application to be sent to 121 George Street. At the same time I was posted to the Ministry of Finance in Jesselton (Kota Kinnabalu), and this to my mind, was further providence. There is (was) no Church of Scotland presence in North Borneo at that time and one of the ministers used to come over from Singapore every six months to conduct services for the Church of Scotland members resident in North Borneo (Sabah).

While in Sandakan, I had attended St. Michaels Church (Church of England) and took my turn at reading the Lessons at the evening service. On arrival in Jesselton I attended the cathedral and continued to read the lessons at the evening services. It was here that I met Cannon Rusted. "Rusty" was also the Headmaster of the secondary school and when he learned of my hope to join the ministry he loaned me books.

Following the advice given I sent a CV to the Secretary for Education of the Ministry at 121 George Street and received a prompt reply.

Most of what was required of me could be attended to when I returned to the UK the first step being that I would be required to attend a selection school.

When I returned a particular book to Rusty I mentioned that the most interesting thing about the book was that it had made it quite clear God was not only transcendent but also imminent. Rusty looked at me for a moment and then said, "You have learned that from reading only one book, when the day comes for you to be Ordained I want to know and I shall attend the Ordination".

In 1968 I returned to the UK and when I reported to 121 George reet I was given instructions to proceed to Glasgow and attend the ection School. I did and in the course of time I was informed that I had been selected and there followed a list of conditions with which I had to comply.

I entered New College in October 1969 as a mature student and after two years I reported to the Rev. George Elliot as his Probationer Assistant at Ness Bank Church, Inverness. I became Sole Nominee for the Charge of Ballantrae in Ayrshire and was Ordained and Inducted to the Charge on the 21st of September, 1972. Rusty was there.

Rusty had returned to Croydon where he was Canon Emeritus and in the Diocese of the Archbishop of Canterbury, Archbishop Ramsay. When Rusty asked for leave to attend my Ordination he had to explain to the Archbishop the background for his request. On hearing what Rusty had to say the Archbishop gave his approval and added, "And give that young man my blessing also". I suppose that makes me one of the few Ministers to be Ordained with the blessing of the Church of Scotland and the Church of England.

I was at Ballantrae from September 1972 until March 1982 when I was introduced to the Terminable Appointment to the Kelso Old Parish. The Kelso Old Parish was restored to full status on the 16th December 1984 and I was Inducted to the restored Charge. During the refurbishing of the interior and the exterior of the church building I was granted extensions of service having reached the age of 70 in order to permit my continued supervision of the refurbishing. I retired on the 31st of December 1988 and continued as Locum Tenens until the Induction of my Successor on the 25th of August 1989.

During 1987 the television "Highway" programme featured the Kelso Old Parish Church and Sir Harry Secombe referred to my three careers when I was able to reply that the Church was the most demanding and satisfying. The programme was televised on the 28th of February 1988 while I was in hospital receiving a hip replacement.

I am still involved in Pulpit Supply and Pastoral duties and shall continue as long as I am able and required.